Boldly Going Somewhere

RON & AIMEE COOPER

Charleston, SC
www.PalmettoPublishing.com

Boldly Going Somewhere
Copyright © 2021 Ron & Aimee Cooper

All rights reserved
No portion of this book may be reproduced, stored in a retrieval system, or transmitted in any form by any means– electronic, mechanical, photocopy, recording, or other– except for brief quotations in printed reviews, without prior permission of the author.

First Edition

Paperback ISBN: 978-1-68515-209-3
eBook ISBN: 978-1-68515-781-4

Dedication

Ron: This book is dedicated to our fellow travelers—those who dream of a wild adventure and then go make it happen. To me, that starts with Aimee, who makes every day of my life special.

Aimee: I dedicate this book to my husband; the thrill-seeking, optimistic oddball who talked me into a first date in an RV. Let's raise a glass to all the explorers out there!

Contents

Acknowledgements	vii
Big Bend	1
Monkey on Your Back	5
Why Did We Do It?	7
I've Met a Man and He Lives in a Motorhome	10
Picking Our Prairie Schooner	13
The Squeak	15
Less Is More	19
Squid Sucker	23
Getting Started	25
Black Tank	29
Settling Into Our New Lifestyle	32
The West Coast Wholly Granola Ride	42
Red Rock	44
Home Is Where You Park It	48
Driving an RV in America	52
The Google and Google Maps	56
Michigan's Upper Peninsula	60
Catch and Release	65
The Life of Pie	69
Love and Cherry Pie	74
Oh, We Got Fat!	76
Swim Your Way Across the USA	80
Jaws	85
Leech Lake	88
The Economics of Living on the Road	90
Monotony	94
You Manage What You Measure	97
Fight Club	101
Wild Things	105
Night of the Conch	111
Seasons on the Road	114

Metal Tent	120
The DelMarva Peninsula	123
New England Isn't a State	127
Exploring Our Family Roots	130
Red Scare	136
Tour de America	139
The Cycle-Ology of Bike Riding	146
Good Vibrations	149
The Singing Cowboy	153
Amarillo, Texas	157
Easy Bake Oven	161
Motorhome Meals	165
Sisterhood of the Traveling Ants	168
Horse Country	171
Talking Trash	174
New Orleans	177
Can I Buy Your Ghost a Drink?	181
The Great Oyster Shooter Incident	185
Holidays on the Road	188
Quilt Junkie	192
Truth or Consequences	195
Mobile Wild Kingdom	199
Romance on the Road	202
Rest Stop	206
Texas Hill Country	208
And a Color TV!	213
Cross Country Routes	216
O Canada	224
Signs, Signs, Everywhere the Signs	232
Companionship on the Road	236
Idiot Light	242
The Best Of…	248
What's Next	264
Lessons of the Road	268
About the Authors	269

Acknowledgements

Wandering around America was an amazing experience, but it wasn't always easy. Fortunately, our friends and family were incredibly supportive, even when they questioned our sanity. Many of them opened their homes to us as we journeyed around the country. We spent Thanksgiving with Walt and Suzan Strader in North Carolina and with Rick and Diana Roof in Virginia, explored the Delmarva Peninsula with Deb Keller, and enjoyed spring in Kentucky with Spencer and Sonia Clark. Charley Brown invited Ron and our son Michael to do a business project with him while we were traveling, which let us get together several times and kept Ron mentally challenged. Visiting our daughter Wende let us explore Long Island, and we got to celebrate our daughter Kimberly's wedding in Massachusetts. Ron's brother Russell and sister Robin and our daughter Dakota all made trips to visit us on the road, so we got to share the joy of discovering new places with our family.

Writing about our experience took longer than the trip itself and we owe a second debt of gratitude to many of the same people for encouraging us, reading our drafts, and providing honest feedback about how to improve the book. It was a little like getting advice as first-time parents; not always easy to hear but ultimately extremely helpful. Our daughter Wende and Suzan Strader, who are both published authors, took the time to explain publishing to us. Our daughter Kimberly did a detailed proof-read and made over 200 corrections to our spelling and punctuation. (We are so grateful to have kids that are smarter than us!)

Finally, to Katie, Colby, and the entire team at Palmetto Publishing, thank you for guiding us through the publishing process. Your patience and good humor made it easy and fun.

Big Bend

—*Ron*—

We are floating on our backs in the Rio Grande, with one hand in Mexico and the other in the United States. The river is less than 50 feet wide here, and as we look up, we can only see a thin sliver of blue sky between the 1,500-foot-high cliffs on either side. A week ago, we had never heard of Santa Elena Canyon or Big Bend National Park. Located in a far-flung corner of Texas 300 miles southeast of El Paso, Big Bend is so remote that it gets few visitors, but it sounded interesting, and that was reason enough to drive here. After two years and nearly 100,000 miles on the road, we have learned that our best experiences are the things that we discover by chance as we wander around America.

Earlier that day, music filled the cab of Gypsy, our 29-foot motorhome as we drove down the two-lane road into the park. Big Bend includes a huge swath of the Chihuahuan desert, so outside was a classic Western landscape of dry arroyos dotted by cactus and desert wildflowers in bloom. We could almost picture the outlaws hiding here in the mountains that make up Texas' southern border with Mexico. Avoiding the roadrunners that darted across the asphalt in front of us, we reached the Rio Grande and stopped to take a hike along the river. The Grand Canyon may be deeper, but Santa Elena Canyon is so narrow that we felt surrounded by the sheer rock, and its shade was a welcome relief from the rising heat of the day.

After our swim, we head back and climb into Gypsy. Sweaty and hungry, we each take a quick shower and change into clean clothes, then we make lunch, grateful that we have a bathroom and a kitchen with us at all times. We drive around Big Bend watching the local wildlife, who are clearly unafraid of humans. A herd of javelina pigs have made their home in a campground along the river. They are living in a campsite next to a sign that says *No Animals Allowed*. "Well," Aimee laughs, "I guess the javelinas haven't learned to read."

Heading toward our campground, we see a sign for Terlingua, an old mining town. It once produced most of America's mercury, then became a ghost town and is now an artist community of about 50 people. Terlingua's current claim to fame is that it hosts the country's longest running chili cook-off, which started in 1967 to settle an argument over who made the best chili. The first contest ended in a tie, so they held another competition the following year and a tradition was born. For four days each November, over 10,000 people arrive in Terlingua eager to find the best chili. We are six months too early for this year's contest, but the local watering hole advertises its "award-winning entry," so we buy some for dinner that night.

We pull into Maverick Ranch RV Park, where we will be staying for the night. After hooking up our water, sewer and electricity, I take my bike off the back of Gypsy and go for a ride, then Aimee and I have a swim in the campground pool. Aimee builds a campfire, and we eat Terlingua chili over spaghetti noodles as the sun sets and the mountains around us turn purple. After cleaning up, we sit outside watching the stars come out. According to the National Park Service, Big Bend has the darkest skies in the continental United States, and the Milky Way is a dense band stretching from horizon to horizon. We gaze in awe for over an hour before going inside to bed.

The next morning, I make coffee and straighten up Gypsy's living area while Aimee makes the bed and takes her shower. She does her morning yoga while I shower and unhook the electrical, water and sewer. In less than an hour, we are back on the road. We have done this over 500 times on our trip, so we know the routine very well.

We drive back to Terlingua, where the old Starlight Theatre doubles as a restaurant. Almost everyone comes in for brunch on Sunday mornings, so it is a great place to chat with the town's folks. After we fill up on BBQ'd local game meats and homemade Mexican vanilla ice cream, Aimee visits with the local artists and buys a painting to hang in Gypsy as a memento of our visit.

Then we face our biggest daily decision. Where should we go next? East toward San Antonio? West to El Paso? North to Amarillo? We have no specific destination or schedule, so we can go wherever we like. Aimee turns on some tunes and we head north, enjoying the desert's mild spring weather. A few miles outside of town, we stop to let a herd of wild Barbary sheep cross the road in front of us. The babies are curious, stopping in the middle of the road to stare at Gypsy until their mothers nudge them to safety on the other side of the road.

As we drive, we talk about politics, about our kids, about what it would be like to live in the desert, and about anything else that comes to mind. Mostly, we just enjoy the feeling of complete freedom together. We have spent nearly two years wandering around America, letting random chance guide us to the people and places that make our country so special. We have no idea what we will find next, but we have learned to appreciate the unexpected. We take every back road, follow every hand-lettered sign, and stop at any place that looks remotely interesting. We are experiencing America by Boldly Going Somewhere.

Monkey on Your Back

—*Aimee*—

Traveling with another person 24 hours a day in an enclosed space is an excellent way to get up close and personal with their vices. However, an RV trip is NOT a good time to address your partner's failings. Woe to the traveler who says: "You really should be drinking less coffee."

Ron had gotten used to my need for a morning espresso over the years, but he had no clue what a monkey I had on my back until we headed out in Gypsy. Each morning, I would snarl and grouch until we got rolling, then I'd look up the closest Starbucks and tell Ron to "Step On It!" so that I could get my four-shot latte. This worked reasonably well until we left the West Coast. I made the mistake of assuming that every town in America would have a Starbucks. Fool that I was. I now know that while there is a Starbucks in every state, their numbers dwindle to nearly non-existence in many places. Soon, I had to settle for a latte from almost anywhere. Espresso was a more exotic request than just a cup of coffee and often confused people. "FOUR SHOTS? Are you sure you want that?" I heard that question so often that I developed a standard response: "I grew up surfing in California, and we needed a strong coffee before we hit the waves."

One Sunday morning, we were driving on Highway 50 across Nevada and discovered that there were no open stores for the next 80 miles. Ron was wisely silent. He knew that I was twitchy. Near noon, we finally reached a small town with a single diner. Ron went inside and returned with two tiny cups filled with watery coffee.

"Best they could do. The waitress said that nobody has espresso around here," he said, trying to sound cheerful. "Tell you what. When we get to Reno, I'll get you an eight-shot latte!"

Smart guy. Many is the husband who would have pointed out that this experience was a sign and an opportunity to address my serious caffeine habit. That spouse would now be a lonely skeleton on the side of desolate Highway 50. Instead, Ron struck a pose reminiscent of the easy stance lion tamers take inside the cage. He knew that I might kill him, so he remained calm and nonthreatening.

Actually, caffeine was a vice that we both shared. Ron isn't a coffee drinker, but he loves an icy cold Coke. Only Coke and not even ordinary Coca-Cola will suffice. It must be in the iconic green glass bottle and made with cane sugar rather than corn sweeteners. This type of Coke isn't even made in the U.S. anymore. It has to be imported from Mexico. Unfortunately, not many stores carry "Hecho en Mexico" Cokes. Out of self-preservation, I Googled "Mexican Cokes near me" and what do you know? There's an app for everything. Now I can locate a Mexican Coke damn near anywhere.

Ron is as fussy about his vice as a wine connoisseur. His Coke needs to spend fifteen minutes in the freezer so that it is cold enough to have a scrim of ice, but not so cold that the syrup has frozen and separated from the water. He would get just as grouchy when deprived of his daily frosty Mexican Coke in a bottle as I did without my morning latte. It reminded me of…me!

Once, Ron drove all around the small town where we were staying, searching for my favorite brand of tequila. He finally found it at a defunct upholstery shop that had been converted into the "State Liquor and Package Outlet." Did Ron stop to question my desire for Patron Silver in the middle of nowhere? Nope. And I can tell you that he enjoyed a warm night's sleep, nestled next to his happy, snoring wife. In the morning, he bought my four-shot latte, and I loaded his Coke into the freezer. That, my friends, is what companionship looks like. So, I say: Embrace each other's quirks. A motorhome is too small for righteousness.

Why Did We Do It?

—Ron—

Why did we spend two years wandering around America in an RV? It's a question that we asked ourselves many times. Up to that point, Aimee and I had lived fairly typical lives. We had each worked for many years at large companies including General Electric and The Sharper Image. We had both been divorced, then found each other, got married and raised our combined four children together. After living in Los Angeles for several years, we moved to Northern California's wine country where I had grown up and where many of our family members and close friends were living. We bought 25 acres and built our dream home with plenty of room for the kids. It seemed like the perfect setting for the rest of our lives.

Nine years later, our children were grown and had moved away to different parts of the country. Taking care of our big house was getting more difficult as we got older. It felt like the property owned us. We decided to sell it and surprisingly, the buyers wanted it fully furnished. Suddenly, we found ourselves with very few possessions and even fewer responsibilities. It was a great opportunity to try something totally new.

Have you ever wondered what it would be like to wander around America with no destination or schedule, just to experience the country? How it would feel to get up in the morning, pick a direction and drive, not knowing what you would find—scenic beauty, quaint restaurants, and interesting people? Would you enjoy "walking lightly" across the land, staying a day or two in a place before moving on?

The idea intrigued us. During our business careers, we had visited almost every city in the US, but we wondered what the rest of the country was like. We wanted to find the places that are symbols of America. We dreamed of small towns with family-run restaurants, shady parks and public pools filled with splashing kids. We wanted to see our country's natural scenery, the mountains, deserts, lakes, and coastlines. We wondered if we could spot antelope, buffalo, bighorn sheep, moose, flamingoes and manatees in the wild.

We owned a motorhome and had taken many trips with our kids as they were growing up. It had been a great way to spend time together seeing America, fueled by snack food as we cruised Historic Route 66 with the sounds of the Temptations blaring from the cassette player speakers. Our planned routes were always subject to change and some of our best experiences were completely unexpected. Someone would point out an interesting road sign, I would yell "Coming out of warp!" and hit the brakes and another adventure would begin. The trips were wonderful, but after a week, the kids were always ready to get back to their normal routine. What it would be like to live on the road for a year or more, just the two of us?

While many people live in their RVs, most full-timers stay in a location for six months or more, often working there to pay for their campsite. Others spend the winter in their RV at a warm weather location, then return home in the spring. Our concept was different. We wanted to see as much of America as possible, so we would be driving almost every day, wandering like legendary gypsies, albeit with modern plumbing. The idea was a little scary because we didn't know if people would be friendly to passing strangers, but we decided that we had to give it a try.

We certainly did not take our trip to write a book about it. I love to tell stories, but when I try to write I'm like a kid cleaning his room—every part of the process is a chore. Writing together was even more difficult, because Aimee and I have very different writing styles and had experienced living on the road in different ways. Ultimately, we decided to take advantage of our different perspectives by writing separately. My chapters focus on external things like locations and activities, while Aimee's chapters describe what it's like to have a relationship while living in a small metal tent that is constantly on the move.

Despite the challenges, telling our story brought the memories back to life for us, and we hope that it helps people who are considering a similar trip. By reading about what it is like to live on the road, it may be easier for you to take the plunge and have the experience of a lifetime.

Our title "Boldly Going Somewhere" is a nod to Star Trek, our favorite TV show, and the inspiration for our travel strategy.

I've Met a Man and He Lives in a Motorhome

—Aimee—

"I'll never forget what Aimee told me about Ron after their first date." said my Maid of Honor Erica as she began her toast at our wedding.

It was 2001 and I sat in a beautiful outdoor tent, wearing my wine-colored wedding dress, and smiling at the speech that I knew my friend was about to give.

"'I've met a man and he lives in a motorhome.' That's what Aimee said to me about Ron, and I'll never forget it."

Erica went on to describe to our wedding guests how Ron and I had met on a job interview. He was the CEO of an Internet company, and I was interviewing for the VP of Human Resources job. I decided not to take the job after Ron and I realized that we had a lot of personal chemistry that could be awkward in a work environment. Erica explained how Ron and I had talked over the phone, how I had accepted his invitation for dinner and how Ron had showed up for the date in his motorhome.

"So began their adventures together; hopefully the beginning of many more," she finished with a flourish and downed her champagne.

It was all true. Ron had been living in Southern California at the time, flying up to his company's office in Redwood City each Monday and back home on Friday. Rather than stay in a hotel, he had purchased a motorhome as a place to live on the nights when he was in town. He also used it to hold business meetings, calling it his "mobile command center." It might have seemed strange anywhere else, but in 1999 Silicon Valley was in the middle of the Internet craze and things were as groovy as in the late 60's Summer of Love. Everyone was having office Nerf Gun battles and taking Segway Scooters to work. Having a CEO who lived in an RV and used it as an office was pretty tame. In any event, it was his only vehicle in Northern California, so he arrived at my house driving a 29-foot RV.

I didn't mind. After a string of dates with men who had fast hands and smarmy attitudes, Ron was a breath of fresh air. Besides being smart and funny, he was a down-to-earth family man who loved kids. Usually when I revealed that I was a single mom, a prospective beau would pause and then say, "Well, that's all right," as if having a child was a flaw that might be overlooked if I was attractive enough. When Ron asked me out and I told him that I had a daughter, his immediate response was, "Great! Bring her along!"

As an added benefit, the motorhome was like a playground for my four-year-old. She climbed into the loft area over the cab, made herself a nest and claimed it as her own. Later that evening, when Ron and I shared a goodnight kiss, her little blond head appeared hanging upside down, grinning as she broke up our romantic moment.

That night was the beginning of a relationship that would come to define us. In the months that followed, we dated and grew closer. Dakota and I got used to seeing Ron roll up in his motorhome wearing a business suit and tie and off we would go together. We could have taken my car, but having a full bath, kitchen and bedroom at our disposal turned out to be a tremendous luxury.

After we married in 2001, I brought my daughter to live in Los Angeles with Ron's three kids. Ron eventually left the Internet company and stopped living in his motorhome, but we still used it frequently. We took our kids on road trips through the Southwest, seeing Route 66, the Grand Canyon, Area 51 and Las Vegas. On holidays, we would take the RV to visit family in Northern California and make midnight runs down I-5, stopping only for gas and Dairy Queen sundaes and pulling up to our house as the sun came up. A couple of times when we were forced to evacuate our house during the LA fire season, we packed up the entire family, including the dogs and headed north to camp on the beach until the danger had passed. When we coached our kids' basketball teams, we used the RV as our team bus to take them to their games. Sometimes Ron and I snuck away in the RV to for a date night, enjoying some private time together as we watched the stars or a meteor shower in the mountains behind Ojai.

Having an RV was a big part of our history together, so it wasn't that much of a leap to consider living in it for our next big adventure. I guess my Maid of Honor had it right all along.

Picking Our Prairie Schooner

—Ron—

Having committed to try living on the road, we had to decide what type of vehicle would work best for our trip. We weren't exactly pioneers going into an uncharted wilderness, but we still wanted to have the right covered wagon.

A trailer was the most economical option, since we already had a vehicle that could tow it. We also liked the flexibility of a trailer. We could leave it at the campground while we used our SUV for local sightseeing. On the other hand, pulling a trailer big enough to live in would be a challenge. I had pulled horse trailers growing up, so I knew that driving a large trailer through the mountains, in the cities or anyplace with strong winds could be very stressful. The other drawback of a trailer was that we couldn't access its living area while we were driving. That meant that Aimee wouldn't be able to use the bathroom or fix me a snack as we rolled down the road. It was a small thing, but we had grown used to it during our motorhome trips.

We also looked at the large "A" Class motorhomes that are seen cruising majestically down the freeway. They are basically a house on wheels, over 40 feet long with multiple beds, a full kitchen, large bathroom, huge TV and even a built-in washer & dryer. They are great for staying in one place for a long period of time, but nearly impossible to drive on narrow roads, which didn't fit our vision of exploring the backroads of America.

In the end, we chose to stay with the Fleetwood 29-foot Class C motorhome that we had used for our trips with the kids. It was small enough to navigate narrow country roads, but it had plenty of room for the two of us, with a queen-size bed in the back, a couch in the living area that folded out into a double bed and a large loft above the cab. Its 10-cylinder gas engine combined power and reasonable fuel economy. I had owned this model for 15 years and was comfortable driving it even on city streets, so we would not need to tow a car. However, our motorhome was nearly 20 years old and had over 140,000 miles on it. Nicknamed the Desert Weasel for its many trips through the Southwest (or the Dessert Weasel for the many snacks that were eaten during those trips), it had been a faithful vacation vehicle, but we had serious concerns about living in it as we drove another 100,000 miles. Fortunately, Aimee found a newer model for sale that had been driven less than 3,000 miles and was in mint condition. Its owners had bought it with visions of camping under the stars with their kids while still having real beds, a kitchen, and a private bathroom. When they realized that they were only using it once or twice a year, they decided to sell their expensive toy. We grabbed her and named her "Gypsy" in keeping with the carefree lifestyle that we were seeking.

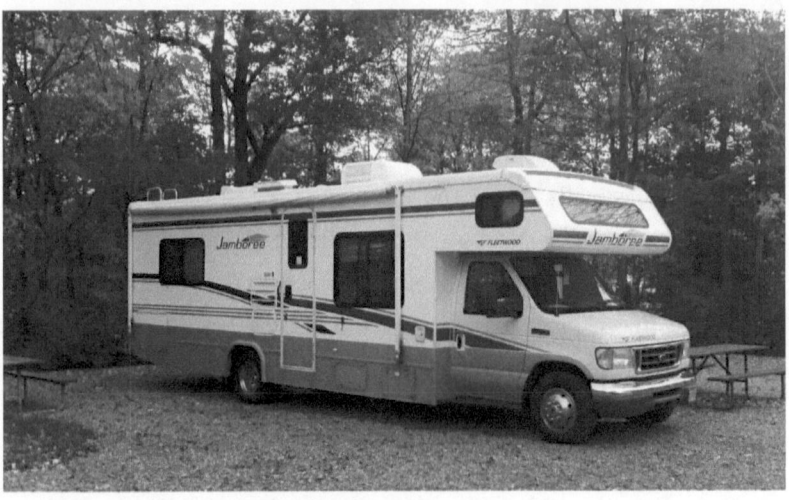

The Squeak

—Aimee—

I'm sure most RV owners would agree that one of the more maddening things is "The Squeak." The Squeak is an intermittent noise that you hear while driving, but it cannot be readily located. It seems to come from nowhere and everywhere at once. When we got our first motorhome, I would literally creep around while we were driving down the road, listening for odd noises and pressing on things while yelling to Ron, "Does that make it better?"

These noises are caused by the basic physics of mass, velocity, and momentum. Think of an RV as a doll house on wheels. It's somewhat flimsy, two sizes too small and full of household items. And every motorhome, like every boat or car, has its own idiosyncrasies.

The first time we took Gypsy out on the road everything rattled. Metal pans clattered and glassware made ominous musical noises in the cupboards. Things upended and slid around inside the refrigerator. Eventually, we learned how to stack pans with no-slip materials between them and stock the fridge so that the eggs and milk stayed put, but we still experienced The Squeak on a regular basis.

Objects that are making noises are primarily doing it because they are on the move, so where you put things is critical. Once, a can of tuna flew past my head when Ron hit the brakes to avoid hitting a squirrel that was crossing the road. I had foolishly loaded a cabinet that faced directly toward the driving area with canned goods and pasta sauces. I had congratulated myself for putting the tuna in between the pasta sauce jars to keep them from clinking against each other, ignoring the fact that a stomp on the brakes would not stop the cans and jars from moving at whatever speed and direction we had been going. When Ron saved that squirrel's life, everything in the cabinet including the tuna can continued cruising forward at forty miles per hour, popping the cabinet latch and raining cans and jars all over Gypsy. From then on, I learned to store heavy objects in the side cabinets of the kitchen. What happens to objects in the side cabinets when we hit the brakes? They shift sideways, not forwards! Let me give a shout out to my high school physics teacher, Mr. Wasserman: Thanks!

"Objects may have shifted during flight" is also a phrase to remember in a motorhome. You must assume any cabinet that you open will have something fall out of it, often landing on an unsuspecting spouse. I learned to open cabinet doors slowly, with my other hand ready to catch that can of chili as it dropped out.

Packing an RV with an understanding of the forces of mass and velocity is truly important. You can't just leave things on your tables or counters and expect them to stay put. Let's say you like to have a bottle of fragrant hand soap and a box of Kleenex on the bathroom vanity. You had better find a way to secure them or expect a nasty surprise when they migrate across the countertop. I wanted to have actual art prints on our walls, but how do you attach a picture to the bedroom wall that was constantly bouncing around? Industrial double-sided Velcro and Command Strips is how. I loved those giant Command Strips!

My tiny bedside closet was located ten feet behind the rear wheels, which made that area of the RV act like a giant springboard. The first time we hit a bump in the road, the closet door banged open, my hanging clothes jumped off the closet rod, and everything came flying out onto the floor. I wanted to blame Ron's driving, but the fact was that you just can't jam a full wardrobe into a closet the size of a large suitcase. Fifty pounds of clothing moving at fifty miles an hour will inevitably burst the closet latch. I ended up ditching most of the hangers in favor of folded clothes stacked on the closet floor.

Sometimes, we just tried to ignore a new squeak that we failed to find, but it was hard to enjoy each other's company with a constant annoying noise. Our earlier experience with motorhomes had also taught us that an unusual noise can represent something significant. At one point, "The Desert Weasel" had developed a strange whistling noise around the cab area. Ron and I could feel air blowing in but couldn't locate precisely where it was coming from. We thought that perhaps the weather stripping was getting old. After all, the rig had been used for years to take the kids out on camping trips and was getting a bit elderly. The noise got louder over a period of a few months. I got very worried when I started to see a bit of daylight in the seal between the cab and the boxy part of the rig that your RV superstore may refer to as "The Coach." We went to a Camping World, where the technician told us that the screws holding the cab to the coach had mostly been sheared off by some tremendous force. Had we driven over some terribly bumpy highway? We shrugged as if it were a mystery.

It wasn't really a mystery. Ron's favorite trick in the Desert Weasel was to load our kids and their friends on the rear bed and drive at 40 miles an hour over a local set of railroad tracks. The tracks had a steep rise followed by a dip in the road, which created a perfect springboard at the back of the RV. The joyfully screaming kids were launched into the air, their shoes flying off in every direction. To them, it was like a magic trick, and they would beg Ron to do it over and over again. Putting that much torque on the RV as we did the "diving board maneuver" must have sheared the screws. I probably shouldn't be admitting that we ever did something so clearly nuts and ultimately expensive, but what wouldn't you do to bring that much joy to a kid? We quietly paid to have the cab repaired and took it a little easier on our "Fun with Physics" approach to parenting after that.

Over time, Gypsy's squeaks become as familiar as a creaky board in a house. Every so often there would be another sound that had to be identified and silenced. A small breath of air and a whining noise in the back? Someone left the bedroom window ajar. An annoying rattle from the kitchen? It's probably a loose rubber grommet on the stovetop. Loud thump as we leave our campground? The sink cover had fallen to the floor. As I said, it was part of Gypsy's unique character and charm.

So don't be deterred if you are thinking about buying an RV, every conveyance has these quirks. I bet the Space Shuttle has a squeak.

Less Is More

—Ron—

Our next big challenge was packing for the trip. Like most people, we loved stuff and believed that "more is better." Our American Dream had always included a big house filled with stuff. Two or three cars? Check. Multiple computers? Check. Wall-sized TV? Check. Staggering array of kitchen appliances? Check. But having lots of stuff wouldn't work when we were living in Gypsy. There simply wasn't room. Gypsy was bigger than a Conestoga wagon, but tiny compared to what we were accustomed to. We couldn't take it all. Hell, we couldn't take 10 percent of it. We had to downsize every part of our daily routine and get honest about what we really needed. In the process, we learned a lot about ourselves.

We made list after list as we debated what we would need on the road. Books? Yes. My favorite electric griddle? Nope. Extra bedding and blankets? Some. Cell phones for each of us? Absolutely. We wanted to be pioneers, but not Robinson Crusoe.

Gypsy needed certain equipment to operate, including a freshwater hose, sewer hose, and leveling blocks. It was important to have spares of these items, as we learned after spending three hours in a wilderness campground one evening trying to repair our sewer hose. We also needed some outdoor gear, like folding chairs, cots, a cooking grill, and campfire tools. We managed to squeeze it all into Gypsy's outside storage compartments, but everything else had to fit inside.

Gypsy's interior had roughly 200 square feet of living space, with most of it taken up by the bed, couch, dining table, shower, cabinets, and built-in appliances. There wasn't much room left for storage. Gypsy's designers were clearly aware of this problem and had tried to use any available space to create additional storage. We pictured their engineers in white lab coats, chattering enthusiastically about their latest creative storage ideas. "We have an extra 2 inches above the sink, so let's put in a spice rack." "Let's cut slots for sharp knives in the countertop directly behind the stove, where you can reach for them while the burner is on." "There's some space in the wall behind the kitchen table, so let's put a two-foot-deep nook there." These were all real storage areas in Gypsy. Even the bed could be lifted up to access a 25 square foot compartment, which was really helpful, except that it took both hands to hold it open, so reaching in to get something meant possibly smashing a finger. Even with her creatively designed storage areas, packing Gypsy took some major ingenuity.

We began with clothing. We needed clothes for all kinds of weather, but our bedroom had just three feet of closet space and four tiny drawers. Our jackets alone took up half of the closet space. No more looking at rows of clothing, deciding what to wear that day. I went from thirty pairs of pants to five—two pairs of blue jeans, two pair of Dockers and one pair of dress slacks. Shirts, shoes, gym clothes, even underwear and socks went through the pruning process, and I was amazed at how hard it was to leave good clothing behind. It was even worse for Aimee, who had built up her wardrobe lovingly over many years. After what we thought were extreme measures, we still had twice as much clothing as we had space. It was time to think outside of the box. We had each brought a carry-on suitcase for those occasions when we needed to leave Gypsy overnight. I put my everyday clothes into one suitcase and stored it in the loft above the cab where it was easy to reach. Since we did laundry almost every day, it held plenty of clothes for my needs. We filled the other suitcase with our off-season clothes, although we quickly found that "off-season" is as much about location as the calendar. Albuquerque in May is shorts weather, but a few hours' drive north into the Rockies and it's time for the heavy coat and gloves.

Next was the kitchen. At home, we had lots of cabinets and counter space. My KitchenAid full stand mixer, which had made many chocolate chip cookies over the years, proudly stood on our kitchen countertop. We even had a large pantry that let us stock up when things were on sale. By contrast, Gypsy's kitchen storage consisted of four small cabinets, three tiny drawers and a miniature refrigerator. Counterspace was equally limited and difficult to use for storage because items tended to shift around when we were driving. We pruned our kitchen items as diligently as pioneers setting out in their Conestoga wagon. All the dishes had to be stackable inside each other. Our cookware collection was reduced to two skillets, two saucepans and a stock pot. The only kitchen appliance to make the cut was a toaster oven that we wedged into the corner behind the sink while we drove. All our non-refrigerated food items had to fit into five feet of shelf space. No more deciding which cereal sounded good— now it was Shredded Wheat or nothing. We also got creative on food storage. We put the fresh fruit and bread in the oven while we were driving and pulled them back out on the counters after we stopped each night. This got us a strange look from a Canadian Customs officer when he found our oven full of bananas during his inspection.

Then there was the bathroom. We were used to a large, luxurious master bathroom filled with make-up and other mysterious skin and hair care products. There was no way they would fit in Gypsy's tiny bathroom. Fortunately, Gypsy had a split bathroom with a separate shower across the hall from the vanity and toilet area, which made the shower and the vanity area a little bigger. This design also meant that when the door to the vanity area was opened, it closed off the bathroom and the bedroom from the living area. This gave Aimee a place to shower and dress in private each morning, an important part of being able to live together in tight quarters. The shower had two small shelves and the vanity area had two tiny cabinets. Not a lot to work with, but we had used dopp kits for our daily toiletry items during our many years of business travel, so we each made one and tucked them into a corner on the floor. That left the cabinets for our medications and miscellaneous items. Now the storage compartment under the bed proved its worth. Aimee's hair care items went there, along with the other bathroom products that we didn't need every day but could be crucial. For example, the vanity cupboard was only big enough to store one extra roll of toilet paper and while we were willing to cut back on a lot of things in our new lifestyle, toilet paper wasn't one of them.

Finally, we needed room for our books and important papers. We used to have bookshelves throughout our house and a dedicated home office. Not possible in Gypsy, so we improvised. Our home office became a laptop and a small file box stored in the loft. We crammed 20 books in the nook behind the kitchen table and swapped them at the campgrounds along our route. It was fun to see what other campers were reading as we went across the country. We wondered why there were so many romance novels, but I'm sure that they had similar questions when we left Aimee's horror novels behind.

When we had finished packing, we had everything that we thought we really needed, just not as nearly as much of it as we were used to. After a while, we found that we didn't miss the extra stuff. Daily tasks like cooking and clean-up were easier with fewer possessions and everything was within arms' reach.

After we finished our trip, we spent three months traveling overseas using only our two carry-on suitcases from Gypsy. We watched people in airports with their huge stacks of luggage and wondered how it would ever fit in their rental car. We had spent two years living small and learned to enjoy it—pretty amazing by American standards.

Squid Sucker

—*Aimee*—

It was not the prospect of hours of driving together, getting lost or breaking down in the middle of nowhere that worried me about our trip. It was Ron's snoring.

Have you ever accidentally sucked up some loose change or bobby pins while vacuuming? Take that horrible rattling noise and add the deep sucking sound an octopus or squid might make if you repeatedly ran it over with a vacuum cleaner and you might come close to the noises that my husband makes in the night. It might be bearable if his snoring was regular, but it isn't. It's randomly punctuated by giant snorts and gagging noises. Sometimes there is a minute or two of blissful silence and I think "Okay, now I can relax," but soon it starts up again even louder than before.

Ron's snoring was the stuff of legend. People sharing a hotel room with him slept in the bathtub or outside in their cars to avoid it. On camping trips, Ron was not allowed to set up his cot within 50 feet of other people. The kids said that they could hear him snoring when they were staying at a friend's house down the street.

Even though he does not believe that his snoring is as bad as people say, Ron has tried numerous snoring solutions over the years, including "snore guards," which are basically a prizefighter's mouth guard designed to keep the jaw wedged open and allow more air in. I call them "snore mufflers" because they dampen the noise but don't stop the snoring. Worse, Ron often spits out his snore guard during the night. Not surprisingly, a snore guard is less effective when it is lodged in someone's armpit rather than in their mouth.

You're probably asking yourself, "Why didn't he get a CPAP machine? He clearly has sleep apnea!" It seems easy to suggest that. However, Ron hated the idea of basically wearing SCUBA gear to bed. Those of you who are married will understand that you can make suggestions to your spouse, but ultimately your partner's health decisions are theirs to make. Instead, Ron would say to "gently tell him that he is snoring, and he will stop." Surprise! The gentle reminder strategy did not work.

At any rate, the idea of trying to sleep in a metal can next to my Squid Sucking Snorer was more than daunting. What would I do, curled up in a tiny RV bed next to my deafening husband? At home, we had a large Master bedroom with a king-size bed and lots of bedding, allowing me to build a wall of linens between us to muffle the sound. If necessary, I could even move to our guest bedroom and catch a few hours of shuteye, Ron's snores dimly echoing through the walls. In Gypsy, there would be no place to go. I was terrified.

I ended up trying a variety of things. I would shout "IS YOUR MOUTHGUARD IN?" at ungodly hours. Ron would fish around in the bed until he found it and jam the muffling device back in. I also developed my own brand of mixed martial arts in the bed—punching, kicking, and wrestling Ron into different positions until I found one that allowed him to breathe quietly. A few times, I even tried sedating myself with a late-night cocktail or a shot of Nyquil (don't judge if you haven't been there.)

Gypsy did offer one big advantage—her HVAC system that was like a huge white noise machine. I eventually slept with the fan on at gale force levels with a circle of pillows surrounding my ears like a muffling crown. I also started going to bed before Ron in the hopes of drifting into deeper sleep before he began snoring.

Eventually we worked it out. The white noise, mouthguard and early-to-bed pattern all helped. Having a workout regimen also seemed to reduce his snoring. After a while, it rarely kept me awake.

Ironically, Ron says that I now snore. He says that it is "charming." I tell him to nudge me gently and I'll stop. I think it will work.

Getting Started

—Ron—

We began our new life on the road with a shakedown trip around California. We had driven much of our home state before, but it was always on a schedule. Now we were free to go anywhere we wanted at whatever pace suited us. We rented a storage space for the few things that we were leaving behind and took off, stopping only to sell our last remaining car at a local dealership. Aimee said that we were like Cortes burning his ships after arriving in the New World—there was no going back.

The first night, staying at the San Francisco RV Resort in the seaside town of Pacifica, we faced the first challenge of our new lifestyle: Juno was determined to sleep with us in our bed. On our vacation trips, she had always shared the couch bed with our daughter Kim. Juno would gradually spread out during the night, and in the morning, it was fun to see whether she had pushed Kim entirely off the bed. Juno felt that sleeping with humans was her right, but after much discussion, we eventually we got her to sleep on couch as long as she had Apache for company.

The next morning, we headed south on Highway 1 to explore the California coast. In Santa Cruz, we walked along the beach boardwalk and rode on the rickety wooden roller coaster and classic carousel, then played PacMan and Space Invaders in a huge video game arcade, feeling like we were kids again. We toured Monterey's Cannery Row and world-famous Aquarium. Outside of Hearst Castle in San Simeon, we stopped at Elephant Seal Beach, with its colony of over 100 elephant seals. The huge males were raucous as they competed for the attention of the females, and Apache wasn't sure whether he should chase them or run away in terror. In Morro Bay, we rented a kayak to explore the birds and sea life, including a sea otter that let us paddle right up next to him as he floated on his back eating his breakfast. We walked around downtown Pismo Beach, a classic beach vacation town filled with small shops, food stands and saltwater taffy. We ate barbequed tri-tip in Santa Maria, where it was first introduced to California by Mexican vaqueros. We stayed at Hobson County Park, a small campground on the ocean between Santa Barbara and Ventura. I rode my bike on the paved Rincon Bike Trail that ran along the shore next to the 101 freeway, then went body surfing in the ocean to cool off. Later, we sat around our campfire and watched the sunset. It felt like the first week of summer vacation, full of fun with no end in sight.

Nearing Los Angeles, we spent a night at Malibu Beach RV Park, which was expensive, but the location was worth it, situated on a bluff overlooking the Pacific Ocean, with the lights of Los Angeles off in the distance. We walked down the hillside path to the local seafood restaurant, then sat around our campfire enjoying the view and the evening air. In the morning, we ate breakfast outside and watched whales and dolphins cruise by in the ocean below.

We took a detour to Agoura Hills, where we had lived before moving to Sonoma County, and ate lunch at the Agoura Deli, my favorite delicatessen in America. Everything on its enormous menu is delicious, from the New York style bagels to their signature Santa Maria style skirt steak. To top it off, they make the best éclair that I have eaten anywhere in the world. Afterwards, we sat in the park and talked about how much we had enjoyed living in Southern California, swimming in our pool, or going to the beach nearly every day. It had been a great part of our lives, but we were ready to start living a different chapter. Aimee played Willie Nelson's "On the Road Again" and we headed out.

We drove east through Los Angeles and north on Highway 395 along the eastern edge of California, with the snow-capped Sierra Nevada mountains on one side and the desert on the other. We camped on Mount Whitney in a site that was surrounded by trees and backed onto a creek, all for five dollars a night. In one day, we had gone from glamping in Malibu to dirt camping in the mountains, and both were wonderful. Further north, we took Route 158 to the beautiful glacial Silver Lake and spent the night at a campground set in the trees by the lakeshore. The dogs were eager to chase the local wildlife, but neither wanted to try swimming in the icy-cold water. For Juno, lying next to the campfire was a much better idea.

We turned west on State Route 89 and State Route 4 through several old gold-mining towns and entered the Delta, a 1,150 square mile estuary nicknamed "California's Holland." The Delta's 700 miles of slow-moving waterways and 250 islands have long attracted people as a place to relax and enjoy its leisurely nature. Erle Stanley Gardner, creator of Perry Mason, wrote a book called *Gypsy Days on the Delta* describing the tranquil pleasures of life on a houseboat there and I was eager to see it for the first time.

When we arrived at 5pm, I wondered if we were in the wrong place. It was hot and muggy, with clouds of mosquitos everywhere. The muddy water of the river wound through barren fields dotted with old buildings, rusty vehicles and endless litter. Our campground could be kindly described as "weathered" and most of its spaces were occupied by ancient trailers that would never move again. The beach at the campground had signs warning against entering the water. We retreated to Gypsy, locked the doors, turned on the A/C and went to bed.

We woke up the next morning to a different world. Peace and tranquility infused everything. The moisture of the river brought a softness to the air and filtered the morning light. The insects sang but did not bite. The foghorn call of a barge carrying its cargo to San Francisco Bay seemed like part of the natural setting. Now, the Delta urged us to rent a houseboat, put out a fishing pole with a piece of cork and float gently through life. As we drove away, I the wondered how many other "off the beaten path" jewels were out there waiting for us.

We headed back to Sonoma County, pleased with our experience so far. We had driven 1,200 miles in eight days, averaging three hours a day, which had given us plenty of time to stop and explore. On vacation, we had always been forced to choose what things we had time to see, but now we could stop at any place that looked interesting. The dogs had enjoyed riding with us and behaved themselves when we stopped. Living in Gypsy's small space had its challenges, but we were adapting and had already begun to think of it as home. Our youngest daughter was attending Oregon State University in Corvallis, so we bought a little house there to give us an address, then we packed up Gypsy, loaded the dogs and hit the road again. We were ready for more.

The Mystic Inn, Mystic, Connecticut

Driving down the New England coastline, we stumbled upon the Mystic Inn, set on a knoll overlooking Mystic Sound. Our room had a wood fireplace and an oversized jetted soaking tub, perfect for soaking out the kinks of the road. The restaurant on the property featured a phenomenal Happy Hour food menu and Mystic Soup Company across the street made the best soup that we found on our trip. We walked around town, then took food back to our room for long baths and naps in front of the fire. It was a postcard of a New England seaside getaway.

Lake Quinault Lodge, Washington

We were driving the Olympic Peninsula when we came across this historic lodge. Built in 1926, it looks like a large rustic estate house, with the exterior covered with shingles, the interior made from natural woods and a huge fireplace as the centerpiece. They had a last-minute cancellation, so we got a room and spent the day lounging on the lawn and swimming in the lake. We ate dinner in their restaurant that looked over the water with the mountains in the background. The Roosevelt Classic Pot Roast, named in honor of the President's visit in 1937, was worth the trip all by itself.

Kimpton Marlowe, Boston, Massachusetts

We wanted to visit Boston without subjecting Gypsy to the city's suicidal drivers, so we decided to stay in a hotel. We picked the Kimpton Marlowe because it had good access to the major roads, but it had everything else that we wanted as well. They let us park Gypsy in their secure parking area so that we could get to our things easily and not worry about whether she was safe. The hotel's décor is spectacular, from the elaborate entryway to the traditional bar club room with overstuffed chairs that urged us to order a cognac from the bar. Our room was luxurious with a beautiful view of the city. We ordered room service and spent a night being pampered. In the morning, the hotel let us use one of their kayaks to paddle on the Charles River, then we walked around the historic downtown area. It was such a perfect way to see Boston that we went back the following year.

Many Springs Resort, Flathead Lake, Montana

This was the best "off the beaten path" lodging of our entire trip. We were driving around the back side of Flathead Lake to see the cherry orchards when we passed an old, faded sign for the Many Springs Resort. We were curious, so we pulled over and called the phone number. After many rings a lady answered and told us that they had rooms available. We drove down their steep, narrow driveway to find a wonderful lakeside inn with a fantastic restaurant. We booked a large room with jacuzzi tub right on the lake. We swam in the crystal-clear water off the dock, then ate in the restaurant and watched the sunset over the lake and the surrounding mountains. It was such a spectacular place that we went back and spent several days there relaxing toward the end of our trip.

Providence Biltmore, Providence, Rhode Island

It was Aimee's birthday, and she wanted to see the final resting place of H.P. Lovecraft, one of her favorite authors. We decided to celebrate by staying in Providence so that we could experience the atmosphere of the area where he lived and worked. I booked a room at the Providence Biltmore, the grand hotel of Providence. Built in 1922 by the designer of NYC's Grand Central Station, it is listed in the National Register of Historic Places and featured in many movies and TV shows. From the amazing architecture of its two-story entrance to the luxurious comfort of its rooms, spending a night at the Biltmore was like living in 1940's grand style. We ordered a traditional Delmonico steak dinner from the hotel restaurant and pretended that we were Clark Gable and Carole Lombard in a romantic movie.

The Hilton, Marco Island, Florida

A sudden tropical storm hit Marco Island and knowing how hurricanes and tornados love RV parks, we decided to park Gypsy in a sheltered place and stay in a hotel for the night. When we got to the Hilton, it looked so nice that we used my Hilton Honors points to spend two days enjoying the luxury of an Executive Room. We watched the storm rage around us, thankful that Gypsy was safe in the hotel's sheltered parking lot. Aimee took a video of the storm on her phone that was picked up by the local TV news and it was fun watching the broadcast, yelling "Aimee took that video!" After the storm passed, we swam in the huge pool, walked on the beach and made several visits to the hotel restaurant.

Red Cliffs Lodge, Moab, Utah

This was our first hotel stay during our trip. We had spent the day wandering around Moab and were headed toward Grand Junction, Colorado. On a whim, we decided to take the small Highway 128 that wound along the Colorado River. We had gone 14 miles when we saw a sign for Castle Creek Winery. "A winery!" I exclaimed. "I didn't know that they had wineries in Utah!" As it turns out, it was one of six wineries in the state. While we were there, we saw a brochure for their sister property, the Red Cliffs Lodge. "A bathtub!" said Aimee. "Please!!" We went over and found that they had large hacienda-style rooms overlooking the Colorado River, a fitness center, a huge pool, a working cattle ranch, a horse stable and a restaurant that featured buffalo ribeye steaks. And they were dog-friendly!

Best Scenic Drives

Highway 12 from Lewiston, Idaho to Missoula, Montana

We found this road by accident when we were making our way through Oregon on our way to Yellowstone National Park. Aimee loves Pendleton blankets, so we decided to stop in Pendleton to see how it all started. After taking the factory tour and buying several items, we decided to drive the back roads and ended up staying in Clarkston, Washington at a great RV park on the Snake River. From there, the shortest route to Yellowstone was on Highway 12 for 200 miles along the Clearwater River to Missoula, Montana. It is a beautiful scenic drive through the mountains, with several places to stop and swim.

The Blue Ridge Parkway, Charlottesville, Virginia

We had heard so much about the Blue Ridge Parkway that we were afraid that it would not measure up to its reputation. Still, no road trip would be complete without this classic drive, so we gave it a try. We left Charlottesville just after Thanksgiving and the fall colors were breathtaking. Winding through the dense forests of the Blue Ridge Mountains with the leaves falling and creeks babbling along the road was almost too perfect to believe. We even got to protect a mama bear who was walking down the middle of the Parkway while her cub tried to keep pace from off the road. We drove slowly and honked the horn until her cub got upset and started crying, at which point she decided to go back into the woods.

Oak Creek Canyon from Flagstaff to Sedona, Arizona

We found this route in a book of America's Most Scenic Drives when we were taking the kids around the Southwest. It was so beautiful that we made a detour to see it again and it had the best red rock scenery that we found on our trip. Starting 6 miles south of Flagstaff, Highway 89A winds for 12 miles through the Oak Creek Canyon, providing spectacular views of green vegetation set against the red rock with a ribbon of blue water running down the center. Its only drawback is that the road is very steep and difficult to drive, dropping over 2,000 feet in eight miles through a series of hairpin turns. When we reached the bottom, we stopped to play in the water at Slide Rock State Park and let Gypsy's brakes cool off.

Overseas Highway through the Florida Keys

This was another classic route, over 100 miles long with the Atlantic Ocean on one side and the Gulf of Mexico on the other, with the water often only a few feet away from the road. Pelicans lined the pier posts or flew alongside us like guides showing us the way to the next fish restaurant. Every few miles there was another beautiful beach where we could take a break from driving and picnic, swim or take a nap. And we never got tired of the spectacular sunsets.

Northern drive through Yellowstone and on to Cody, Wyoming

While the most popular drive through Yellowstone is the route through the center of the park that includes Old Faithful and the Park headquarters, we preferred the northern route because there was more wildlife available to see. Leaving the park from the northeast corner we then took the winding road through the canyons to Cody, Wyoming. It is 175 miles of rugged natural beauty, with huge meadows, rivers, red rock canyons all teeming with wildlife.

Best Places to See

The House on the Rock, Wisconsin

This was the epitome of Americana, a huge complex structure built on a massive 200 ft high rock that has more visitors than any other place in Wisconsin. Its history is a combination of fact and legend, including a story that it was built to spite Frank Lloyd Wright, whose home is nearby. Inside is a series of rooms with every sort of collection imaginable. Dolls, guns, nautical equipment, chandeliers, model airplanes, automatic music machines and the world's largest indoor carousel. Even the hallways that snake between the rooms are filled with items. Outside is an elaborate set of Japanese gardens. We walked nearly 3 miles doing the tour, so we also got our workout for the day.

Rock & Roll Hall of Fame, Cleveland, Ohio

After years of hearing about it on TV and the movies, the Rock & Roll Hall of Fame was high on Aimee's list of things to see on our trip. Situated on the shores of Lake Erie, the building was designed by I.M. Pei, famous for designing the Louvre Pyramid. We wandered through seven floors of exhibits about rock, soul, gospel and country music. We tested our knowledge at the interactive "One Hit Wonder" and "Songs that Shaped Rock & Roll" exhibits. Just before we left, we had our picture taken and put on a fake cover of Rolling Stone Magazine. While we were standing in line with about 30 other people, we realized that we were both quietly singing Dr. Hook's "Gonna get my picture on the cover, gonna buy five copies for my mother." The other people looked at us and suddenly they all burst out with, "Wanna see my smiling face on the cover of the Rolling Stone!" The cameraman just said tiredly, "Gee, I've never heard that before."

Basketball Hall of Fame, Springfield, Massachusetts

Basketball is my favorite sport. I played for over 45 years and coached each of my kids' teams. Aimee also loves the game and we coached together for several years. So, it's not surprising that the Basketball Hall of Fame was one of our favorite stops on our trip. It is a shrine to the sport, its exhibits covering all levels of the game for both men and women. We walked around, soaking up the history of the game from peach baskets to the Splash Brothers. There is even a regulation hardwood basketball court and we spent an hour shooting baskets. No scouts approached us, although Aimee's talent and 6' height got some appreciative looks.

Grand Coulee Dam, Washington

This was our favorite man-made sight and a tribute to American determination. Located in the middle of a barren landscape nearly 100 miles from Spokane and over 200 miles from Seattle, it was the world's largest hydroelectric dam when it opened in 1942, and it is still the largest power station in the United States. Over 8,000 people worked on its construction, building roads and support buildings as well as the dam itself. The temperatures were below freezing for nearly 6 months of the year and most of the workers' housing lacked electricity, yet the dam was completed in just seven years. It provided irrigation to over 1,000 square miles of farmland and its electricity was critical to winning WWII. Walking through the exhibits and hearing the stories of the workers made us feel proud and humble.

What's Next
—Ron—

It's been three years since we finished our trip. We came back to our house in Oregon and spent several months adjusting to a more stationary lifestyle. We joined a health club and got on a first-name basis with our neighbors and the people at the local Starbucks. Juno and Apache have both passed, but our four chickens keep us busy. Dakota and Josh got married and moved to a town two hours away, so we see them about once a month. Wende has two daughters and Kim has a son, so we are experiencing the joy of being grandparents. After the solitude of the open road, we are enjoying the familiar routine and the regular relationships that come from living in one place. Having neighbors and fellow gym members who know us provides a sense of belonging that was difficult to find when we were moving around almost every day.

Looking back, we got to experience America in a way that few people can. Our trip let us see, taste, and touch a huge part of the country in a very personal way. We drove in each of the lower 48 states, visited over half of the National Parks, swam in all 5 of the Great Lakes, rode a bicycle in 26 states, worked out in over 200 YMCAs, stayed in over 500 campgrounds, and ate at over 1,000 places including every type of local cuisine. We drove Gypsy nearly 100,000 miles on every back road that we could find, stopping in innumerable small towns and in quite a few big cities.

While we did not set out to discover any great truths, the experience left us with some lasting impressions: First, America is a vast place and most of it is still very empty. People who believe that our country doesn't have room to grow should travel outside of the cities. They would see that the amount of vacant, unused land far exceeds the developed areas. With good planning, we could easily double our population and still have room to spare. In doing so, we could also double our economic strength as well as our cultural and creative richness.

However, we have not been good stewards of the America's natural beauty. For all the wonderful places that we saw, there were also some incredibly ugly scenes, from abandoned buildings to vast areas stripped of their trees. Most of America's major rivers are unsafe for swimming. Finding a moose has become a rare event due to human encroachment on their habitat. In North Dakota, the scenic beauty of the northern Great Plains has been replaced by the grotesque effects of the Bakken oil field boom, with derricks everywhere and natural gas flares lighting the night sky like a post-apocalyptic landscape. Like most people, we had heard about the damage to America's natural environment, but it was heartbreaking to see it in person.

Still, we were amazed at America's people. We were strangers in a somewhat worn RV, yet everywhere we went, we were welcomed by folks who were genuinely friendly and helpful. Americans are good people no matter where they live. When I accidentally left my wallet in a shopping cart at a grocery store in Wisconsin, someone took it to Lost & Found with all its contents intact. When I was feeling particularly homesick, a farmer in an extremely rural part of Virginia invited me to pet and feed his Clydesdale horses. When Aimee was feeling tired and lonely on Mother's Day, a family restaurant in northern Utah re-opened its doors and made us a fabulous dinner even though we arrived as they were closing. A repair shop in central Wisconsin mobilized its entire team to fix Gypsy so that we could get to Massachusetts in time for our daughter Kim's wedding. Across the country, we saw people's fear of different ethnic groups, but we also saw their appreciation of having diversity in their local restaurant choices. We heard a lot of frustration about unreasonable rules, unfair treatment, and our political leaders' inability to get things done, but people still believe that America is something special that they want to be a part of. America's spacious skies and purple mountains' majesty are magnificent, but its people are the most beautiful thing about our country.

The trip also changed us in ways that we could never have predicted. While living on the road was often hard, the thrill of wandering became addictive. The unknown made each day exciting, with surprises and potential wonders around every corner, and it helped us balance our innate need for order with the joy of adventure. We learned to listen better to our body's rhythms. Before, we had always just "gutted it out" when we were tired or sick, because our jobs or our kids needed us. After all, we would say, there was plenty of time to sleep in the grave. On this trip, however, with no set schedule and only ourselves to answer to, we could stay up late and sleep until noon, or get up early to watch the dawn, then drive while the world around us was waking up. We discovered the joy of an afternoon nap. We got better at meeting new people and hearing their stories. We are both pretty private people by nature, so it was an adjustment to open up to strangers, but we were amazed at how much we enjoyed learning about their lives and sharing some of ourselves in return. Most importantly, sharing this amazing experience, including learning how to get along in a small space for two years, made us closer as a couple. It gave us memories to share and stories to tell, perhaps the most valuable gift that we could receive.

Although we have appreciated the comfort of living in a house during the Covid pandemic, we miss life on the road and look forward to going back out again. We will do some things differently on our next trip. We will make more stops, and when we find an interesting place, we will stay longer to explore it rather than moving on almost every day. When we are driving, we will take even more back roads and stop at more unusual places. We will spend more time meeting people and getting to know them. We will eat at more local food joints, even though it will make the battle of the bulge that much more difficult. We will plan less and wander more, because the biggest thing that we learned from our travels is that our favorite place is the one that we haven't seen yet. Every mile that we drove took us someplace that made us appreciate America even more.

The United States has over 4 million miles of roads, the largest road system in the world. We only drove 2 percent of it, so there are still lots of places to go and things to see. Hopefully, we will meet you along the way, and share stories of the road over a piece of homemade pie or a fresh Maine lobster. After all, anything is possible when you are Boldly Going…Somewhere.

Lessons of the Road

1: There is always something interesting to see.

2: Not everything that you see is pretty.

3: Have a route plan.

4: Route plans are made to be changed.

5: Motorhomes sometimes require special treatment.

6: People in cars sometimes hate motorhomes.

7: Unexpected discoveries are the most fun.

8: It's amazing what you talk about when you are driving down the road together.

9: You can find Americana anywhere.

10: The best part of exploring America is the people that you meet.

About the Authors

Ron and Aimee Cooper are retired business executives with four adult children and three grandkids. They have always enjoyed travel and after decades of climbing corporate ladders and getting kids through college, they decided to take off in a motorhome to wander around America looking for adventure, with no specific itinerary and only a vague idea of the places that they wanted to visit. Two years and 100,000 miles later, they had quite a story to tell.

They are back now but they're planning their next adventure. ...

They welcome feedback at rcoop913@aol.com

www.ingramcontent.com/pod-product-compliance
Lightning Source LLC
LaVergne TN
LVHW041624060526
838200LV00040B/1423

Black Tank

—*Aimee*—

If you're enjoying a sandwich while you read this book, you might want to stop. Things are about to get real.

One of the conveniences that an RV offers its occupants is a private toilet, which beats the heck out of using gas station restrooms or having to walk from your campsite to the community campground toilets in the middle of the night. Like everything else in a motorhome, however, an RV toilet has some unique characteristics. It is basically a marine toilet with a lever or pedal that adds a tiny amount of water to the waste materials, which then drop into a tank below. In RV terms, this is called the Black Tank. Most RVs have an instrument panel that indicates how full your various tanks are, including your black tank. Gypsy's instrument panel had a set of five lights for the black tank, indicating empty, one quarter, half, three quarters and full. Most people use their black tank for a few days before emptying it into a sewage drain, but I would get nervous when the display read anything higher than half full, so we generally cleaned out our tanks every time we left our campground. That way we always hit the road with empty tanks because you never know what might happen. Some campgrounds had campsites with dedicated sewer connections, so we could hook up our hose and flush as much as we liked. Other campgrounds had a central sewer dump that the campers would drive up to when their tanks got full. In state and national parks, tank dumping was often an impromptu social gathering, people chatting with each other as they waited in the long line for their turn.

When it comes to how and when you may use your RV toilet, every family ends up making their own rules. Some people prefer to skip the whole process of cleaning the system and dumping human waste, opting to use campground restrooms instead. Some folks only use their RV toilet for "number one," preferring more serious business to be done at the campground community bathroom. Some folks allow the toilet to be used while rolling down the highway and others consider that a strict "no-no" because of the danger of flying objects. We owned an RV throughout our child-rearing years and developed a very egalitarian set of rules. You could use the RV toilet anytime, anywhere and for anything, including while we were rolling down the highway, as long as you kept it clean and fresh. As a result, I was comfortable using our facility on a superhighway or a winding mountain road, bracing one foot against the tiny bathroom wall to steady myself, and timing my pants-pull-up for straightaways. Perhaps as I get older, the pleasure of bathroom gymnastics will fade, but for now, I'm a bit smug about this hidden talent.

Most importantly, RV toilets require a special toilet paper. Like many ladies, I absolutely love the thickest, softest toilet paper that money can buy. At home, I am a devotee of Charmin Ultra Soft and I detest the flimsy, scratchy toilet papers that is reminiscent of high school bathrooms. With some amount of sorrow, I must report that bad things happen when you use the wrong paper in an RV. You may only use RV toilet paper or suffer the inevitable clog in your sewage tank. This special paper is so thin and flimsy that you could read your cell phone through it. I suspect it is made from a paper paste that dissolves upon contact with moisture. So sad.

Despite your best efforts, a clog is nearly inevitable, and nothing tests your personal relationship like a clogged black tank. It's easy to let the accusations fly, blaming your mate for failure to flush properly, excessive paper use or a love of Mexican food. "It was the burrito!" Don't succumb to the frustration. Now is the time for team problem solving.

Early on, we clogged up fairly frequently and ended up with fun watersports activities like snaking a garden hose through the bathroom window and ramming it down the toilet to clear the blockage. Ah, the memories. Me dressed in waterproof pants and boots while Ron yelled instructions through the RV bathroom window over the sound of the spurting water. Later, we bought a black tank wand, which is a lovely-sounding euphemism for a tool that turns a garden hose into a high-pressure sprayer. The wand fits down the toilet hole and removes everything that the spray encounters. I also started adding Blue Chem each time we dumped the tank. Blue Chem is basically lye and lubricants, so use with caution, but it worked wonders. My final suggestion—Scott RV toilet paper offers a good combination of comfort and no clogs. We never needed the wand again. Yay team!

Next time you have to use the "facilities," I suggest that you look lovingly at your roomy ceramic toilet and enjoy your Charmin Supersoft Mega Roll. Go ahead and give that roll a muscular spin and listen to the whir of premium, snowy white paper spinning off. You are truly in the lap of luxury.

Okay, you can go back to eating now.

Settling Into Our New Lifestyle
—Ron—

When we began our trip, we sent regular emails to our family and friends, describing where we had gone, what we had seen, and how we felt about our new lifestyle. That kind of journal seemed awfully boring for a book, but I decided to include parts of it as a chapter, because it describes the adjustment process that we went through in learning to live on the road. There was a big difference between vacation trips and living in an RV, especially since we were on the move almost every day. It took us a while to understand how to enjoy our new lifestyle. I've described what we learned as "Lessons of the Road," which may sound a little corny, but they helped us remember the things that made living on the road easier and more fun.

We started our journey by heading east on Highway 20 toward Bend, Oregon. It was our first time driving through the Cascade Mountains and it was beautiful, the road winding through the forest along the Santiam River with waterfalls every few miles. At one place there was a platform hanging nearly halfway across the river so we could look straight down into the water as it tumbled through the rocks. We stopped in Sisters, whose natural setting, recreational activities, and small-town ambiance had made it a popular tourist destination. We saw a sign for the Sno-Cap Diner, which looked like the burger joints that I had loved when I was growing up, so we had to try their cheeseburgers and blackberry milkshakes. Afterward, we tried to walk off lunch, but when we came upon Angelina's bakery with its homemade scones and cinnamon rolls, we decided that we were kids again and counting calories was for grown-ups. One day on the road and already we were losing the Battle of the Bulge.

The next day, we headed south on Highway 97 through central Oregon's high desert, with not much to see other than scrub brush. It was not a route that we would have taken when we were on vacation, but since we had never been there before, it was today's drive. Along the way, we learned **Lesson of the Road #1: There is always something interesting to see.** In this case, it was several large prairie dog towns along the highway. It was mating season and the male prairie dogs apparently showed their bravery by standing in the middle of the road and staring down the oncoming traffic. At first, I tried to avoid them by swerving Gypsy across both lanes of the road, her tires and Aimee both screaming. Soon, we discovered that prairie dogs knew to jump out of the way just in time. What we had thought would be a dull drive ended up being more thrilling than a roller coaster ride. We stopped in Alturas, California just south of the Oregon border and stayed in Sully's RV Park, a tiny campground located next to the city park. We bought dinner from Antonio's Cucina Italiana and ate in the park while the dogs got their exercise by trying to find the local deer that left their scent behind. Enjoying the quiet evening, we told each other how easy camping our way around America was going to be. We were so naïve!

The next morning, we drove through the northeast corner of California and got a first-hand look at the effects of the drought. Goose Lake, Eagle Lake and Honey Lake were all at less than half of their normal water level, with wildlife crammed together in a habitat that was much too small for them. It was tough to watch their struggle and it gave us **Lesson of the Road #2: Not everything that you see is pretty.**

We continued south down Highway 395 through Reno and Carson City, then eventually into Death Valley, where we stayed at Oasis Resort's Furnace Creek Ranch RV Campground. The RV sites were pretty basic, but there was a big pool and plenty of room to walk the dogs. The next morning, I rode my bike on the road that cut through the alkaline valley floor, watching the local wildlife gather anyplace that had been irrigated.

Soon it was over 100 degrees and we spent the rest of the day at the pool or inside Gypsy with the air conditioning on full force.

The next morning, we left early to catch the sunrise at Zabriskie Point. It was a beautiful sight as the rocks turned different colors when the morning sunlight hit them. We took the eastern road out of the valley to Shoshone, an old desert town with its quaint Crowbar Café and Saloon, then drove south to Joshua Tree National Park. Forty miles of our route was on unpaved road, which Aimee said was poor planning on my part, but I replied that it was part of having a carefree lifestyle. We hiked Joshua Tree's desert trails, enjoying its spectacular natural scenery of the Mojave and the Colorado deserts. In one place, we could see 20 miles of the San Andreas Fault as it cut through the Coachella Valley. That night we stayed in TwentyNine Palms at a charming RV park with a pond filled with fish and birds, including one mama mallard who moved her 8 newborn ducklings around like a miniature armada. At bedtime, we let Juno out to do her business, but when she didn't return, we got worried. We had visions of her being hit by a car, encountering a rattlesnake, or getting caught in the pond weeds. After an hour of sneaking around the campground trying to call her without waking the other residents, we found her with a group of college students who were on their spring break. They thought Juno was cute, Juno thought their food was delicious and we were tempted to leave her there.

As we contemplated where to go next, we discovered **Lesson of the Road #3: Have a route plan.** As parents and businesspeople, we had always been pretty organized and we needed some kind of goal or guiding concept to feel comfortable. It didn't have to be ambitious, just a theme that would give us a purpose as wandered around. The weather was getting warm and we liked the idea of being near good swimming locations, so we decided to follow the Colorado River, which travels 1,500 miles on its path from the Rocky Mountains to the Sea of Cortez, and passes through 11 national parks including the Grand Canyon on the way. We pictured ourselves telling people that we had "traced the path of the Colorado River back to its headwaters" and sounding like we were wilderness explorers.

We stopped at several campgrounds on the Colorado River between Blythe, California, and Lake Mead outside Las Vegas. Our two favorite places were River Island State Park outside Parker, Arizona and Big Bend of the Colorado State Park near Laughlin, Nevada. They both had beautiful scenery, nice camping sites and sandy beaches that provided great access to swim in the river. The water was clean, and the current could either be peacefully slow or dangerously fast. In some places, it would provide a quick trip to Mexico if you weren't careful.

When we reached Lake Mead, we discovered that other than the Grand Canyon and Lake Powell, most of the Colorado River's route further upstream was inaccessible in an RV, which didn't sound like a lot of fun. We spent the night at Nevada's Valley of Fire State Park and were so impressed with the red rock spires that seem to erupt from the surrounding flat desert terrain that we decided to alter our course and explore the red rock country, having learned **Lesson of the Road #4: Route plans are made to be changed.**

The next day, we headed into Utah and Zion National Park. They had to stop the oncoming traffic for 30 minutes to let us through the entry tunnel and we discovered **Lesson of the Road #5: Motorhomes sometimes require special treatment** and **Lesson of the Road #6: People in cars sometimes hate motorhomes.**

We got off the major roads and drove Utah's high country on Highway 12 and the old Highway 95, rarely meeting any other people but seeing some spectacular scenery. We hadn't realized that many of Utah's parks had petroglyphs, but after we saw some amazing ones at Capitol Reef National Park, we looked for them wherever we went as we drove through the red rock country of southern Utah and northern Arizona. Rejoining the Colorado River outside Moab, Utah, we were heading northeast along the river toward Colorado when we saw a sign for Castle Creek Winery. "A winery in Utah?" We had to try it. While we were tasting, I noticed a brochure for the nearby Red Cliffs Lodge and we decided to take a look. It turned out to be one of the best stops on our entire trip, with western-style suites looking over the Colorado River, a full fitness center, a huge pool and a restaurant that featured fantastic buffalo rib eye steaks. It gave us **Lesson of the Road #7: Unexpected discoveries are the most fun.**

We heard that there were some interesting dinosaur sites in northwest Colorado, including a town called Dinosaur, so we took a detour from red rock country to check it out. The town seemed to have a dinosaur statue on every street corner, but no fossil exhibits or dig sites. The whole build-up was to attract people there so that they could sell them rafting trips. We had better luck at the Carnegie Quarry Exhibit Hall in Jensen, Utah. Its Wall of Bones had approximately 1,500 dinosaur bones displayed in the ground where they had been found. Touching the 150-million-year-old bones of a Stegosaurus, we felt like we were paleontologists on an actual dig.

Highway 191 north into Wyoming went to a place called Flaming Gorge National Recreation Area that sounded like more red rock and a place to swim, so away we went. The road looked like it had been built to support a mining operation, but coming down through the mountains on the other side was a spectacular drive. It was close to dusk and wildlife was everywhere, as we saw pronghorn antelope, Rocky Mountain elk, yellow-bellied marmots, mule deer and wild turkeys. We stayed at Lucerne Campground overlooking Flaming Gorge Reservoir, sitting out after dinner under the clear night skies. In the morning, the pronghorn antelope showed up to give Apache a workout. He had no chance of catching them—when the antelope got too far ahead, they would stop and wait for him so that he wouldn't give up too quickly. By the time we were ready to leave, Apache was more than willing to lie down and rest.

Yellowstone National Park was only 300 miles away and neither of us had never been there, so it seemed like a natural destination.

Driving the back roads through the farm country of Wyoming and Idaho, we saw thousands of horses, most of them laying down in the spring sunshine. We fed apples to some of them, but quickly realized that we would never reach Yellowstone if we stopped to feed them all. Aimee jokingly suggested that we build an air gun so that we could shoot apples into the pastures as we drove by. Since there were often 20 or more horses in one pasture, she wanted it to fire apples continuously like a machine gun. We named it The Appling Gun and had a long discussion about its design and use. What is the ideal muzzle velocity so that the apple will reach the distant horses without hurting the closer ones? If we are driving, how do we factor in Gypsy's speed? After spending an hour discussing ballistics as we drove through the countryside, we realized **Lesson of the Road #8: It's amazing what you talk about when you are driving down the road together.**

Most people visit Yellowstone to see Old Faithful, hot springs and mud pots at the world's largest super volcano. For us, the best part was the wildlife. We saw a young bear cub climb a tree, then watched a herd of ten thousand antelope grazing in a meadow. At one point, a herd of bison with a fuzzy newborn calf swam across the frigid Yellowstone River, then crossed the road right in front of us, the calf stopping to nose Gypsy's bumper before scampering back to his mother.

Leaving Yellowstone, we took Highway 212, then Highway 296 to Cody, Wyoming. The road was twisty and steep in places, but it was scenic on a massive scale as it wound through huge mountains, red rock formations, river valleys, plateaus, and alpine meadows. From Cody, we found the one back road that wasn't closed due to snow and headed northeast into Montana. Even in May, the snow was over six feet deep on either side of the road. We imagined being part of a wagon train traveling through the area at ten miles per day and were glad to be in our warm, fully stocked motorhome.

In Billings, we stayed at the first KOA ever opened and we could see why they became popular. The campground backed onto the

Yellowstone River with large RV sites, clean laundry and showers, a playground with a basketball court and lots of trees and grassy open space for kids and dogs to run. It was a perfect kind of place for a family to spend a week outdoors and showed us **Lesson of the Road #9: You can find Americana anywhere.**

I was going to Las Vegas to play in the World Series of Poker, so we started heading west to let Aimee spend the time visiting our daughter in Oregon. We could have made the drive in a couple of days, but we were in no hurry. At one point, we stopped to stretch our legs and found ourselves in the middle of a prairie dog town. Apache nearly went crazy trying to chase them, only to find that they had perfected a system for dealing with would-be predators. All the prairie dogs within 25 feet of Apache would hide inside their burrows, while the prairie dogs that were further away stood up at the entrance to their burrows and chattered at him. When Apache ran toward one of them, it would pop down to safety while the prairie dogs in burrows behind Apache would pop up and start chattering. It looked like a massive game of Whack-A-Mole, but the prairie dogs were completely safe.

Further west, Aimee noticed that Highway 93 ran 400 miles down the length of Idaho along the Salmon River, passing through several national forests on the way to Twin Falls. It looked scenic, so away we went. We were a few miles outside Missoula when I saw a handmade sign for homemade pie. Whipping a U-turn that made Gypsy's tires screech, I pulled into Glen's Cafe, a family-owned coffee shop. The owner Glen, who was 85 years old, told me that he had always wanted to have a place to offer his wife's homemade pies, along with burgers using the beef from his cattle ranch. As we talked, his daughters arrived with freshly baked apple, cherry, huckleberry, and lemon meringue pies. Discovering America couldn't get any better than this!

That afternoon, we saw a sign at a family farm offering RV spaces on the Salmon River. I called the number on the sign and the lady who answered said that they were closed while her husband recovered from a hip replacement. I was planning to get my hip replaced and asked her what the rehab was like. After chatting for a bit, she opened the gate to let us stay for the night. The next day, we were driving south on Mother's Day, and I was looking for something special for Aimee, so we stopped at JC's Country Diner, a family-owned place that was the top-rated restaurant in Tremonton, Utah. It had just closed early so that the employees could be with their families, but when they heard that there was a road-weary mom in the RV, they made us a great take-out dinner. We had a picnic in a nearby park and talked about **Lesson of the Road #10: The best part of exploring America is the people that you meet.**

We headed west on Highway 50 into Nevada and endured its well-deserved reputation as "the Loneliest Highway in America." We spent one night in a campground where the only other tenants were itinerant mine workers. The water was brown and smelled so strange that we used the water in Gypsy's tanks to be safe. The next morning, we hit every coffee shop listed on Google looking for Aimee's espresso, only to find that each one was either closed or out of coffee. "Out of coffee!" screamed my caffeine-deprived wife, "How can a coffee bar be out of coffee?" When we finally found a place that was open and in stock, I ordered three giant lattes with extra espresso.

After 550 miles of desert, we were ready for something different, so we decided to take Highway 120 over Tioga Pass into Yosemite National Park. It is the highest highway pass in California, and even in late May we had to wait overnight for the snow to melt enough to let them open the road. I have visited Yosemite many times over the years,

but its rugged beauty still takes my breath away. We drove its entire length, watching small pockets of spring emerging from winter.

Leaving Yosemite, we took Highway 41, then Highway 49 through Angels Camp, home of Mark Twain's tale of "The Celebrated Jumping Frog of Calaveras County." We continued north over the Golden Gate bridge, then took Highway 1 over Mount Tamalpais and up the coast. We had never driven this route in a motorhome because the road is very narrow in places, but after the back roads through the Rockies, this didn't seem all that difficult. After stopping in Sonoma County to visit family, we took Highway 101 north through the redwoods and back to Oregon.

Once we arrived back at our house, we took stock of our experience so far. We had been living in Gypsy for eight weeks, far longer than any of our vacations. We had travelled 8,000 miles, enough to cross America and back, yet we had barely made through the Rocky Mountains. Our serpentine route looked like a Family Circus cartoon showing Billy's path home when his mom called him for dinner.

We had enjoyed driving the highways and two-lane country roads more than the freeways. The freeways were faster, but we didn't get to see as much and there was too much competition from the other drivers, especially the trucks. On the smaller roads we could relax and enjoy the scenery. We also preferred the towns to the cities. They were easier to navigate, and we enjoyed seeing their history on display as we drove down their main street.

We had developed a comfortable daily routine. Early morning was breakfast, showers and clean up Gypsy, then drive for a while, stopping anywhere that looked interesting. Lunch was our chance to try out a local restaurant, then back on the road for more sightseeing and adventures. We tried to get in by 5pm so that we could hook up while it was still light outside and explore the campground. We would buy dinner from a local restaurant or Aimee would cook while I did office work, then we would sit outside before we settled in for the night.

We made some changes, including buying leveling blocks and a better mattress for our bed. After two months of sleeping on a thin, hard mattress and trying to not fall off the bed when the campsite was uneven, we had learned that comfort is more important when you are living in a motorhome versus just taking a week's vacation. We also bought an Italian coffee pot for making espresso in Gypsy. Tense morning drives looking for a latte for my caffeine-deprived wife was just too risky. Our most difficult adjustment was to leave the dogs behind with our daughter in Oregon. We enjoyed having them on the road, but Juno was having trouble climbing in and out of Gypsy. She needed a more sedate living arrangement, and our house with its woodstove was her idea of heaven. Apache could handle the travel, but he was much happier being with Juno.

Soon, we were ready to go out again. We had become comfortable with our new lifestyle, and our Lessons of the Road were useful reminders of how to enjoy living on the road. The most important lesson was that there was always something interesting waiting ahead.

The West Coast Wholly Granola Ride

—Aimee—

Although life on the road was mostly about the adventures inherent in the travel itself, I frequently found that the interactions with people from different places and all walks of life was just as entertaining. They were often enlightening, and I learned a few things about my own outlook on life along the way.

On our way back to Sonoma County after 8 weeks on the road, we stayed in the quiet and tiny seaside town of Olema, California along Highway 1. When we pulled into the only RV park in the area that offered full hookups and laundry, we were told that there was one spot available "as long as we didn't mind the noise."

They explained that a group of cyclists was staying at the park on the last leg of a "Climate Ride" from Oregon down the coast to San Francisco. It was their last night together and apparently riding for clean air and clean water included the right to drink themselves into a stupor. They had set up in the open bandstand area behind the RV sites and the park was rocking and rolling with over two hundred twenty-something-year-old cyclists partying like mad.

Rather than get irritated with the thumping music and slideshow, Ron and I decided to appreciate the vibe and join the fun. We grabbed a couple of bottles of wine and served any adult who wandered over to our campfire and picnic table. Talking to our drop-ins, we learned that most of these folks were employees of Bay Area Internet companies, and the slideshow they set up was worthy of Silicon Valley. How did someone pull together a collage of funny moments, otter sightings and cycling wipeouts and set it all to music so quickly?

As the evening progressed, guitars came out and off-key sing-alongs filled the air. As we watched the whole dynamic while sitting around our campfire, I wondered how these folks would be able to get on their bikes and ride fifty miles to San Francisco the next morning.

I got up early to drop our trash in the dumpster, passing a long line of unitard-clad cyclists testing their equipment and backpacks while several coordinators with clipboards wandered around. To get to the dumpster, I had to walk through the bandstand area. It looked like the Oxford Dictionary entry for "Mess." There were beer bottles and food wrappers everywhere, sweatshirts lost on the grass and a singularly unfortunate sheet cake that had been half-eaten by a raccoon.

Totally offended, I grabbed a garbage can and started chucking beer bottles into it. One of the coordinators wandered over and said, "Are you with the Ride staff?".

"No, I'm just picking up," I said, tossing the racoon-eaten cake into the can.

"You don't have to do that," she said. "I'm sure the park staff can clean it up."

Perhaps I might have been a tad snarky when I turned to face her and said, "Let me tell you guys something. Saving the climate is great but it starts with picking up your own crap. These guys were pigs!"

I never felt so much like my own mother in my entire life. It was embarrassing and liberating at the same time. Is this what it feels like to grow old? Bitching at people for being young and stupid?

At least the event coordinator had the good sense to look embarrassed. She helped me pick up and then gave me a Climate Ride thermos. I may be trash-righteous, but I never say no to free swag.

Every time I fill that thermos, I think about the complexity of youth, who can be totally committed to protecting our environment, but blind to needing to clean up after themselves. Then I appreciate the simpler truths of being older as I take out my trash bag and start picking things up.

Red Rock

—Ron—

Much of America's beautiful scenery can be found throughout the country. Roughly 40 states have mountains, 23 have ocean beaches, most have forests, and every state has at least one lake. Some types of scenery, however, are more local. Red rocks are only found in a small portion of Utah and the surrounding states.

I'm not sure why I find the red rocks fascinating. Perhaps it's because I grew up watching Westerns, all of which seemed to be set against the backdrop of bizarre red sandstone formations. Maybe it comes from Saturday morning cartoons, watching the Road Runner zoom through the red rocks with Wile E. Coyote close on his heels. Whatever the reason, touring America's red rock country was one of my favorite parts of our trip.

We started our exploration of the red rocks quite by accident. We were driving north along Lake Mead near Las Vegas when Aimee told me to take a small side road. When I gave her a questioning look, she said, "You'll see." Suddenly, strange rock formations seemed to erupt from the flat desert landscape. It was the Valley of Fire State Park, Nevada's oldest state park. We went hiking around the vividly colored rock formations, which included the historic scene of Captain Kirk's death in the Star Trek movie "Generations" and we were hooked. When I asked Aimee, "Where to next?" she said, "Find us some more red rocks." The next day, we headed toward Utah, the mother lode of red rock, with five National Parks—Arches, Bryce, Capitol Reef, Canyonlands, and Zion—that were all top-notch red rock destinations.

Entering Zion was an adventure all by itself. We went through the Zion-Mount Carmel tunnel, which was a mile long and so narrow that oversized vehicles like RVs needed both lanes to get through. We paid a special fee, then the park officials stopped traffic coming the other direction and set up a motorcade to take us through the tunnel. It was like having a Secret Service detail, including the attention of the people in their cars as they waited to use the tunnel again. Once inside the park, we were struck by the contrast of red rock and green plants. Zion's steep canyons have enough year-round water to support a lot of greenery and the combination of ancient stone and living plants was beautiful.

From Zion, we headed to nearby Bryce Canyon. It was smaller than Zion but had amazing pinnacle-shaped rock formations called hoodoos. Created by erosion and frost weathering, these stone spires were up to 200 feet tall. In Bryce Amphitheater, the collection of hoodoos was twelve miles long and three miles wide and looked like an endless sea of fossilized teeth.

We took the narrow two-lane Highway 12 through the mountains and canyons of central Utah to Capitol Reef National Park. It is named for the Waterpocket Fold, a 100-mile-long warp in the earth's crust that folded its layers on top of each other to create strange shapes and brilliant colors. Caused by colliding continental plates, the fold is so steep and rugged that it is nearly impassable, much like ocean reefs can block travel by ship. From Capitol Reef, we drove southeast on the backroads to Canyonlands, Utah's largest National Park, where the Colorado and Green Rivers have formed a vast system of canyons, mesas, and buttes. At the south end of the park, the view of the Colorado River cutting a perfect horseshoe formation through the sandstone cliffs at Dead Horse Point State Park was one of the most spectacular sights of our trip.

Four miles outside of Moab, Arches National Park had over two thousand arches with some truly wild-looking rock formations and amazing petroglyphs. After a morning of hiking around the red rock formations, we had lunch in Moab at Quesadilla Mobilla, "the first gourmet food truck in Moab." Their signature item was called the New

Mexico Identity Crisis, a wrap filled with green chile chicken, spinach, artichoke hearts, black olives, and cheese. It was huge, but filled with vegetables, so we didn't know if we should feel guilty or virtuous.

In the northeast corner of Utah, Dinosaur National Monument's red rock included some amazing petroglyphs as well as the Carnegie Dinosaur Quarry of over 1,500 fossils in their original state.

Wyoming didn't have a lot of red rock, but one place really stood out. Flaming Gorge Reservoir, a 91-mile-long reservoir on the Utah/Wyoming border, was made up of four gorges carved out of the surrounding red rock by the Green River, the largest tributary of the Colorado River. Driving north on Highway 191 through Ashley National Forest and along the western edge of the reservoir, we had a great view of how the river had carved out a path through the rock strata, creating a spectacular contrast between the red stone, the blue water, and the green forest.

Arizona had our favorite drive through red rock country—Highway 89A down the Oak Creek Canyon between Flagstaff and Sedona. Formed by geological action along the Oak Creek fault and erosion from a rare year-round stream in the high desert, the canyon was a wonderfully picturesque blend of red rock, oak trees and running water. At Slide Rock State Park, the creek had worn the rocks into smooth channels making a huge natural water slide big enough to accommodate hundreds of people at a time.

Back in California, our final stop was at Vasquez Rocks Natural Area, located 30 miles outside of Los Angeles. It has been featured in over 400 films and TV shows, including the famous Star Trek episode where Captain Kirk fights a Gorn. For Trekkies like us, having our tour start and end at two famous Star Trek locations made it an even more interesting way to explore the timeless beauty of America's red rock country. We also learned that part of the fun of living on the road was following a route that was defined on a whim. It was a lesson that we had to keep learning, but it was a big part of what made our trip so special.

Home Is Where You Park It

—*Aimee*—

One of the most common questions that people asked us about our trip was "How did you find places to stay?" I'm sure that they pictured us parked in the wilderness next to a glacial lake or sitting in a lonely Walmart parking lot with our doors locked.

This may bother a lot of people, but when we started out, we had no plan whatsoever for where to stay. We mostly played it by ear every night. No surprise if you know my husband, who counted on the fact that there are RV parks and campgrounds nearly everywhere around the US.

I have to say that finding a campground was easier on this trip than when we bought our first RV a decade ago. Back then, we would pull out our "RV Across America" or "Good Sam" list of parks and search the area where we were headed. Picture an enormous telephone book with lists of parks and campgrounds by state and city area. As dusk approached, Ron would be driving down the highway while I desperately tried to read the tiny print in the fading light. Many times, we ended up in the campground that used the largest print in their listing.

Fast forward to this trip. Now there were several apps on my phone that were dedicated to RV accommodations, complete with pictures, amenities, and reviews. Google provided a list of locations in any area and a map of how to get there.

RV accommodations come in three basic types. They are "Campground," "RV Park" and "Trailer Park." Often the actual names of these places could be misleading, so stay with me here.

A campground is a rustic, outdoorsy setting with fairly basic amenities. Campgrounds offer that classic Americana experience:

picnic tables near lakes, a fire ring, tent camping and often scary bathrooms. Most are missing things like cable TV, a pool and "Full Hook-ups," the holy trinity of water, sewage, and electricity that most RVers prefer. There are literally thousands of campgrounds around the US. Some of our most jaw-dropping experiences were in campgrounds, including ones on the slopes of Mount Whitney or along the Pacific Ocean's Highway 1 in California. Almost all National Parks and State Parks have campgrounds. If you really want to see the awe-inspiring vistas that America has to offer, I suggest that you go to the lesser-known National and State Park campgrounds. Everybody knows to stay in Yellowstone, but not everyone knows that you can see herds of buffalo and wild horses in Teddy Roosevelt National Park. Few people have even heard of Hueco Tanks State Park near El Paso, Texas, but its combination of desert and mountain scenery was simply amazing.

RV Parks, by contrast, are meant to offer a comfortable place to stay. They are often found along the major highways and near small towns. There are a few national chains, but most are individually owned mom and pop operations. They generally offer full hookups, cable TV, Internet, and have clubhouses with things like laundry and private showers. Some RV parks are really fancy, with huge brick pads to park on and pool complexes that rival a Las Vegas resort. One of the most spectacular RV parks that we stayed at was located in Key Largo along a strip of sandy beach. It had a huge pool, fitness center, hot tub, and kayaks for their campers to use in the ocean. We stayed there three times, eating grouper and watching the sunset over the palm trees from our poolside chairs.

The final category is "Trailer Parks." No knock on the many Americans that live in trailer parks, but they are not generally designed for people who are on vacation or out to see America. Trailer parks may have a few spots for people just passing through, but their focus is not camping. They provide a community for their long-term residents.

Before we got more savvy on how to do Internet research, we often just drove into a park and eyeballed it. If it looked like no one's unit had moved since the Nixon Administration, we said "no, thank you" and rolled on down the road. One night near the Idaho and Wyoming border, our choices were limited, and we ended up at a ten-unit trailer park next to a creek. The neighboring trailer had a stovepipe sticking out of a hole that they had punched in the side of their trailer, with puffs of smoke gently wafting into the night air. Outside were two freezers set up next to what looked like a game processing table. It was a little scary, but it was available. Sometimes you take what you can get.

The hardest state to find an RV campsite? Nevada. Highway 50 really is the Loneliest Highway in America. We drove and drove and then drove some more. In the middle of Nevada as dusk fell, we finally spotted a tiny trailer park along the highway with one or two lonely trailers in its eight spots. There was no one at the office, so we left our $18 in an envelope and parked on a lumpy gravel site that was totally bare bones. We skipped hooking up when we saw the brownish water that trickled out of the spigot. Turns out most of the park's clientele were seasonal workers for a local mine. But hey, the stars were fantastic. It's all about enjoying what you <u>do</u> get and not what you don't.

So now the million-dollar question: Did we ever stay in a Walmart parking lot? Sorry to disappoint, but the answer is "No." We never had to. We always managed to find a place of one kind or another to stay in. I guess we could have and maybe we should have just once so that we could say that we did. We have friends who drive their RV between California and Kentucky who love to stay in Walmart parking lots because it's free. They say that not every Walmart will let you park overnight, and you have to ask permission from the manager. Personally, I treated it like a challenge for Ron. "If we can't find a spot, we'll just have to stay at a Walmart," I'd remark. Consequently, no Walmart. One day I'll switch it up and challenge him to stay at a Walmart as often as possible, and we'll see what happens.

Driving an RV in America
—Ron—

Starting out, we were a little concerned about driving our motorhome around the different parts of America. Could we safely manage the freeways and the major cities? Would the country roads be uncomfortably narrow? Gypsy was going to be our home and we didn't want to end up living at a repair shop. We soon discovered that driving an RV around America was its own kind of adventure.

At over 10 feet tall, 30 feet long and 11 feet wide including the side mirrors, Gypsy was larger than most vehicles and her size often presented a challenge. Driving over a narrow bridge in Cape Cod, we scraped our tires against the curb on the passenger side while a UPS truck coming the other way hit our driver's side mirror. Afterward, we had to stop to let our blood pressure come down. After several near misses at overcrossings and gas stations, I learned to avoid any place that did not have at least 12 feet of clearance. Even parking could be a challenge, as Gypsy was too tall for most indoor parking garages and needed several spaces to park on a curb or in a parking lot.

When in motion, Gypsy had different characteristics than a passenger vehicle. She weighed three times as much as an average car, but had a similar braking system, so it took her a lot longer to stop. Her height meant that we had to be careful driving in a crosswind or sudden gust would push us into the next lane. Her rear axle was 11 feet forward of the rear bumper, so when we turned, the rear corner would swing out several feet in the opposite direction into the adjoining lane, giving "lane sharing" a whole new meaning.

Gypsy seemed to bring out the aggressiveness in other drivers. No matter how fast we were going, cars would sit on our bumper, then pass us and swerve back into our lane as if there was a prize for missing our front bumper by the smallest possible margin. They did not seem to understand that if they hit the brakes, they would find an RV in their back seat.

We had to learn the rules of the road for each state, and some of them were completely new to us. In many parts of New Jersey, it is illegal to make a left-hand turn. Vehicles that want to turn left must make three right hand turns on the surface streets in a maneuver called a Jersey Jughandle. The local drivers do it at high speed and pedestrians crossing the street in front of them are either quick or dead. Then there is the Texas Turnaround. If you are driving on a freeway and want to get to something on the left side of the road, you must pass it, exit on the right onto a multi-lane access road, make a U-turn under the freeway, get back on the freeway going in the other direction and exit again onto the other access road to reach the destination. If this sounds complicated, imagine trying it while cars are whizzing by on both sides like a NASCAR training course.

Whenever possible, we drove on the two-lane highways and back roads where the pace was slower, and the scenery was better. We enjoyed looking for signs to local attractions and watching people's expressions when they saw Gypsy. But for some reason, animals found the challenge of crossing in front of an RV irresistible. With squirrels, for example, we decided that God must have given big fluffy tails to the really dumb ones to compensate for their apparent lack of brains. And sometimes the country roads could also be scary. When we drove through northwest part of North Dakota, it was in the midst of a huge oil boom. There was a frenzy of activity to bring in materials to create new wells and take out the oil. With limited pipeline and railroad capacity, almost all the transport was done by truck over narrow two-lane roads that had very little room for error. The truck drivers were paid by the load and drove at breakneck speeds. We were told that they routinely took drugs to stay awake so that they could get in as many loads as possible per day. We felt like we were trapped in a scene from Mad Max, with 18-wheelers flying by in both directions as gas flares lit up the sky.

We did take Gypsy into several cities and quickly learned that each city had its own personality. Boston drivers were openly aggressive as they careened through its narrow colonial-era streets. One native proudly described it as a nonstop game of Chicken. Driving in Seattle's maze of one-way streets and roads that crossed over the top of each other was like playing 3-D chess. Washington, D.C.'s drivers came from all over the country, so it was a melting pot of driving techniques, including Boston/New York aggression, Southern gentility, Midwest politeness and West Coast love of freeway speed. Despite the ensuing chaos, Washington, D.C. was one of our favorite cities for driving because it had wide, multi-lane boulevards and lots of curb parking to accommodate Gypsy's length. The biggest challenge was that its street layout combined a traditional American grid with a Paris-like hub and spoke system, so the side streets came in at strange angles. Many times, we tried to turn left and found that we were nearly making a U-turn across several lanes of oncoming traffic. Fortunately, Gypsy's size caused most drivers to back off—they did not want their brand-new BMW hit by a motorhome.

One pleasant surprise driving Gypsy around America was the ferries. We took ferries in several parts of the country and had good experiences each time. On the ferry from the rural eastern end of Long Island to New London, Connecticut, they gave us special assistance loading and unloading Gypsy. We then spent the ride enjoying the Long Island Sound scenery, happy to skip New York City's traffic. No tailgaters, no sudden lane changes and no blaring horns, except for the tugboats. The ferry from Cape May, New Jersey to Lewes, Delaware was like riding a roller coaster as we were crossed the mouth of the Delaware Bay where it meets the Atlantic Ocean. It was exciting, but we always felt safe and we saved 175 miles of driving. When a flash flood closed the I-10 freeway between Louisiana and Texas, we took back roads to the Cameron ferry at the mouth of the Calcasieu River. The ferry was only big enough to fit ten cars, and we wondered whether they would take us, but once they got over their shock at seeing Gypsy, the operators were very helpful and got us safely across the swollen river.

Our most challenging place to drive? Long Island. Gypsy was banned from most of the bridges to Long Island because her propane tanks were considered a Hazmat risk. Strangely, we were allowed on the Verrazzano-Narrows Bridge, the longest suspension bridge in America, so we joined the more than 200,000 vehicles that cross it each day. Judging from the other drivers' terrified looks, not many RVs drive onto Long Island and we quickly found out why. Long Island is over 110 miles long and has the same area as Rhode Island, but 8 times as many people. This combination of distance and density means that there are a lot of cars, all filled with New York drivers. "Why do their cars even have turn signals?" asked Aimee. "They never get used. They should get a second horn, because they must wear out the one that they have pretty fast." Once we got onto Long Island's scenic parkways we began to relax, until we discovered that they had been designed by a man who didn't want trucks or buses on his roads, so he put in overpasses with clearances so low that only automobiles could get under them. Which was all fine, except that he neglected to put up signs to inform the blissfully ignorant RV drivers. We survived, thanks to some quick thinking on Aimee's part, as you will see.

The Google and Google Maps
—Aimee—

I don't know how we would have lived on the road without the Internet. We had taken family road trips before there was an Internet and it was like watching TV without a remote. (Before you say how lazy that sounds, try getting up and going to your TV every time that you want to see what's on a different channel. It's amazing how quickly we become dependent on things.) Before the Internet, each road trip required lots of research and we had a special library of travel books describing the best routes to take, places to eat, interesting stops and places to stay. Our directory of RV campgrounds was bigger than the phone book (back when we had phone books.) "Captain Daddy" Ron would get up early each day during the trip and make a plan for what we were going to do that day. Over breakfast, he would eagerly share his plan with the girls, describing the stops in great detail as they looked at him with bleary eyes. His plan rarely survived the first dose of reality, as usually half of the stops were out of business or closed for the day. Ron would then try to improvise while three young girls told him how lame it was to be trapped in an RV with their parents for a week of "vacation."

With the Internet, planning a trip was a breeze. No more straining to read the tiny print of the RV Campground directory. No more phone calls to politely ask the campground host whether their facility was a resort or a "port in the storm." There were Internet sites that specialized in RV parks, complete with ratings, pictures, and reviews. When one RV park's website touted its "atmosphere," the reviews let us know that it was located next to a sewage treatment plant.

The Internet was also great for doing things on the fly. We didn't have to even pretend that we had our day planned ahead of time. I would search for interesting places online while we were driving, and we would adjust our route based on what I discovered. When we needed gas, I would use an app that compared prices in our area. If we were getting hungry, I would research restaurants in the nearby towns.

To Ron, the Internet was also a great way to answer random questions and avoid boredom while he was driving. Wandering through the pastures of Idaho, he wondered how many horses there were in America. Were there more horses than dairy cows? A few keystrokes later, I informed him that there were roughly 9 million horses and almost exactly the same number of dairy cows. "What movie has the line 'Mary Ellen Moffett—she broke my heart"? Jaws. A family member had dubbed this random Internet research "milking the cat," which was certainly an interesting visual.

We were fans of every aspect of using the Internet, with one exception—Google Maps. If you are thinking of taking an RV trip of your own, I have some advice for you: Never Trust Google Maps. Google Maps is a fantastic and helpful technology, but blindly placing your trust in it may send you driving off a cliff to a wonderful chorus of "Re-Routing." Google Maps is particularly dangerous to RVs. Why? Height!

When was the last time you paid any attention to those height markings on bridges and overpasses? You should if you travel in an RV. You will need to know how tall your rig is to the inch. Gypsy is ten feet six inches tall. Google does not know this, and Google does not care. It will insist that you drive under a seven-foot railroad bridge and get frustrated when you abruptly change direction. Have you noticed that Google's audible speech function gets snippy when you don't follow its directions?

While visiting our daughter Wende on Long Island, we foolishly let Google send us onto the Cross-Island Parkway, despite the signs that read "Passenger Vehicles Only." Confusing…hmmm…Aren't we a passenger vehicle? We drove along as the stone overpasses seemed to get lower and lower. I was getting seriously nervous and finally looked up a trucking website. It said that the next overpass was six feet four inches high, which is four feet lower than Gypsy's roofline.

"Get off, get off!" I yelled at Ron. "There's six feet four coming up!" To his credit, he immediately swerved over into the right-hand lane at 65 mph in rush hour traffic and exited in the nick of time.

It turns out that there are two types of commuter highways on Long Island: expressways and parkways. Expressways are your classic four-lane, "get there now" roads that Californians think of when they say "freeway." On the other hand, parkways were designed in the 1930's by an urban planner for a charming afternoon ride in a jalopy. They have no shoulder and their route meanders to create a scenic effect. People could enjoy nature while driving serenely under the low-slung arched stone overpasses at 30 miles an hour. Nowadays, expressways and parkways are both jammed with New York traffic, but parkways still only allow cars. Woe to the RV, bus or truck that fails to catch on quick. Look up "Truck Stuck under Parkway Overpass" if you want to see what could have happened to us.

Did Google care? No. It continued to insist that we "PROCEED TO THE ROUTE" the entire time. I may have suggested loudly at that point that Google Maps go perform an act with itself that heretofore no computer has achieved.

The lesson of this story? When it comes to the Internet, Trust but Verify.

Michigan's Upper Peninsula
—Ron—

One big reason that we took our trip was to visit the "off the beaten path" parts of America that most people don't see. We quickly found a flaw in our plan—how do you find out where the unknown parts are? We thought about searching on the Internet, but that felt like cheating. Instead, we wandered around and hoped for the best. Not much of a strategy, but it seemed to work, as we came across quite a few places that were relatively unknown and really interesting.

One of the most unusual places that we found was Michigan's Upper Peninsula. Physically, it is separated from the rest of the state by Lake Michigan and Lake Huron; instead, it is attached to the upper part of Wisconsin. Despite being twice the size of New Jersey, the U. P. has only 300,000 inhabitants and they are very isolated—the only city within 200 miles is Green Bay, Wisconsin. The people who live in the U. P. call themselves "Yoopers" and they have their own dialect, their own unique types of food and a fiercely independent outlook. They have tried to become a separate state several times and generally view non-Yoopers as people from a foreign country. The Upper Peninsula was once a rich mining area, producing more mineral wealth than the California Gold Rush. At one point, it was the largest source of iron in America and supplied 90 percent of the country's copper. Its economy is now driven by tourism, as people go there to enjoy its 1,700 miles of shoreline on the Great Lakes, the longest freshwater shoreline in the country. Heavily wooded with a wide variety of wildlife, it is a sportsman's and naturalist's paradise, which sounded perfect to us.

Most people get to the Upper Peninsula by going north from the rest of Michigan across the Straits of Mackinac that connect Lake Michigan with Lake Huron. We took what the locals call "the back door," driving north along the shores of Lake Michigan in Wisconsin. We toured Green Bay, originally called "Bay of the Stinks" because of its swamps. (Green Bay also invented soft, flushable toilet paper, earning it the nickname "The Toilet Paper Capital of the World." Coincidence?) After stopping at Lambeau Field to pay homage to the Green Bay Packers, we entered the U.P. at the sister towns of Marinette, Wisconsin and Minominee, Michigan on the state border. We ate lunch in a café, where we were introduced to pasties, one of the staples of the Yooper diet. Pronounced pass-tees, pasties are shortbread or rye dough wrapped around various types of filling, usually some combination of meat, potatoes, and vegetables. If a calzone and a meat pie had a love child, it would be a pastie. Pasties are traditionally associated with Cornish miners from England, but Yoopers have their own version due to the influence of its Finnish population.

The Finnish influence was also evident in the wide availability of fruit wines. Yoopers make wines out of almost every type of fruit that grows locally and most of them have a high alcohol content. At the Garden Bay Winery, we sampled their signature drink, the Yooper Stooper, made from a blend of raspberry, blackberry, strawberry and blueberries fermented to 36 proof. It was advertised as "delicious and very relaxing" which was pretty accurate judging from the nap that I took immediately afterward. I wondered how the locals could drink it and still function until Aimee informed me that the U.P. has twice as many bars per person as any state in America. The area's most famous book is the story of a father and son taking a road trip together to sample 109 bars across the Upper Peninsula. Clearly, Yoopers take their drinking seriously.

We drove north through the Hiawatha National Forest toward Lake Superior. The center of the Upper Peninsula is a huge forest, with almost no people but full of lakes and rivers. Ernest Hemingway wrote a famous story about fishing on the Fox River and called the area "the best trout fishing in the country," so we decided to give it a try. Hemingway must have caught all the fish, because the only bites that we got were from the mosquitos. The Upper Peninsula's mosquitos are big, fast and always hungry. Our bug spray didn't seem to bother them and we decided that its scent just made us easier to locate.

Driving east through the forest, we saw a sign for "Root Beer Falls." Intrigued, we pulled in and discovered that its official name was Tahquamenon Falls and that it was the setting for the poem The Song of Hiawatha. It had been nicknamed Root Beer Falls for the golden-brown color of its water, caused by the tannins from the cedar swamps that drain into the river. This marketing trick seemed to work, as we saw more people there than at any other place since we had entered the Upper Peninsula. We hiked the trails that ran along both sides of the river, enjoying the shade and the sound of the rushing water.

Further east, we reached Lake Superior at Whitefish Bay, made famous in the Gordon Lightfoot song "The Wreck of the Edmund Fitzgerald." We went swimming and found that the bay was so shallow that we were nearly a mile out from shore before the water got up to our chest. However, the view was truly amazing. Looking out, the water stretched out as far as we could see in every direction. When we turned back toward the shore, it was an unbroken wall of forest. If not for the paved road, it could have been a thousand years ago. As we drove along the shoreline, we were constantly reminded by the size of Lake Superior. How many lakes have a lighthouse? Lake Superior has over a hundred.

We stopped in Sault Ste. Marie, a small town that straddles the border between the US and Canada. Set on the Saint Marys River that connects Lake Superior and Lake Huron, it has scenic walkways along the river and lots of restaurants. There seems to be an unwritten rule that the town's restaurants must serve whitefish, because we saw menus offering whitefish in every way imaginable. We ate at the Lockview Restaurant, which offered eight different whitefish dishes and when we jokingly asked why there were no whitefish desserts, the manager looked genuinely thoughtful. Later, we walked over to see the ingenious Soo Lock system that allows 10,000 ships per year to navigate the twenty-one-foot difference in water level between Lake Superior and Lake Huron. The lock has no pumps—all the water movement is done by gravity as they use the gates to raise or lower the water in the lock to match the lake that the ship is going toward. It was so intriguing that we watched several ships pass in each direction to convince ourselves that it really worked.

We headed south and finished our tour of Yooperland by riding the ferry to Mackinac Island located between Michigan's Upper and Lower Peninsulas. A picturesque island that started as a fort in 1780, it is now a major tourist destination that attracts over a million visitors each year. It reminded us of Williamsburg, Virginia with its beautiful colonial homes, historic hotels, quaint shops, and restaurants. Motor vehicles are not allowed, so everyone walks, bikes or rides in one of the horse-drawn carriages. At every stop, the island's 500 inhabitants help them spend their money pretending that they are living in an earlier time. We wandered around, enjoying the sights and the food, but a little overwhelmed by the crowds. It was quite a shock after the solitude of the Upper Peninsula. The 300 people that shared the ferry with us was more than the total number of people we had seen in over a week. After a couple of hours, we headed back to Gypsy and drove over the Mackinac Bridge to the main part of Michigan.

The Upper Peninsula was one of the most enjoyable parts of our trip around America. We often talk about our time there, eating pasties and drinking potent fruit wines while fishing on the Fox River, walking through the endless forests, wading out into Whitefish Bay, enjoying Sault Ste. Marie's quiet beauty while watching the ships pass through the lock. We listen to Da Yoopers, the U.P.'s most famous band sing "Second Week of Deer Camp" and roll on the floor laughing. Looking back, we passed through Yooperland too quickly and would happily return.

Catch and Release

—Aimee—

As I stood waist deep in the icy waters of the Fox River, struggling to keep my balance, it occurred to me that this was exactly as I had pictured it. I steadied myself in the rapidly flowing waters, batting away several hungry mosquitos. I baited my line from a pocket in my fishing vest, carefully brought my pole back and cast the line away in a beautiful arc, the lure sparkling in the sun as it dropped straight into a blackberry bush.

"Shit!" I muttered, cursing the underbrush, and trying not to scare the trout that surely lurked below. Ten minutes of retrieval and one slip into the fast-moving water later, I was ready again. This time, the hook did not catch my vest or my hat and the cast was lovely. Splonk! The baited lure, sure to attract any trout, landed perfectly in a dark pool under the overhanging branches fifty feet away and began to drift slowly toward me. Today, I would finally catch my first trout.

An hour later, I climbed up the embankment of our remote fishing spot in Michigan's Upper Peninsula, greeting Ron as he emerged from the bushes further downstream.

"Well?" I asked.

"Nope. You?" he responded, using an economy of words. He looked half frozen.

"Nope. Couple of good bites though," I lied. We both needed hope.

We silently loaded our gear into the fishing box, stripped off our wet clothes and started Gypsy's engine and heater. Once I got warm, I turned to Ron.

"I love that you'd try anything with me," I said.

"I'm actually having fun," he said. "We get to see some of the coolest countryside and rivers doing this. But instead of 'Catch and Release' fishing, I'm going to call it 'and Release' fishing because we seem to skip the 'Catch' part."

"Har, har!" I said, but the name stuck.

I had been bitten by the fishing bug in Kalispell, Montana near Flathead Lake, which has some of the most incredible rivers for fishing in the West. As we drove through its lush grasslands and tall mountains, we often saw people fly fishing or casting for trout. It occurred to me that I wanted that serenity. I wanted to stand at dawn, my breath fogging in the cool of the morning, silently using my skills to snare a trout that we would cook over a campfire for dinner that night.

Like any foolish first timer, I was convinced that all I needed was the right gear to become successful angler. I dragged Ron into a fishing store, mesmerized by the amazing selection of rods, reels, lures, bait, and clothing. Good lord, some of the poles cost thousands of dollars. I could hear Ron doing the math. "We could buy a hundred trout at Whole Foods for what this gear costs!" he exclaimed.

We ended up buying some basic poles and equipment for cast-fishing, since fly-fishing seemed to require both extreme skill and phenomenal amounts of cash. Some of the fuzzy, bug-like lures called "flies" were shown under a locked glass display like jewelry, with beautiful lighting and price tags that were conveniently turned over. If you had to ask the price, you couldn't afford fly fishing. I did manage to talk my way into a super-technical looking fishing vest with about twenty tiny pockets. I told Ron that "it's so I can carry all my gear easily." Truth is, I just thought that I looked totally cool when I wore it.

Over the next few months, I learned how to <u>not</u> catch a trout. I now know a thousand ways to <u>not</u> catch a trout. Turns out that trout are wily, elusive creatures who disdain fishing lures and scents guaranteed to draw them. I have sat shivering on a lakeside pier and watched the trout as they circled in the clear water below, totally ignoring my baited hook. I have crept through bramble bushes and poison ivy on the barest word of a local fisherman about a good fishing spot. I have stood silently while mosquitos drank my blood so as not to disturb the fish. I have risked grizzly bear attacks and backed away from skunks stealing my bait, all in the pursuit of these tasty bastards, all to no avail.

We bought fishing permits in every state and county that had the slightest possibility of finding fish. My very favorite was a permit to fish Duck Lake just east of Glacier National Park in Montana. Ron and I had heard that the trout were abundant there, but the lake is located on land belonging to the Blackfeet Nation Indian Tribe, and it is notoriously difficult to acquire permission to fish. Throwing caution to the wind, we drove Gypsy to the only official-looking building on the reservation, hoping to obtain a permit. There were a lot of folks in dress clothes roaming in and out of the building. It turns out that a wedding was about to begin, and we were crashing it. Thinking quickly, Ron offered the guests several bottles of wine from our stash to commemorate the occasion. They were delighted with the gift and happy to send us down the road to the local bar where the owner sold permits to people who were "in the know" for five dollars. There you have it, Ron can make friends everywhere. The next morning, we got up at the ungodly hour of 5am to fish the "can't miss" lake at the best time of day. And we still struck out.

We eventually got pretty laissez-faire about what we were fishing for, trying our luck in any river with a fishing sign. Once, we stopped at a fishing hole along the muddy, brown waters of the Missouri River to try casting under the highway bridge. On our way back up the bank, we saw an information board describing the kinds of fish that were in the river. The board listed a variety of strange fish including the paddlefish, a prehistoric gray creature with a long saw-toothed snout. I probably would have screamed in terror if I'd found one of those monsters munching on my lure.

Did we ever catch a fish? Yes. We caught two sun perch in Wisconsin from a rowboat. They were too small to keep, so we tossed them back. We caught one trout from a bridge in Traverse City, Michigan when he got so hung up in our gear that Ron had difficulty removing the hook. We both agreed to set him free, and I felt like a criminal for sending an injured fish back into the water. I hope he's there to this day, scarred and grizzled, teaching little trout how to avoid getting caught.

I don't regret my feverish year of fishing. I think back on the bug bites, bramble bush scratches and waterlogged sneakers and I wouldn't trade those memories for anything. I still have my gear and I pull it out once in a while and head off into the dawn or dusk to fish. I learned the greatest truth about fishing: it is Nature that you are there to enjoy, the quiet at a time of day that few people see. Ron and I spent many evenings sitting together amiably on creek banks and railroad trestles, watching the sun go down and waiting in the dying light for the fish to start feeding. I loved every minute of it.

Ron is just lucky that it wasn't duck hunting that interested me. We'd own twenty decoys and a cabinet full of guns.

The Life of Pie
—Ron—

I grew up in the era of "eat your dinner if you want dessert." We were fairly poor, so dessert was often imitation ice cream with chocolate syrup, but on special occasions, there was pie.

In my family, pie was more than a dessert. It was almost a religion. Anyone who made good pies held a place of honor at our family gatherings. Each Thanksgiving and Christmas, we would scour the grocery stores to find tart cherries packed in water for cherry pies. I started picking wild blackberries when I was 7 years old, enduring the pain of the bush's thorns for the delicious taste of blackberry pies. For apple pie, the big question was which type of apples to use. Granny Smiths or Pippins were recommended in most cookbooks, but our favorite was the Gravenstein, an obscure apple that had the perfect combination of sweet and tartness. We had an ongoing debate over pumpkin pie—sweet or spicy filling? Our family holidays included both, because it wasn't Thanksgiving or Christmas without pumpkin pie. Lemon meringue pie was also tricky, because some people liked a sweet filling, while others preferred more tartness, but we all agreed that chocolate meringue pie, with the meringue still warm from the oven, was fantastic. How important was pie? For my 50th birthday party, my family made 50 full-size pies and I tried every single one of them.

So, it should come as no surprise that we were always on the lookout for homemade pies as we drove around the country and found that sampling pies provided its own delicious tour of America. Most places in America had their own signature type of pie and sampling them was a tasty way to get to know an area. It was also a great way to meet the local folks and hear their stories. In Florence, Montana, I sat with the owner of Glen's Café as he told me how his late wife had started their tradition of selling homemade pies. Just then, his two daughters brought in four pies that they had just finished baking, still steaming from the oven. One of them was a huckleberry pie, which I had never tried before. I quickly discovered why huckleberry is the state pie of both Montana and Idaho. It was so good that when we went back through Montana, we detoured 100 miles to have their pies again.

I had never been a big fan of blueberry pie, but people kept telling me that Maine blueberries were different. Driving on one of Maine's tiny back roads, we stopped at a little country store that featured homemade blueberry pie. One bite changed my whole concept of blueberry pie. Smooth and tart at the same time, with a flaky crust, it was amazing. The store owner explained that while blueberries in most places are cultivated, Maine blueberries are grown wild. The soil in Maine is so rocky and acidic that the blueberries need a fungus to help them get nutrients and the fungus makes their fruit smaller and tarter than cultivated blueberries. We drove away with an intriguing botany story and a delicious new pie experience.

Another delicious surprise was key lime pie. I had never found it to be particularly appealing, but we kept hearing that the only place to find authentic key lime pie was in the Florida Keys, so we made a point of trying it at several places along the Overseas Highway from Key Largo to Key West. We were richly rewarded, because the difference was incredible. The key limes were grown locally, so they were fresh and had fully ripened before being picked from the tree. The graham cracker crust was light and crunchy. If the pie had a cream topping, it was freshly made, not canned or frozen. Our favorite key lime pie came from the Midway Café & Coffee Bar near Highway 1 Mile Marker 80 in Islamorada, but we had several great ones, each a little different. People were happy to share their secrets for achieving key lime pie perfection, and we had many lively discussions on the art of making pies.

Aimee loves chiles and had always wanted to try a chile pie, so we searched throughout New Mexico for them. Chile pies were once very common, but apparently now they are only made by grandmas and a few bakeries. Our favorite was the New Mexico Pie Company, who made green chile apple pie and red chile cherry pie. Both combined the sweetness of the fruit and the spiciness of the chile, with a slight afterburn. Served warm with ice cream to put out the fire, it was delightful.

Aimee and I had family from Louisiana and Texas who loved pecan pie, but we always thought that it was too gooey and sweet. When my brother Russell flew into New Orleans to join me for a bicycle ride, he suggested that we try the Camelia Grill, a local diner that was famous for its griddle-seared pecan pie. Served hot, the slight char of the pecans went perfectly with a scoop of vanilla ice cream. When I asked the cook how he made such a great pecan pie, he just smiled and pointed at his grizzled gray head, indicating that the secret was the result of many years of hard work and not to be shared.

Texas's hill country was a great pie destination. We found several good bakeries, but two of them really stood out. Tiny Pies in Austin was run by a mother and daughter who started making individual-size pies so that their kids could take them to school in their lunches. Tiny Pies had over fifty types of pie, making it really tough to choose because they all looked so good. Approximately 80 miles west of Austin, in the little town of Fredericksburg that is famous for its spring wildflowers, I stumbled across the Fredericksburg Pie Company, another family-run bakery that offered 25 different types of homemade pie. They would bake early each morning, open the store at 10am and sell out before lunch time. After sampling four different pies, I could see why.

The ultimate discovery in our search for great pie was Pie Town, New Mexico. Located at 7,800 feet atop the Continental Divide on Highway 60, it was truly in the middle of nowhere with Albuquerque 160 miles away to the east and Phoenix 290 miles to the west. We were wandering around the back roads of New Mexico and Aimee saw that the world's largest telescope array was only 60 miles west of us. "And about 25 miles further is a place called Pie Town that seems to be an entire town dedicated to pie," she said, and we were off in a flash. Pie Town had less than 200 people, but three places that competed to offer the best pie. I tried to pace myself, but there were too many tasty looking choices. I tried a dozen types of pie and went on a strict diet for several days after we left town.

Boston Cream pie in Massachusetts, apple pie in Michigan, marionberry pie in Oregon. We tried to sample every homemade pie that we could find and while we didn't get to nearly enough of them, touring our country's pie destinations was one of my favorite ways to experience America.

Love and Cherry Pie
—Aimee—

This may not seem like a story about living on the road, but it is. Living on the road is all about being happy in your marriage. Being together 24/7 puts a lot of pressure on a relationship. You are constantly going to new places where everyone is a stranger. You only have each other to lean on, so learning how to adapt to each other's needs so that you stay friendly is essential. One of my biggest lessons about that came from making a cherry pie.

I consider myself a pretty darn good cook and baker. I spent months mastering sourdough breadmaking from home starter, chasing the recipe for the perfect French croissant and baking all sorts of things for family holidays. However, my biggest challenge was cherry pie. It was my white whale.

When Ron and I got married, I was given a pie plate that had their family recipe for cherry pie hand painted in charming script onto its glossy bottom. It was both an enchanting and terrifying gift. I knew that I would be expected to produce this pie for special occasions from here to eternity. As a cook and an amateur anthropologist, I made it a point to hang out with Ron's mom in her kitchen the following Thanksgiving so I could take notes on her process. She was considered THE family standard for cherry pie. After the holiday, I quietly set about making a cherry pie to her specifications, but with a few modernizations. I just could not understand why pouring milk over the final pie crust would, in any way, help the pie. Nor did I favor using flour in the filling as it discolored the fruit. Big mistake.

When I surprised Ron with a cherry pie, whipping it out as he returned home from a business trip, he smiled broadly and served himself a generous portion (good sign.) After he took his first few bites, I couldn't restrain myself.

"Well? How is it?" I asked, totally trolling for compliments.

"Pretty good," he replied around a mouthful of pie.

Now, "Pretty good" is Ron-speak for "Not bad." "Pretty good" is what you tell the waitress when she asks how the pie was at the local coffee shop.

Pretty good...not *Really good*. And in my world, that meant Total Failure.

That's when it hit me. I wasn't being asked to create a Martha Stewart Cherry Pie or a Julia Childs Cherry Pie. I was being asked to re-create a cherished childhood memory. Cooking isn't always about the perfect ingredients and a precise method. Cooking is about love and the memories of being loved. When I made those little deviations from Mom's pie, it stopped being Mom's pie.

Now when I make cherry pie, I'm proud to make it her way.

Oh, We Got Fat!

—Aimee—

When we set out on our trip, we were so excited. It was the enthusiasm and lightheartedness that anyone would have at the prospect of a long vacation. But therein lay our mistake. We treated it like a vacation, eating for fun and skipping any semblance of a workout regimen.

It wasn't that noticeable at first. We were pretty fit when we started out, so stops for coffee and homemade cinnamon rolls didn't seem to be a problem. Our camping breakfasts often included bacon, eggs, and pancakes before we headed out for the day. If a roadside dive had a great meatloaf and chicken pot pie, why not get them both and their great mashed potatoes, too? We ate like every day was a day at Disneyland, or maybe more like Disneyland with wine. After all, nothing beat sucking down a great Pinot Noir while a couple of ribeye steaks were grilling over the campfire.

We did a lot of driving, which meant a lot of sitting and not much exercise to offset our new eating routine. It's amazing how you can fool yourself into thinking that a lap around the campground at dusk can undo several stops to taste the local pies.

Six weeks, ten weeks, three months went by as we ate our way across the USA. Gypsy didn't have a full-length mirror or a scale, so the self-deception was easy.

While we were visiting the Rock and Roll Hall of Fame in Cleveland, we had our picture taken and put on a mock cover of Rolling Stone Magazine…and what a cover it was! When I saw the printout, I literally shrieked. Oh my God! We had gotten fat! Really fat! So very fat!

I must admit that there were more than a few hours of self-pity and recrimination. "It was your love of pies that did this!" "Oh, yeah? Who keeps making pancakes every morning?" Eyes were narrowed. Lips were tightened. Words were exchanged. I swore that I would burn the photo and the negatives and possibly kill the photographer.

Ron tried the "It was just a bad camera angle" approach for a while, but we knew better. It's not like we hadn't noticed adding few pounds, but we had quietly moved from "a few extra pounds" squarely into the "There's more of you to love" category.

Eventually, we got down to the business of creating a new plan. In a stroke of creative genius, we called it "The Plan." It involved a unique two-step process. Eat Less and Work Out More. Innovative, right?

Step One: Eat Less: We changed our breakfast menu to yogurt with nuts and berries. We agreed to eat out no more than once a day and only if we found something really interesting, so no more casual eating. When we saw something that looked really tasty, we tried to split it. Dinner would be strictly an eat-in affair involving local foods. I got adept at cooking in Gypsy's micro-sized kitchen.

Step Two: Workout More: Workouts became an everyday thing. I revived my morning Yoga routine, despite the campers who laughed at the sight of me stretched out on top of a picnic table in my tights. Ron enrolled us in a YMCA program that would take us as guests anywhere in the country, so we that could put in an hour of weights, cardio and stretching every day. Soon, we saw a lot of YMCAs—ones in ancient brick buildings with old-timey cast iron barbells, modern YMCAs in two-story "green buildings" with brand new equipment and pools, Christian YMCAs with daily prayer boards and inner-city YMCA's complete with daycare centers. In one New York YMCA, we had to be checked against a national database of sex offenders before we were allowed inside. We also started talking long hikes in the National Park System. It wasn't pretty at first and we turned back on trails as often as we finished, but the pounds began to come off. I started to fear selfies less.

Ron started riding his bike more and he really enjoyed the many bike trails around the country. We realized that we were creating a lifestyle that was sustainable instead of treating the trip like a party.

Don't get me wrong, we were not perfect. About half of our 5,000 trip photos have food in them.

This is not an advertisement for some dorky weight loss program. I still eat cinnamon rolls. I still love red wine. There are days that my jeans fit great and days that I am afraid to step on the scale. The real moral of this tale is that a long RV trip cannot really be approached like a permanent vacation. The excesses and vices that you allow yourself on a week-long getaway to the Florida Keys will most definitely haunt you if you indulge that behavior for months at a time on the road. Part of your trip plan should be fitness and meals......and maybe a full-length mirror.

Swim Your Way Across the USA

—Ron—

Even before the "Oh my God, we've gotten fat" moment in Cleveland, Aimee and I had set a goal to swim in as many places as possible during our trip. We both love to swim and thought that swimming in different places would make for some adventures and maybe even a story or two. Little did we know.

At the top of our list was to swim in each of the five Great Lakes. At home, we swam a mile across our local lake at least once each summer, so we thought that we were prepared, but we quickly learned that the Great Lakes are very different. For starters, the Great Lakes are far bigger and deeper than we had imagined. Lake Superior is the largest lake in the world by surface area and second largest by volume. Even Lake Erie, the smallest of the Great Lakes, has nearly three times the volume of the next largest lake in the U.S. The Great Lakes are so big and deep that they have tides and currents, which made swimming in a straight line a real challenge since we couldn't see the opposite shore. It was strange to look out over the waves and see water all the way to the horizon and realize that it was not an ocean. The Great Lakes' size also means that storms arise suddenly and are very dangerous. When we first reached Lake Superior, we walked out on a jetty that extended 400 yards into the lake during 40 mph winds and were shocked by the size of the waves. Despite our vow to swim everywhere, we chose not to jump in.

The Great Lakes are also cold with a capital C. Growing up, we frequently swam in the Pacific Ocean and Lake Tahoe, so we thought that we were used to cold water, but when we swam Lake Superior in August, it took us over an hour to get warm after we got out. We were the only swimmers who weren't wearing wetsuits, which should have been a clue. We learned to gauge the temperature by listening to how loud a person screamed when they jumped into the water, and soon we had our own rating system: Cool, Chilly, Cold, Mighty Cold and "Jeezus, That's Cold!"

Finally, the Great Lakes have some scary creatures living in them. Sharks, sea lampreys and leeches have all been found there, along with the occasional piranha, apparently from people illegally dumping their aquariums. Then there is the snakehead fish, a "voracious predator" with rows of nasty teeth. It has rudimentary lungs and can walk across land for up to four days, so it can reach you even after you get out of the water. At least thinking about what might be nibbling my toes took my mind off the water temperature.

Despite the challenges, we managed to swim in all five Great Lakes. Our most unusual Great Lakes swim was in Whitefish Bay at the eastern end of Lake Superior. It is featured in one of our favorite songs, Gordon Lightfoot's "The Wreck of the Edmund Fitzgerald," so we had to give it a try. Unbeknownst to us, a recent storm had moved enormous amounts of sand into the bay. We waded out from the shore for over a mile and the water was still barely up to our waist. After an hour, we gave up and slogged our way back to shore.

Along with the Great Lakes, we swam in every lake that we could find and had some truly memorable experiences. Maine's Rangeley Lake on the Appalachian Trail had a beautiful view of the autumn leaves turning in the mountains. The water was also turning—to ice, so it was a short swim. Minnesota had so many lakes that we could have been there for months trying to swim in each one. Aimee picked campgrounds that had a lake so that I could grab a quick swim in the evening or early morning when I could enjoy the peaceful feeling of swimming alone. At least I thought that I was alone. More on that later.

We were eager to swim in Louisiana's Lake Martin near the town where Aimee's mom grew up. Its water was clear and still, shaded by trees and hanging moss, with turtles basking on the occasional log. Then we noticed several alligators and decided that we didn't want to come home missing an arm or a leg.

Our favorite lake for swimming was Flathead Lake in Montana about an hour south of Glacier National Park. It is one of the cleanest lakes in the world, as snowmelt from the Rockies replaces its entire water volume every three years, compared to every 200 years for Lake Superior and every 650 years for Lake Tahoe. As a result, the water is incredibly clear and cold. We stayed at Many Springs Resort, which had rooms overlooking the water and a jacuzzi soaking tub for getting warm again after we got out. The people at the resort's restaurant thought that we were brave or crazy. Probably a little of both.

We also wanted to swim in all the major rivers in America. We started with the Colorado River, and it gave us some spectacular swimming experiences, with clear, cool water and an exciting current. Our favorite swimming spot was at River Island State Park near Parker, Arizona. An island had diverted part of the river and created a swimming area that was protected from the swift current and from the ski boats that roared up and down the river's main channel.

Our other favorite river for swimming was the Columbia. We swam in several places along its 1,200-mile length from the Canadian Rockies to the Pacific Ocean. We spent two nights swimming at Steamboat Rock State Park just below the Grand Coulee Dam, another two nights at Lake Roosevelt National Recreation Area and a night at Kettle Falls just south of the Canadian border. Each place had beautiful swimming spots with clear water and a gentle current tamed by one of the river's 14 dams. At a peaceful little park near the dam where the Columbia merges with the Snake River, we had a very pleasant swim until we discovered that it was also a favorite spot for sea lampreys to breed. More on that later, too.

Finding places to swim in the major rivers east of the Rockies was more difficult, as the water was often polluted or had a current that was too treacherous for us. We did manage to swim in a couple of reservoirs along the Missouri and in Lake Itasca at the headwaters of the Mississippi in northern Minnesota. We also stopped along the Rio Grande River in several places, looking for a spot where the water wasn't a dark muddy brown, as we didn't like the idea of swimming in water where we couldn't see below the surface. Finally, in the Santa Elena Canyon at Big Bend National Park, we found a place where the water was clear. The river wasn't very deep, so it was more floating than swimming, but staring up at the tiny sliver of blue sky between the 1,500-foot cliffs on either side was an amazing experience.

Swimming in Florida's rivers was totally different than anywhere else on our trip. Florida is the flattest state in the U.S., with 345 feet between the highest point and the lowest point, so there was barely any current in its rivers. In many cases, the water came from hot springs, so it was warm, especially near its source. In Manatee Springs State Park, for example, the hot spring pumped out 100 million gallons of warm water each day into a large natural pool before it flowed into the Suwannee River. The waterway was a natural habitat for manatee, alligator, turtles, fish and the occasional adventurous swimmer. We had to try it, although it was a bit unnerving being nibbled on by the fish and wondering what else was lurking under the surface looking hungrily at our toes. The water was 72 degrees in January, which warranted a new entry on our temperature scale—the "AAHHHH!"

Living on the West Coast, we had swum most of the Pacific Ocean from Baja to Washington, but we wanted to try the waters along the Atlantic coast and the Gulf of Mexico. We started outside of Maine's Acadia National Park, which in October got a "Jeezus that's cold!" rating. Massachusetts' Cape Cod was somewhat warmer, but the locals still gave me strange looks when I went into the water without a wetsuit. As we worked our way south to Florida, the water got warmer and the waves seemed small compared to the Pacific Ocean. "This is more of bathtub than an ocean. Anybody could swim here!" I told Aimee as I paddled around Florida's New Smyrna Beach. Then she showed me an article describing the thousands of sharks that live there, resulting in over 300 shark attacks each year. After that, I shut up and stayed close to the shore.

When we couldn't find a lake, river, or ocean, we looked for one of America's 300,000 public pools and had some great experiences. In the Midwest, every town seemed to have a large community pool, many with old-style springboard diving boards. My favorite was in Oswego, Kansas. The town had less than 2,000 people, but their Olympic-sized pool was open to the general public for a dollar. I spent several hours doing cannonballs, going off the high dive and feeling like a kid on summer vacation.

Swimming our way around America was more than floating in gentle currents and enjoying the afternoon sunshine. It also meant lots of hikes down rocky trails and enduring endless bug bites, all so that we could jump into icy cold water. At times, we wondered if we were living some kind of crazy dare, but we enjoyed it anyway. There was a sense of being truly alive as we walked back to Gypsy, sharing a towel, and talking about the next adventure.

Jaws

—Aimee—

When I'm swimming in lakes, I have to push aside the thought of being eaten alive. The movie Jaws probably had that effect on everyone my age. I envision a lurking lake monster, its tentacles rising from the dark waters to wrap delicately around my calf and yank me down into the depths below. Despite being a strong swimmer, I regularly stop to tread water in lakes and peer down below my feet to see if any tentacles are present. If a lake weed tickles my feet, I have to resist the urge to dogpaddle desperately away in terror, flattening out on the surface to avoid its rubbery caress.

Rivers worry me less, which is totally dumb. I am fairly educated about water-borne creatures, so I know that many of America's shark attacks occur in rivers that connect to the ocean. Still, I find a river's flowing water and shallower depths comforting. I shouldn't have. Or at least, Ron shouldn't have.

Now if you're getting excited, thinking that Ron may have been bitten by a shark, you're out of luck. He was bitten all right, but it was even weirder.

One hot afternoon in the Tri-Cities area of Washington, we stopped at the junction of the enormous Columbia River and the muddy Snake River. We camped there in a lovely Army Corps of Engineers Park just below a dam. We pulled on our swimsuits and happily carried our towels over to a sunny, designated swim area. There were lots of people about, kids crashing in and out of the water and adults with umbrellas and folding chairs. It looked like a perfect day at the beach, and we went straight into the water. The current was pretty strong as we got further out into the river towards the floating string of buoys that designated the edge of the swimming zone. The water was deep enough and dark enough that you couldn't see or touch the bottom. Ron being Ron, he had to swim out under the rope into the center of the river. I waited in the safety of the swim area. On his way back, he yelled, "Ow!" and spun in a circle in the water.

"Something just bit me!" he said.

Like any good wife, I immediately discounted what he said.

"Like a fish?" I replied, thinking he had been nibbled by a minnow.

"No, something just bit my arm. Look!" He held his arm up out of the water to show me a perfect ring of tiny red marks about an inch and a half in diameter.

"Holy Crap!" I said, backpedaling in the water. "Let's get out of here!" I started swimming back to shore before he could respond, imagining a thousand tentacles, each with a ring of teeth, reaching up from the depths to get me.

Yes, I left him behind. There is a rule in scuba diving that you do not need to be faster than an attacking shark, you just need to be faster than your dive buddy. I am ashamed to say that I turned and fled like the hounds of hell were on my heels. Michael Phelps would not have beaten me to shore that day.

When Ron emerged from the river, I handed him a towel in the hopes that it might look like I had swum back so fast just to get him a dry towel. Fortunately for our relationship, he was too concerned with the bite on his arm to notice that I had abandoned him in his time of need.

"Let me look at that," I insisted. I am, after all, our trip medic. "That looks like a circular animal bite. I can see little teeth marks in the ring." Now that I was safely on land, I was very interested in what could have done it. "Did you see anything when it happened?"

"No, I was just swimming when I felt this eel-like body go by and then a sudden chomp on my arm. It was there and gone in a second."

"Eel-like?" Hmmm. After all, we were in the Snake River. I had heard that it was originally named for the sea-lampreys that migrated upriver to spawn. Could Ron have been bitten by a lamprey? Fascinating!

It was fascinating because I had never heard of a lamprey biting a human and because, well, it wasn't me that had been bitten.

Like any good researcher, I went right to Google and found that the local dam had a "Lamprey Ladder." That's right—they actually built something to help the sea lampreys get access to the Snake River where we were swimming. While adult lampreys only feed on cold-blooded creatures like fish, immature lampreys will bite anything they bump into. Google included pictures of lampreys biting rocks, boat motors, and yes, even the odd swimmer. Ron was probably chomped because he was alone and far out in the river, away from the noise and tumult of the swim area. I also think Ron is especially tasty to blood-sucking creatures. Mosquitos adore him.

The wound took a long time to heal. Lampreys have an anti-coagulant saliva in their toothy little mouths that keeps blood flowing and interferes with their victim's normal healing process. After a few days, the bite was still red and ugly. It looked like the kind of rash surfers get from bumping into live coral. Just when I started thinking that we were headed to the Emergency Room, it began to heal. A shame, really. It would have made a fantastic story— "The Great Lamprey Attack."

I would like to say that I am more careful now to check out our swimming holes before we jump in, but that would be a lie. I just let Ron go in first.

Leech Lake
—Aimee—

I know I'm tough on Ron in my stories. I really do find our marriage a constant source of hilarity, mostly at my patient husband's expense. However, this entry is all on me, as you will see.

Minnesota has a billion, zillion little lakes. Minnesota has more lakes than any other state except Alaska, and I swear that there is more water than land. Its roads curve and meander around the lake-pocked landscape. It's a paradise for camping, as every little lake seems to have fishing and an RV park.

Since there are so many lakes, you can imagine that the naming conventions get a little wonky and after a while I stopped paying attention when I picked a campground for the night.

One day, we grabbed a campsite at dusk, and I hardly noticed the fact that we were at a place called Leech Lake Campground. Busy with my chores, I briefly figured it was a joke or named after someone like that guy Robin Leach in "Lifestyles of the Rich and Famous."

It wasn't until morning, when Ron was out swimming in the lake, that I mused about its name and looked it up on Google. Oh hell! It was actually named after the many leeches known to inhabit Minnesota lakes and the neighboring Great Lakes. There were pictures of swimmers exiting the local lakes with rubbery black leeches attached to their legs. Ugh, barf!

Hopelessly fascinated by this horror, I clicked on "Video of Mass Leech Migration in Lake Superior." It showed an enormous black cloud of over five thousand leeches wriggling and swimming underwater toward the camera. They resolved into detail as they approached the camera lens, little black, worm-like parasites with open mouths. It was worth a full body shudder as I closed YouTube.

When Ron returned, I casually asked, "So, how was your swim? Anything interesting happen?"

"No, it was great. No one else was swimming, so I had the lake all to myself."

"Uh, there's something I should tell you about this lake," I said.

"What?" he said, eyeing me somewhat suspiciously.

"Um, it's called Leech Lake because it's full of leeches!" I blurted out.

"And you didn't think to check that out before I went swimming?" he asked, his tone implying that I had been secretly running an evil science experiment on him.

"I thought it was just a last name or something. But you have to see this video. It'll gross you out!"

"Yeah, I'll be sure to do that after I take an antiseptic shower," he said, stripping off his swimsuit and twisting and turning to check every crevice of his body.

I got lucky. No leeches.

I asked a few local campers about leeches while we packed up that day and I got this "Yeah, we get 'em here" reaction. "If you get one, pick it off." They were totally relaxed about it. They treated leeches in their lakes like we treat rattlesnakes in California. When asked, we always say, "Yep, they're around, don't step on them," which absolutely unsettles the European tourists who have seen a lot of Westerns where the guy dies by snake bite…slowly.

To me, leeches were new and horrifying. To Minnesotans, they are just a small nuisance.

After that, my loving husband would occasionally ask if I had fully researched where we were staying. He would then pause and whisper in a low voice "Leeeeeeech Laaaaake."

The Economics of Living on the Road

—*Ron*—

While we were excited about the idea of wandering carefree around America, we didn't want to go broke in the process. We saw some RVs and trailers that would never move again, except maybe to the junkyard. We couldn't tell if they had gotten that way for mechanical or financial reasons, but we didn't want it to happen to us. Our earlier RV trips with the kids had been vacations, focused on having as much fun as possible in a limited period of time. Cost was less important than the adventures and the memories that we created. This time, we were going to be out for a long time and would need to find a rhythm that we could afford, while still having a grand adventure. When we started, we had only a vague idea of what that meant, but gradually we began to understand the economics of living on the road.

Our biggest cost was housing. The cost of an RV site varied dramatically depending on the campground's location, amenities and the time of year. For a full-service site with power, water, sewer, and cable TV, we paid as much as $250/night in December in the Florida Keys and as little as $25/night in March at a campground in rural Alabama. We could get even lower cost at more rustic campgrounds, where the offerings ranged from water and electricity at the site and a central sewer dump location to pure "dirt camping" with no services at all. Some of the rustic campgrounds also had spectacular scenery. In California's Mount Whitney National Forest, we paid $5/night for a gorgeous site in a grove of trees with a creek running just behind us.

Overall, we averaged $40/night for RV campgrounds during our two years on the road. We also stayed in hotels a few nights each month when we wanted to visit a city or simply enjoy being able to soak in bathtub, so our total housing costs averaged $1,700 per month.

Our second big cost was transportation. Gypsy came equipped with a 10-cylinder Ford E450 engine that averaged 9 miles per gallon of gas, which wasn't great but considerably better than larger motorhomes. We drove about 900 miles per week, so we bought about 450 gallons of gas each month, including a small amount of gas to run the generator. Fortunately, gas prices stayed low during our trip, averaging about $2.20 per gallon, so we averaged $1,000 per month for gas. We paid another $30 per month for the propane that powered our hot water heater, stove, furnace and refrigerator. Then there were Gypsy's maintenance costs. Over two years and 100,000 miles, we did 10 oil changes, two full tune-ups and replaced each of our tires twice. We also had one major repair and several minor repairs. Our annual maintenance costs were a little over $3,500 or about $300 per month. Gypsy's vehicle insurance and AAA added another $100 per month, making our total transportation costs just under $1,500 per month.

Our food costs varied, depending on how often we ate out at restaurants. At first, we tried almost every coffee shop, pizza joint, café, bakery, and ice cream parlor that looked interesting. They all looked interesting, which put pressure on our wallets and even more pressure on our waistlines. Finally, when Aimee decreed that we were going on a diet, we limited our restaurant meals to lunch or special occasions and cut back on the snack stops. We bought food from the local grocery store or at a farm stand and cooked in Gypsy. After we made these adjustments, our total cost for food averaged about $1,000 per month.

Our cost for activities also changed after we committed to a fitness plan, because getting a workout became one of our major activities every day. For a while, gym fees were one of our bigger costs. Our hometown gym membership included guest privileges at other gyms, but the guest fee was typically $10 each, so we were spending over $500 per month in gym guest fees. Eventually, we found a YMCA in Florida with a $50/month couples membership fee that included free guest privileges at YMCA locations nationwide. We ended up going to over 200 different YMCAs, and seeing some of America's original YMCA buildings was one of our most interesting activities. We also bought a Senior lifetime pass to the National Parks, so we had 48 great stops that were virtually free. Otherwise, we relied on Aimee's research and the winds of fortune to find interesting things to see. These chance encounters were a great part of wandering around the country and they were rarely expensive. Our total cost for activities averaged $500 per month, which was surprisingly low for the number of adventures that we enjoyed.

One place that we didn't scrimp was our cell phone package. It was the only way that people could reach us and often the only way that we could use the Internet. Most RV campgrounds offer free wi-fi service, but we found that their bandwidth was rarely up to the combined demand of the people staying there, so we almost always used our phone as an Internet hotspot at night. We also used it while we were driving to get directions, look up places that we wanted to stop or simply to satisfy my curiosity about things. "Which state produces the most turkeys? Which country has the highest per capita consumption of ice cream? How about pizza?" (By the way, the answers are Minnesota, New Zealand, and Norway—see what Aimee had to put up with?) We paid $300 per month to get unlimited data with the broadest possible coverage, and it was worth every penny.

Finally, there were our general living costs like medical insurance, clothing, and personal care. These were about the same or even lower when we were traveling than when we were living at home. We didn't buy many clothes on our trip because we tended to wear comfortable things most of the time; besides, we didn't have room to store a lot of clothes. We were on the move too much for Aimee to use a regular hairdresser, so she did it herself. We still had some costs for our Oregon house, but we offset them by renting out a couple of rooms to students. Overall, our other living costs were about $1,500 per month, mostly for medical insurance.

When we added it all up, the average monthly cost of our trip looked like this:

$1,700	for lodging, including campgrounds and hotels
$1,500	for transportation, including gas, maintenance, AAA and insurance
$1,000	for food, including restaurants
$ 500	for activities
$ 300	for cell phone and Internet service
$1,500	for other expenses, primarily medical insurance
$6,500	Total expenses per month

Our costs were higher because we drove a lot of miles and stopped at so many places. It would have been less than $5,000 per month if we had done fewer miles by staying in each place for longer periods of time and skipped the hotels.

Was it worth it? Absolutely. It wasn't that much more expensive than living in our house in Oregon, and the memories of living on the road were truly priceless.

Monotony

—Aimee—

Living in an RV for a long time can be both intense and dull at the same time. When we started the trip, I expected a new adventure around every curve in the road, and that was true…up to a point. Our adventures weren't always a white-water rafting trip or a hike through Joshua Tree National Park. We spent a significant portion of it just driving. When we were stopped, a goodly amount of our time was spent doing the things that everyone does: shopping for groceries, making the bed, fixing dinner, paying the bills.

I think adventure is an over-used word today. "Adventure" in popular culture evokes constant excitement and picture-perfect moments. When I talk about the adventures on our trip, I am reminded of those nature programs where all of the action is boiled down into a one-hour show when the wildlife photographers actually spend months in trees to get each moment on film. A real adventure, the gritty, long-term, life-changing kind isn't always memorable. Every day isn't a postcard or an Instagrammable moment. Hell, it isn't even fun a lot of the time. People regularly said to us, "Wow, it must be so exciting to see something new every day." I'm going to share the darker side of our trip. It had a lot of monotony.

I'm not saying the trip wasn't fun or exciting, of course it was. But my chair could get really flat as we drove miles of endless road. There were stretches of mind-numbing boredom as the same desert or cornfield rolled by for hours. We often had the same schedule day after day and sometimes it had me climbing the walls.

A true adventure isn't predictable. It includes overcoming adversity, and we had our share. Breakdowns, getting lost, arguments and injuries were all part of the trip. I have sat on the side of the road, wondering how we could get someone to replace a tire on our 14,000-pound RV while silently consoling myself that it was Ron's fault that I was in this predicament.

We got lonely too. At home, the Starbucks barista knows you. "Hi Aimee! Grande four-shot latte?" If you're used to the comfortable, well-known layout of your local grocery store, then you might appreciate that every couple of days, Ron and I had to grab groceries in a new place. The aisle layout was always completely unfamiliar and what was available differed by geography. The checker inevitably asked if we had their rewards card and, of course, we didn't have a rewards card for Piggly Wiggly or Stop and Shop. You miss your community and its cast of characters. Other states have different accents and terms for things. You don't get to know your neighbors. It made us miss home.

Since everyone in the family wanted regular updates, we tried our best to tell them about all the cool things that we saw and generally left out the more mundane parts. Who really wants to hear that my big adventure included trimming my toenails or deep cleaning the bathroom last night? Barf.

Of course, there was also the strain of being with the same person all day, every day. I love Ron and he is a great partner, but after that many days of constant companionship, anyone would get on my nerves. "Have I ever told you the story about…" he would say. "Only about a thousand times," I would think, but even if I said yes, he would often tell it again anyway.

I admit that there were several emotional breakdowns. "Can't we just go home?" I asked Ron on more than a few occasions. Once he said, "We're having such a great time; why don't we do this for another year?" I totally lost it. "I'm done. I want my house, my kitchen, my yard!"

I have to say he was the tougher of the two of us on staying the course. He always took the long-term perspective. "We can go home if you really want to, honey, but this is an adventure and we may never get to do it like this again," he would explain. "It sucks!" I'd yell. "I hate (insert whatever state we were in at the time)!"

"Well, let's move on to somewhere new. Where do you want to go next?" he'd say, picking up his phone. Damn Google. Next thing I knew, he had me talking about a swamp adventure or a museum I had read about that was just down the road and wiping away my tears.

Morning would come and I'd settle my butt on the flat, corduroy seat, adjust the sideview mirror and we'd roll wheels. I guess adventure isn't what's happening now, it's really about what will happen next.

You Manage What You Measure

—*Ron*—

When we told our family and friends that we were planning to drive around America for a couple of years, they questioned whether Aimee and I would be able to get along living in an RV. Actually, they said things like "You'll drive Aimee crazy!" and "Don't expect anybody to blame Aimee when she kills you." There was even an informal pool for how long we would last before we gave up and settled back down to something more normal. Two months? Maybe. Two years? No way.

As it turned out, they were partially right. Living in close quarters and moving around almost every day did put stress on our relationship because it was easy to fall into a rut. Early on, we established a daily routine that included breakfast, breaking camp, a couple of hours of driving with stops if we found something interesting, lunch at a local café, more driving with stops until we reached our next campground, setting up, making dinner, some quiet time around the campfire, then into bed. It was nice to have a predictable schedule, but after a while the sameness of it made began to wear on us.

We were four months into the trip and driving through Ohio when the crisis occurred. We had finished breakfast when Aimee gave me "the look." Now, if you are married, I don't need to describe it any further. All husbands know what "the look" means. Not seeing a way to escape, I asked fearfully, "What's wrong?"

Still glowering, Aimee replied, "This isn't working for me." Perhaps the scariest phrase in the marital handbook. Trust me, when your spouse says, "This isn't working for me," what comes next is not going to be pleasant. It's roughly the same as when the girl you are dating says, "I just want to be friends." Neither one is likely to have a happy ending. I needed to find a creative solution and I had no time to spare.

Thomas Edison claimed that genius is 1 percent inspiration and 99 percent perspiration. In this case, creativity was 1 percent inspiration and 99 percent desperation. Thinking quickly, I fell back on an adage from my career in business. "Well, you manage what you measure," I said. "Let's put together a rating system for each day's activity?"

Somewhat to my surprise, Aimee agreed to give it a try. I asked her what things would make a day good or bad for her, then added a few of my own. An hour later, we had the following list:

- Plus 1 point for espresso (otherwise, it was unlikely to be a good day no matter what else happened)
- Plus 1 point for finding a good local place to eat
- Plus 1 point for each fun activity
- Plus 1 point for interesting sights while driving
- Plus 1 point for a good work-out
- Plus 1 point for a nice place to stay at night
- Plus 1 point for fun evening activities (playing guitar, a walk under the stars, etc.)
- Plus 1 point for romance (which could mean a lot of things)
- Plus 1 point for a good night's sleep
- Minus 1 point for equipment problems
- Minus 1 point for business calls or meetings
- Minus 1 point for getting lost, unless it led to something interesting
- Minus 1 point for injuries
- Minus 1 point for fights, having a bad attitude or getting the blues

Yes, there were more ways to get a plus than a minus. Anyone who won't rig a game to keep their spouse happy is a fool.

We started each day with a score of 5. Getting to 10 would be an outstanding day, while dropping to 0 meant that we needed to do something different. We had a pretty consistent morning routine, with breakfast, a walk/stretch and a drive, so lunchtime was our chance to make adjustments. Did a nearby town have an interesting local restaurant? Was there a gym, pool, or place to take a hike nearby to work off lunch? In the mid-afternoon, we would take stock again.

Did Google show any interesting places to see in the area? Was there a scenic campground where we can get in early and relax before dinner? Do we want to pick something up rather than cook tonight? We discovered a lot of great places while we were trying to make a day rate as a success.

It may seem silly to measure daily enjoyment, but it helped us stay focused on the quality of our time together. I don't think that there was anything special about the list itself. Mostly, it gave us a way to show each other that we wanted the same things from our trip by paying attention to those things every day. It reminded us to look for positive things and avoid the negatives. We were having a once in a lifetime experience; we wanted to still be happily married at the end of it.

Fight Club

—Aimee—

My sister-in-law, Leilani, once described marriage, "If you are married long enough, there will be days when you are giddy with love for him, and then there will be days where you cannot stand the way he BREATHES."

Other than, "Who will do your hair?" the most frequent question that I got from friends when I described our upcoming trip was, "How will you two get along?"

It was a reasonable question. Ron and I both have very strong personalities. During our marriage, we had spent a lot of time apart because we both commuted to out-of-town jobs. Could we really spend every day together in an RV without experiencing a little conflict? Probably not. Cramped quarters do not generally bring out the best in people. The U.S. Navy wouldn't send out a married couple in a submarine, and NASA expressly forbids married couples from inhabiting the International Space Station together.

So, yes, arguments happened. They were often about the smallest things: driving styles, who hogged the covers, not respecting the other's personal tastes in music, side-seat driving. Probably most couples get irritated by little stuff like this. The RV can really magnify a disagreement because there just isn't anywhere to retreat to. Only a fool would yell "Pull over!" and storm off into the wilds of North Dakota. So, if you're driving, the fight happens while you sit eighteen inches from each other in angry silence until someone breaks the tension.

I can remember Ron getting totally irritated at me for refusing to play songs from the TV series Glee as we drove along. I generally loathed music from Glee and so it went like this:

"Hey, can you play some Glee?" asked Ron while changing lanes on the Interstate freeway.

"Come on, that crap isn't real music," I said, grasping my iPhone protectively. After all, picking the music was my job.

"I think most Glee music is better than the singing by the original 80's artists. If you can call that singing," he retorted, nodding sagely to himself.

"Hey! I went to high school in the Eighties!" I said, emphasizing the "I" so he knew that he was getting over the line.

"Worst decade for music ever," he finished, looking self-satisfied.

There you go…fight club.

What do you do when you're in that situation? You could start trading more insults, which I have to say is truly tempting, but that's a path to a longer fight. I sat there fuming for a good five minutes while his lips got tighter. This was no way to see America together. Time for apologies and a compromise.

We ended up making peace. I created a Glee playlist on my phone that I would play for him when he got tired driving or had the blues. At least all the Glee songs were corralled into one playlist. I resisted the temptation to label it "Crap" and stuck with "Glee" instead. See how enlightened I had become?

The truth is that conflict just leads to a lousy day in the RV. Would I like to take this road trip by myself and listen to Metallica (forbidden by agreement) all day? No, not really, although I did briefly picture myself blaring "Enter Sandman" while I pulled into a truck stop looking every inch like a hot single mama….

Sometimes, I had a little case of side-seat driving, and that also led to a few hot minutes. More than once, I told Ron that he was speeding, and he retorted that he was "Optimizing Traffic." I may have responded that no cop in America was going to buy the "Optimizing" angle.

When my obsessive-compulsive style ran into Ron's devil-may-care philosophy, things could get messy in a hurry. For example, Ron doesn't like to be managed, and he could get a bit testy when I told him that he was folding our towels the wrong way—how strange!

Of course, when you're in a campground for the night and you have a fight, it's easy to consider storming off. I have done it, and nothing is as miserable as standing in a campground laundry room, letting your angry imagination run wild. You think to yourself, "I'll show him. I'll call a taxi and disappear into the night. I could grab a plane out of Madison, Wisconsin in an hour." But then you think, "Where the hell would I go?" and there you have it. The one person you want to miss you badly is right here, in this very campground. So, you suck it up, walk back, and tell him you didn't mean to throw a book at him and then cry. No, you weren't trying to hit his pacemaker; it was just a lucky shot. You blame your hormones or your horoscope, and then you apologize. If he's smart, he apologizes too.

I cannot stress enough the power of a real apology. You don't even have to be right or wrong. You just have to want to make peace. I'd like to say that I had a certain Gandhi-like approach to conflict. Truth is, I don't. I am a real pro at apologizing because I get mad on a regular basis. I'm just as hot-blooded as any other Scottish redhead. Funny, menopause has not made this easier.

As an aside, I do not recommend that you take your wife on a life-changing RV trip if she is just starting menopause. In the same way, I do not suggest that you take up cage fighting with grizzly bears. You may survive, but your odds aren't good.

I have to say that Ron worked hard to maintain peace and tranquility on the trip. It's not that he didn't get mad, but he held his tongue most of the time. Often, he tried to diffuse a day headed for a fight involved by changing the scenery ("Let's roll wheels and find something fun!") or finding a pleasant surprise ("Oh look, a Starbucks! Let me get you a latte.") He was a master at subterfuge for marital bliss.

Over the course of the two years, we got better at respecting each other's sensitive areas, and that helped eliminate the little irritations that could cause strife. We also tried very hard to be kind to each other and we apologized when we weren't. Supreme Court Justice Ruth Bader Ginsburg had the following marital advice: "The secret to a happy marriage is that every now and then it helps to be a little deaf." It goes right up there with "hold your tongue."

I do have some advice for NASA. If they ever put a married couple on the Space Station, they should be prepared for someone to get pushed out of the airlock for not putting away their helmet…that is… until things get sorted out.

Wild Things
—Ron—

One of our big goals in driving around America was to see its wild animals in their natural habitat. Aimee bought field guides of North American birds, mammals, and reptiles, then made a list of the animals that she wanted to see. She kept her binoculars next to her as we drove down back roads where we thought that we were most likely to encounter wildlife.

First on our list was buffalo, the largest land animal in North America. (I know that they are actually bison, and the only real buffalo are the cape buffalo and the water buffalo, but I've heard them called buffalo on TV and movies for my entire life and I can't change. Besides, "Give me a home where the bison roam" just doesn't sound right.) I had seen buffalo in zoos and nature preserves, but never in the wild. As it turned out, it was pretty easy to find them in some of the National Parks. Driving Highway 212 through the northern part of Yellowstone National Park, we saw huge herds of buffalo grazing in the meadows. Later, we watched them swim across an icy river, including a newborn that stuck very close to his mother to avoid being swept away by the fast-moving current. In North Dakota's Theodore Roosevelt National Park, we had to wait for 30 minutes while a herd of buffalo crossed the road directly in front of us, completely unafraid of Gypsy.

The National Parks were also a great place to see bears in the wild. Driving through one of Yellowstone's back roads, we came upon a huge snarl of cars and people. As we eased along, we saw that a young black bear had climbed a tree near the road and was clinging to the side of the tree in a picture-perfect pose. He drew an enormous crowd, with people running down the middle of the road trying to set up their cameras. We felt sorry for the poor bear, who was clearly terrified by the attention.

Grizzly bears were not so timid. We were at the east entrance to Glacier National Park on our way to go trout fishing when we saw a female grizzly bear in a meadow next to the road. I had never seen a grizzly bear in the wild, so I got out and started walking out into the meadow to get a closer look. Then she turned toward me with a hungry look on her face and I made a hasty retreat to Gypsy. It gave me a much better appreciation for why there are bear warnings throughout the park.

Our favorite bear sighting was at dusk along the Blue Mountain Parkway in the Shenandoah National Park south of Charlottesville, Virginia. The road had a lot of blind curves, so we were driving carefully while enjoying the fall colors and the quiet of the late afternoon. We came around a curve to find a mother black bear casually walking up the road while her young cub kept pace in the woods nearby. We were afraid that she would get hit by a car coming the other way, so we tried to encourage her to get off the road. We drove Gypsy up close to her and honked the horn, but she ignored us and jealously protected her right of way, apparently preferring the level paved road to the steep terrain on either side. Fortunately, our honking upset her cub and its squalls brought her off the road. We drove on feeling good that we might have saved a mama from harm.

Finding moose in the wild was more difficult. We drove around most of the Rocky Mountain states with no success until we took a small back road through the Bighorn National Forest on our way from Cody, Wyoming to the Little Bighorn Monument in Montana.

The snow had just begun to melt in the high meadow, and we saw a wild moose grazing on the new grass. After several months of searching, we grinned at each other in delight, feeling like we had won a "Find the Rare Animal" contest.

We often saw roadrunners scooting through the desert as we drove around the Southwest. Having grown up with Looney Toons Roadrunner cartoons, we half expected to see Wile E Coyote giving chase with an assortment of Acme products. No luck, but that didn't keep us from shouting "Beep Beep!" every time we saw one zooming along. At Big Bend National Park, a roadrunner had decided to make the Ranger Headquarters his permanent home, watching from the roof as people took photos. We also had a great rattlesnake encounter in Big Bend Park when we stopped for one who was sunning himself in the middle of the warm pavement. We honked Gypsy's horn at him until he reluctantly left, coiled and buzzing the whole time. Clearly, this was his home, and we were the intruders.

Growing up in California, we envisioned Florida as a combination of sunny beaches and theme parks, mostly populated by Miami Vice types, Disney World visitors and elderly occupants of "God's Waiting Room." Yet much of Florida was a natural wonderland of primal waterways and an enormous variety of wildlife. At Blue Springs State Park 30 miles north of Orlando, a hot spring flowed into the St Johns River. A mile-long boardwalk along the water made it easy to see the wildlife. In less than an hour, we saw alligators, turtles, pelicans, cormorants, eagles and gar, a fish that can grow to over 8 feet long with rows of needle-sharp teeth. Our favorite animal was the manatee, which looks like a walrus without the tusks. An adult can be eight feet long, but they are very gentle and timid. Manatees live in the inland waterways near both coasts in the central part of the state. They need warm water, so they sleep near the hot spring, then swim out to the ocean each day to feed on sea grass. Human germs are dangerous to them, so we rented a kayak, which let us so get close without touching them. As we were paddling along, a baby manatee surfaced next to us and nudged our kayak several times, rolling over in a clear invitation to join him in playing tag.

We also saw a lot of alligators, usually from the safety of Gypsy as we were driving, but we had a couple of closer encounters. We took an airboat ride through the Florida Everglades and got close to several alligators, hoping that the boat was fast enough to get away if we needed to. At Champagne's Cajun Swamp Tours near Lafayette, Louisiana, a guide took us through the bayou in his pirogue boat. We glided slowly through the still water, enjoying the quiet, when we noticed a huge alligator less than twenty feet away. He was sunning himself on a partially submerged tree root and was so motionless that he blended into the background. Being that close to him in a boat that clearly couldn't protect us or outrun him, we felt like prey animals as we tried to sneak past without catching his attention.

Aimee was always on the lookout for interesting birds, and they provided some of our most entertaining moments. On the inland waterways of Florida's east coast, we watched the pelicans as they lined up waiting for the fishing boats to return with dinner. In the Everglades, there were signs warning visitors that the buzzards would eat the weather stripping on their car. We thought that it was a local joke for the tourists until we saw three buzzards sitting on a rental car having their afternoon snack. Nighthawks are generally hard to find, but an entire flock joined us at a campground in eastern Oregon, thrilling us with their aerial acrobatics as they swooped through the evening air hunting for insects. Our best bird sighting was in Hell's Half Acre on the Powder River in the high plains west of Laramie, Wyoming. The campground had osprey living there that hunted in the river and Aimee spotted one flying back to her nest with a fish in her beak, bringing dinner to her babies.

Watching for wildlife as we drove was a constant source of entertainment for us. There was the joy of discovery, that "aha" moment when we would spy an animal that we had never seen before. We often found that it was more an accident than a planned event. We spent weeks in looking for a rare American mountain goat, only to see one peacefully grazing ten feet in front of us outside the entrance to the Mount Rushmore Monument. In Texas, a herd of over twenty Barbary sheep sauntered across the road directly in front of us. We found over a dozen wild javelinas making themselves at home at a campsite in Big Bend National Park. Our first close-up view of a manatee was when we found over a hundred of them camped out near a power plant that kept the water warm in the winter. Want to find a porcupine? Try the dumpster at your campground. Alligators, dolphins, or otters? Take a kayak out and they will find you. Our favorite sightings were the babies, greeting the world with newborn curiosity from the comfort of their mother's side. Finding animals in the wild was more than seeing them, it was being part of their world. We hope that America always has a home for them.

Night of the Conch

—*Aimee*—

We had many exciting wildlife interactions throughout our trip. Otters, bison, manatees. Too many to even list. This one deserves its own story if for no other reason than it was simply bizarre.

One humid night along the Gulf Coast of Florida, we managed to snag a campsite on Fort Meyers Beach. The beach was a typical Florida postcard with endless miles of white sand set against the calm gulf waters. The sunset was spectacular, and we enjoyed walking on the pristine beach at dusk after everyone had packed up and left with their kids, umbrellas, and lounge chairs.

In the waning light, I noticed that the tide was coming in and was starting to cover most of the beach. Oddly, I saw quite a few of the small striped "fighting conch" whose shells you often find washed up on the Florida beaches. These were alive, moving in the water-logged sand at the margin of the tide. The sand around each conch looked bubbly and disturbed. "Super weird," I thought.

By the time darkness fell and we headed back to Gypsy for the night, we were stepping over and around dozens of two and three-inch conch working their way out of the deep sand.

Since I'm 100% fascinated by weird and unusual wildlife, I ate dinner quickly and went back out. Walking around, it was so bright that I hardly needed my flashlight. I looked up and sure enough, there was a huge full moon rising over the palmetto trees. The gentle sound of the Gulf waves was closer than I expected, and it didn't take me long to realize that it was a very high tide, almost reaching the first row of RVs in our park.

The beach was almost completely covered with shallow water and alive with activity. Fighting conch were everywhere, writhing in the shallow surf, turning the water frothy. They crawled over and around each other, collecting in knots around any of the larger female conch. I couldn't walk on the exposed portion of the beach because of all the alien activity going on. It looked like a mosh pit at a rock concert.

I had stumbled onto conch date night. Or more accurately, conch porn.

Like any good researcher, I needed a lab assistant. Running back to Gypsy in the darkness, I banged on the door.

"Get out here! You gotta see this!" I yelled.

"Jeopardy is almost over. Then I'll be right out," Ron said. Now, Jeopardy is part of Ron's holy sacrament of evening relaxation. He must watch Jeopardy each and every weeknight, wherever he is, camping or not. Only a house fire would make him miss it.

I danced from one foot to the other, waiting as Ron yelled, "Genghis Khan!" at the TV as his answer to Final Jeopardy.

"Hurry! You'll miss it!" I said urgently.

"I'm coming, this had better be good," he said, the RV door swinging open and the automatic step whirring out. "I'm really tired from all the driving today."

"There are conches all over the beach and I think it's some sort of lunar mating thing!" I said with my customary enthusiasm over the bizarre.

Ron obligingly grabbed his flashlight and followed me through the rows of RVs. He's gotten used to my quirks over the years and has given up on talking me out of dragging him to see offbeat curiosities.

We made it to the beach, and with his usual aplomb he said, "Yep, that's a lot of conches."

"It's amazing, look at their fighting claw sticking out from under the opening of the shell. I think they are vying for larger females!" I babbled, giddy with the joy of scientific discovery. "Pick one up and let's check."

"You pick one up. I can see them just fine from right here," he said.

Okay, as lab assistants go, Ron is somewhat squeamish. He hates it when I discuss diseases while we are eating dinner and he actively resists any hands-on research that I instruct him to perform.

"Here, I'll grab one and you shine the flashlight on it," I said, reaching for a conch in the scrum of frothy conchs. "Do you think the froth around them is fertilized eggs?"

"Hey, how about you leave these guys alone and enjoy the fact that we're probably the only people who get to see this. It really is cool. Those guys can really move when they want to. Wow!"

Never say that husbands can't be subtly manipulative. With that one comment, he stopped me from interfering, acknowledging that it was cool and complimenting my interest in coming out at night in the first place. One sentence. Bad Lab Assistant. Good Husband.

We walked back to the RV. Ron quietly holding my hand. Me chattering on endlessly about conch mating habits and lunar tides. A match made in heaven.

Seasons on the Road
—*Ron*—

One of our goals was to experience America's seasons in different parts of the country. In northern California, we had four distinct seasons, but they were fairly mild. Spring was awash with colors, as fields of yellow mustard flowers covered the hillsides, wild poppies and daffodils sprang up alongside the country roads and the vineyards came out of hibernation in their annual growth spurt of vines and leaves. Summers were hot and dry, with little rain and temperatures commonly above 100 degrees as the grassy hillsides turned golden brown. In the fall, the days quickly got shorter and cooler, filled with the smell of the harvest in the air as the grape leaves turned shades of red, gold and brown. Winters were rainy, but snow was a rare and exotic event that would cause the schools to close while the kids played outside for an hour or two until the snow melted.

Now that we were mobile, we wanted to catch all the classic settings at their perfect time of year. Summer in the high country of Montana. The fall colors in New England. Winters sunning ourselves on the beach in the Florida Keys or in a snowy mountain retreat. Spring watching the explosion of flowers in the desert. Basically, every post card that you have ever seen of the American outdoors.

At the top of our list was the fall colors on the East Coast. I had lived in Connecticut and outside Washington, D.C., so I had seen them a little bit, mostly as I was raking the millions of leaves that fell each year in my yard. Aimee had only been to the East Coast on business trips to downtown Boston and New York City, so she had not seen the outdoor foliage at all. Wanting to get the full experience, we decided to follow the fall colors down the entire length of the Appalachian Mountains, timing our trip to hit the peak color in each state as we went south. We started in Maine's Longfellow Mountains during late September and drove through the White Mountains of New Hampshire, the Green Mountains in Vermont, the Berkshires of Massachusetts and Connecticut, New York's Adirondacks and Catskills, Pennsylvania's Poconos and the Blue Ridge Mountains through West Virginia, Virginia, the Carolinas, and Georgia. We finished in late November and while the leaves were long gone in Maine, they were still gorgeous in Georgia. I never knew that so many shades of red, orange, and yellow could exist. At times, the colors seem to explode across the landscape, framing the mountains and the water in the background. We took a lot of pictures, but even a perfect photo couldn't capture the crunch of the leaves and the smell of autumn as we walked through the woods. Driving a motorhome may be the best way to see the fall colors, because it provides the mobility to adjust to the local weather and find the spot where the leaves are perfect. Following the autumn colors was even better than we had hoped.

We had planned to spend most of our winters in warm weather locations, but we also wanted to explore some classic winter destinations. I had visions straight out of the movie White Christmas, sipping cocoa and reading a book as I watched the snowflakes drift gently down in the New England countryside, then going outside to build a snowman and coming back inside to warm up again. We quickly learned that RVs aren't made for freezing weather. Gypsy didn't have much insulation, so our living space would quickly go from toasty warm to uncomfortably cold. More importantly, our water and sewage systems were exposed to the outside air, so they would freeze up when the temperature dropped. Thawing a frozen line with a hair dryer didn't fit any of our winter travel fantasies. We also learned that there were very few places in America with reliably warm weather in the winter. Florida was the safest bet and even it could be pretty risky at times. We almost got blown over at our campground a couple of times when storms ripped through the Keys. Still, it was nice to go swimming and get a tan in the middle of winter while watching the weather report on the rest of the country.

Apparently, we weren't the only ones who had set their sights on Florida, because the state was overrun with campers in the winter. The first time that we tried to book an RV park in the Florida Keys for January, I spent three hours looking for a vacancy, then nearly had a heart attack when I saw the prices. After a week, we realized that our dream of lounging our way through the winter months in the Keys sipping Mai Tais and pretending that we were Ernest Hemingway did not fit our budget. We moved to more rustic campgrounds in the less-crowded western coast and interior parts of the state while we waited for warmer weather. The next year we flew back to California to spend Christmas with our family, then took a cruise ship back through the Panama Canal and around the Caribbean for most of January. We felt completely decadent at having a bathtub to soak in and smug in the knowledge that the flight, hotel and cruise cost less than it would have to stay in an RV park in the Florida Keys.

Summer was a different kind of challenge. Each June we went to the West Coast to visit family and so I could play in the World Series of Poker with my brother Russell. Then we would drive across the country to catch autumn on the East Coast. We always started by going through the Rocky Mountains, enjoying its rugged beauty, cool mountain air and alpine lakes. After we left the Rockies, however, we had to drive through the middle of the country in July and August. Our first year we went across the upper Midwest and our impression of summer there can be summed up in one word: MOSQUITOS. Minnesota is called "The land of 10,000 lakes," but it should be called "the land of 10 billion flying hypodermic needles." Now we know why they have a town called St. Cloud—it had clouds of mosquitos that followed us for several miles even after we left town. When we reached Lake Superior, they seemed to diminish in number, but made up for it by being even more aggressive and hungry. We discovered that they would leave us alone for a while after we went swimming, perhaps because they couldn't penetrate the goosebumps that we got from the frigid water.

Our second year we tried a more southern route, dropping down through Colorado, then east through Kansas, Missouri, Arkansas and the upper portions of Mississippi and Alabama on our way to Atlanta. Along the way, we learned why the movies set in the South always show people sitting in the shade drinking iced tea or mint juleps. The combination of heat and humidity was like living in a steam bath. We would take a walk around the campground in the early morning and return to Gypsy with our clothes dripping a mixture of sweat and moisture from the air. We ran Gypsy's air conditioning all night and day, occasionally opening the windows to reduce the condensation on the inside surfaces. We ended up driving a lot of miles each day with our eyes set firmly on getting into the Appalachian Mountains and cooler weather.

Our first year, we thought it would be fun to experience spring in the Rockies. We had grown up watching The Sound of Music, so we expected lush mountain meadows in the bright sunshine with new flowers peeking out and baby animals following their moms around. We got to Yellowstone in early May and quickly learned that spring there is like winter almost anywhere else. We watched buffalo shiver as they swam across an icy river and were very glad for Gypsy's heater. Driving through Wyoming a few days later, almost every road was closed due to snow and the one road that was open had six-foot high snowbanks on either side.

The following years, we were determined to find warmer weather after enduring a winter in Gypsy, so we stayed in the southern part of the country. We spent April Fool's Day in

Memphis listening to Beale Street's blues music, visiting Graceland and Sun Records and eating at Gus's Fried Chicken. Then we drove 400 miles across Tennessee, through Nashville and Knoxville, enjoying the rolling countryside covered with spring flowers. We came back through Kentucky, seeing Colonel Sanders' original restaurant and watching the new foals in Lexington's bluegrass pastures. We spent three weeks in Louisiana, kayaking in the bayous, checking out the river towns, soaking up the New Orleans vibe and driving the barrier islands along the Gulf of Mexico. We wandered around Texas, New Mexico and Arizona searching for desert wildflowers. We spent three spring seasons on the road and still felt like we had just begun to explore.

We were often asked, "Where was the prettiest place that you saw?" but there were so many amazing places that it was impossible to choose. In spring, would you rather watch the desert flowers bloom or the newborn buffalo in the Rockies? Autumn leaves on the East Coast or harvest time in the Midwest farm country? Living in an RV gave us the mobility to experience the diversity that makes America so beautiful.

Metal Tent

—Aimee—

RVs were originally intended as vehicles to take your family away for a weekend of upscale camping in the woods, not as a regular home. Though they have added numerous luxuries over the years, RV manufacturers were slow to understand that many folks live in their RVs full time in situations that they were never really designed for. Over our two years, we had to adapt to the fact that an RV is not a house. It is more like a glorified metal tent.

Gypsy's air conditioning system, for example, just didn't work the same way as one in a house. RVs have air conditioning units on their roofs and some big RVs even have two A/C units. When the weather was hot, we ran our air conditioning frequently and it worked great, even when the temperature exceeded 100 degrees outside. In Death Valley, we left it running through the night while we covered the windshield with a reflective sheet and lowered the window blinds. Even with the sun blazing on our metal exterior the next day, the interior stayed very comfortable.

Very comfortable, that is, as long as it wasn't humid outside. There's an inherent problem with air conditioning in small spaces that have metal walls—condensation. In the hot South, when we ran our air conditioning, the walls would sweat, moisture dripped out of the ceiling intake vents and the windows fogged up. We opened our windows to try to normalize it, only to get walloped with oppressive swamp-like heat. It's very tricky to manage the temperature vs. moisture trade-off in places like Louisiana and Georgia. Sometimes we just had to let it drip inside Gypsy and mopped up as necessary.

Staying warm in cold weather was an even bigger problem. Truly cold weather, that is, not your "Oh what a beautiful October morning!"

cold, but rather the butt-freezing, hat and mittens weather where even hunters think twice about going outside. When it was really cold, we ran our heater, which worked pretty well, but burned propane at an alarming rate. I pictured tiny pterodactyls being burned by the bushel just to blow a little heat onto my frozen toes in the morning. We tried not to run the heater when we were sleeping, instead bundling under five quilts. Still, nights below freezing were a tremendous challenge for Gypsy. Her water lines would freeze up and her septic hoses would freeze onto the outlet valves. I spent one lovely morning squatting in the snow, a hairdryer in one gloved hand, trying to unfreeze our septic lines just so I could flush the toilet. We had to develop tricks to deal with serious cold. We would unhook all our hoses at night so that we weren't stuck the next morning with our water hose frozen to the campsite water spigot. We put anti-freeze in our black tank under the toilet, so the unthinkable "waste-cube" did not occur. I later learned that some newer RV models offer heated waste tanks. Oh, what a joy that would have been!

Hot weather, cold weather—we learned to adapt. There is, however, one sort of weather that no RV traveler wants to be a part of and that is tornado weather. Everybody jokes about how tornados love trailer parks. The truth is that being basically metal tents, RVs and trailers do not weigh enough to stay put in really high winds and are not built to handle the lightning that usually comes with a tornado. If Gypsy had taken a lightning strike while hooked up to an electrical post at a park, it would have surely fried all of her electronics. Once, we were camping on Lake Superior when a huge thunderstorm hit, causing us to do an emergency evacuation in the middle of the night. The waves on the lake were over six feet high and started to flood our campsite while lightning struck repeatedly. It was a recipe for an electrical disaster, so we unhooked Gypsy from the power post and left the area, driving through rising water and giant hailstones while the storm raged about us.

So, how did we avoid being fried to a crisp or whirling away to Somewhere over the Rainbow? Mostly, we watched the weather closely. The biggest advantage of having a metal tent is that you can fold it up and go somewhere else if things look ugly. Since we were constantly on the move anyway, it became part of our routine. If the weather looked like snow showers in Colorado, we could be 200 miles away camping in the desert in four hours. We managed to avoid tornados, blizzards, floods and two hurricanes using our simple formula—Pull Up Stakes and Get Out!

The DelMarva Peninsula
—Ron—

Another unexpected gem on our trip was the Delmarva Peninsula, the strip of land that separates the Chesapeake Bay from the Atlantic Ocean. It got its name because it includes parts of Delaware, Maryland, and Virginia. The Delmarva has a sense of rugged isolation and timeliness that we found fascinating. Its highest point is only 102 feet above sea level, so land and sea wage a never-ending battle for dominance, with wind blowing across the water and through a seemingly endless sea of tall grass in every direction. Driving around, human presence seemed nonexistent. It felt like we had gone back 500 years, except for the paved roads.

We entered Delmarva in Lewes, Delaware after taking the ferry across the Delaware Bay from Cape May, New Jersey. It was a fitting introduction to the area as the strong currents and the wind blowing in from the Atlantic Ocean gave us a clear sample of the Nature's power here. Our ferry was big enough to hold 100 vehicles, but we were still tossed around like badgers in a sack during the ride.

Nestled at the mouth of the Delaware Bay, Lewes is the oldest town in Delaware and one of the oldest in America. Originally founded in 1631 as a Dutch whaling village and trading post, it was permanently settled in 1682 by William Penn. Penn's party included my great-great-great-great-great-great-great-great-grandfather James Benjamin Cooper, so when I stepped off the ferry, I was standing where my family had first arrived in America. Today, Lewes is a beautiful seaside resort town with a well-deserved reputation for being friendly. For example, one local resident's last wish was to have a helicopter drop $10,000 over the local marina as a final gift to his fellow townspeople.

After grabbing a snack from the local bakery, we headed out to explore the local coastline. We were looking for horseshoe crabs, which were on Aimee's Top Ten Must See Animals list. Horseshoe crabs are one of the oldest living animal species on Earth. Valued for their blue blood, which is used in medical testing, the Delaware Bay horseshoe crab population has declined by 90 percent over the past 20 years. Fortunately, one of their best remaining habitats was just outside Lewes in Cape Henlopen State Park, which had been set aside by William Penn as public land over 300 years ago. The park's 5,000 acres includes six miles of shoreline that is a haven for natural wildlife. As we wandered along the beach, we were pleased to find a lot of molts, which are the shells that a crab discards as it grows and a sign that the crab population was increasing again.

After we finished beachcombing, we spent the night at the Jellystone Park Campground in Lincoln, Delaware. It featured a huge playground, several trampolines, and a swimming pool, all in a Yogi Bear décor, which was quite a contrast from our afternoon of searching for living fossils.

It was late October, so the campground was nearly deserted and in the middle of night it had the eerie feel of a horror movie, the playground equipment creaking as the wind moaned across the marshes.

We skipped the northern part of Delmarva, which looked more industrial than we wanted. Several facilities of the giant chemical company DuPont are located there, and we didn't want to risk encountering animals that might belong in a monster movie after being exposed to DuPont's products. Instead, we headed west across the peninsula to the Chesapeake Bay and took a short detour off Delmarva by crossing the bay to visit Annapolis.

Annapolis was one of our favorite places in America. It had an amazing combination of scenic beauty, history, architecture and great food all within walking distance. We strolled through the downtown area, its colonial-style shops flanking a marina filled with vessels that ranged from oyster boats to luxury yachts. We wandered around Annapolis' historic neighborhoods that have more colonial period buildings still standing than any other city in America. We toured the U.S. Naval Academy grounds and the Maryland State House capitol building, which was America's national capitol when the Treaty ending the Revolutionary War was signed.

We crossed back across the Chesapeake Bay Bridge, then headed south on Highway 50 through several small towns that could have been a setting in the James Michener's novel Chesapeake. We stopped in as many as we could to soak up the harbor atmosphere, meet the locals and join in the crab cake debate.

Despite being divided across three states, the people of Delmarva are friendly and laid back, except on one topic—who makes the best crab cakes. When it comes to these tasty morsels, Delmarva's residents have passionate opinions and almost every town has its candidate for "the perfect crab cake." Driving around and listening to the locals, it looked like a new place popped up every week to challenge the established favorites like Woody's in Dewey Beach or the Fenwick Crab House on Fenwick Island. Our vote went to the Hunters Tavern in Easton, MD, whose crab cakes were crunchy on the outside and tender on the inside with a wonderful flavor. They were easily the best crab cake that I had ever eaten, but after seeing how many places were trying reach perfection, we decided that we needed to do a lot more research.

We got off Highway 50 in Salisbury and took Highway 13 to Assateague Island. The island contains Assateague Island National Seashore, Assateague State Park and Chincoteague National Wildlife Refuge, made famous by the Misty of Chincoteague children's books about the wild ponies that swam ashore from a shipwrecked Spanish galleon to live there. We learned that the herd has thrived so well in this isolated environment that its population must be controlled to avoid outstripping the island's resources. On the Maryland portion of the island, the herd is managed by the National Park Service and given contraceptives. In Virginia, the herd is owned by the local Volunteer Fire Department. They put on the annual Pony Penning Days Round-up and Auction that raises over $250,000 for the fire department and local charities. So, to address the same problem, the federal government uses chemicals at a considerable taxpayer cost, while the local volunteer organization creates a community event at a profit. Hmmm.

We spent two days exploring the island's coves and marshes and enjoying the constant symphony in the background. Over 320 species of birds are found there, and their numbers can block the sun during their fall migration. We watched them feeding in the marshes and listened as they filled the air with their raucous cries, joined by croaking frogs and the steady beat of the waves hitting the shore. The Delmarva Peninsula is a place where Nature still rules, and the people who live there have learned to fit in with wild ponies, ancient sea creatures, gigantic flocks of birds and the elemental forces of the sea and land. We loved it.

New England Isn't a State
—Aimee—

I consider myself an intelligent, college educated person with a broad knowledge base, but it's amazing what gaps a person can have and not know it. I once coached our daughter Kim on state capitals in preparation for a school test. I had decided that mnemonic tricks would help her remember and so I tried a string of jokes or interesting facts to help jog her memory.

"He had no Hair?" for Harrisburg, Pennsylvania worked fine.

"Sacred Tomato?" helped her remember California's capital Sacramento.

Then for Columbus, Ohio I tried goosing her with a clue. "The guy who came to the New World….he had five ships."

"Five Ships? Really?" she said, cocking an eyebrow. "Name them."

Thinking about it briefly, I said, "The Nina, the Pinta, the Santa Maria and…..(whoops) the Pentium Four and….Pentium Five… Ha!" I retorted, pretending that I had been making a joke.

She literally fell over laughing at my gaffe. Now she will always know that Columbus is the capital of Ohio, and I will too until the day I die.

Fast forward to our trip. As we drove east across the seemingly endless prairies of eastern Montana and the Dakotas, I told Ron that I was looking forward to visiting New England and seeing the fall colors that I had always heard about but never seen as I was growing up in California.

"Which state are you most interested in?" he asked.

"New England," I answered. Was this guy an idiot?

"Uh, New England isn't a state, honey. It's a region," he said, looking at me like I had a brain tumor.

"Wait a minute," I said, feeling defensive. "What about the New England Patriots? How can a team represent a region? And what about that Barry Manilow song 'Weekend in New England'?" I was exasperated and concerned. Could he actually be right?

"It's a region, honey" he said gently, the way you humor your wife when you don't want her to kill you.

I thought back. Had I ever actually looked on the US map for New England? Where would that pesky state be? Somewhere between New Hampshire and Vermont?

Don't laugh too much. After all, you probably think that Rhode Island is an island. If you do, don't blame yourself. On the West Coast, children are taught about five seconds' worth of East Coast geography, starting and ending with building a replica of Jamestown out of popsicle sticks in the fourth grade. After that, we're on our own. Besides, the East Coast has a bunch of states that are smaller than most counties in my home state. Californians really only know the following geographical areas: The West Coast (that's us!), the East Coast (That's New York) and the Mid-West (several states whose names begin with I, O or M.) Texas and Florida belong somewhere, but we aren't really sure where. We are pretty shaky on what states make up The South and totally mystified by concepts like "Mid-Atlantic States." If you want a good laugh, grab a teenager who was raised in Los Angeles and ask them to name the states on the Atlantic Ocean starting in Maine and going south. Now sit back and enjoy the fun. It will probably go something like this:

"Uh, Maine. Then Vermont? Then there's New York and Delaware. Then New Hampshire and Virginia and…pause…Florida." If you were born and raised in a state that got missed, don't fret, the kid probably will include it in "The Mid-West," which most West Coast people think contains about forty states.

If you're from New York, don't feel superior. You think California contains two things: Los Angeles (which of course includes both Hollywood and Disneyland) and San Francisco. You are surprised to find that the two cities are nearly 400 miles apart, which makes that whole "let's go to Disneyland in the morning and have dinner at Fisherman's Wharf" plan a little unrealistic. The truth is, geography wasn't anyone's favorite subject in school, except maybe when we got to draw maps.

Anyway, driving around the country for two years, I had ample opportunity to fill in the gaps in my knowledge about geography and some other topics as well. Driving past the gazillionth golf course in upstate New York, I asked Ron "Why do you yell the number four when you tee off?"

He turned to look directly at me.

"What?" I asked.

"It's FORE! F-O-R-E." He spelled it for me.

"Huh?" I said. "I thought you guys all yelled FOUR! But I never knew why."

"Fore is a warning to people ahead that a golf ball is coming their way. It's not the number four," He explained very slowly. Apparently, I am the idiot in our relationship. Who knew?

Then there's hacky sack. Apparently, the game is not called Hackensack and it was not named after a city in New York. Or New Jersey. Or New England...

All I know is that after being humbled by my apparently substandard education, I'm never rooting for the New England Patriots again. Get a real state!

Exploring Our Family Roots

—Ron & Aimee—

One of the best things about our trip was that it let us explore things that we found interesting, but hadn't pursued while we were living at home. In this case, it was tracing our family histories. Growing up, we had each spent quite a bit of time with our grandparents and heard a few stories about our more distant ancestors, but we didn't pay that much attention until we got older and became more interested in our family backgrounds. Driving around America, we had the time and the mobility to trace our roots and visit the places where our ancestors had lived.

We started by piecing together our family trees. We called our parents from the road to get names and relationships, then Aimee got on the Internet and started researching. She found birth and marriage records, along with census and armed services documents. There were even some old photos. All of it helped her find where our ancestors had lived, then we started driving the local roads in those areas. We wandered around the fields and bayous of northern Louisiana where Aimee's grandmother grew up. We followed my family's track from their arrival in Pennsylvania, through North Carolina, Tennessee, Oklahoma, and New Mexico to their eventual home in California. Finding the people and the places was like putting together a jigsaw puzzle with lots of missing pieces. We had several missteps, but it was a lot of fun working on it together. We slowly put together our family stories and they were fascinating to us.

Ron's Story

I knew that my family had English and American Indian ancestors and that we called ourselves Okies, but never knew how all these roots came together. As it turns out, the consistent theme was younger sons looking for the opportunity to own land. James Benjamin Cooper was born in 1661 in Stratford on Avon, the town where William Shakespeare had lived fifty years earlier. James was the son of Sir George Ashley Cooper, an English noble, but as the youngest, he was not in line to inherit any of his father's property. When William Penn promised him land, James and his wife Hester joined Penn's Quakers and left for America in 1682. They became major landowners in Philadelphia and had 3 daughters and 9 sons, including William Cooper born in 1701.

As the second-youngest son, William wasn't going to inherit any of his father's newly acquired land, so he moved to North Carolina. He and his wife Mary had seven children including their youngest son Alexander, born in 1730. Alexander was also unlikely to inherit any land, so he moved to Virginia with his wife Mary.

Alexander's son Alexander C. Cooper fought in the Revolutionary War, keeping Tennessee safe from Indians, which was pretty easy as the Cherokee were peaceful and friendly. His son James was born in 1776 and made his own personal declaration of independence when he married Sarah Elizabeth Mavel, a full-blooded Cherokee. This began our Cherokee Indian heritage but probably caused some family controversy because James moved his family to Tennessee, where his son Reuben Nathan Cooper was born.

Reuben Nathan Cooper's son Reuben Winchester Cooper (my great-great grandfather) married Mahala Bumbalough in 1874 when he was 18 and she was 16. They had 9 kids, including my great-grandfather Esrom Cooper before Mahala died in 1890 at the age of 32 during a flu epidemic. Six weeks later, Reuben, who was now 34, married Sarah Lou Huddleston, age 16. Reuben had 9 kids with Sarah for a total of 18 children in 36 years before he died in 1910 at the age of

53, most likely from exhaustion. Along the way, he moved the family to Oklahoma, beginning my family's Okie legacy.

Esrom, who had married Ida Irene Davis before leaving Tennessee, had 9 kids, including my grandpa S.B., the second youngest, born in 1913 in Harmon, Oklahoma. Grandpa worked a trucking route that included Roy, New Mexico, a tiny town 100 miles west of the Oklahoma border. There he met and married Grace Patricks and they had 4 children, starting with my father Richard, born February 14, 1934. The family moved to Petaluma, California in 1939 where they bought 20 acres of steep hillside with the rockiest soil imaginable. The land came with two small houses and the family eventually built seven additional houses. My dad was the first in his family to finish high school or get a college degree. He became an attorney and a real estate broker, buying property in California, Nevada, Texas, and Arizona. His three sons, including me all worked in the real estate industry as a way to acquire property for themselves.

So, my family history is eleven generations of younger sons moving to and across America in search of land of their own.

Cooper Family Lineage (Patrilineal)

Sir John Cooper (1597-1631) m. Ann Ashley (1602-1628)
                             m. Mary Hicks (1589-1639)
Sir George A. Cooper (1621-1683) m. Elizabeth Oldfeld (1624-1683)
James Cooper (1661-1732) m. Hester Burrows (1663-1706) Moved to America
William Cooper (1701-1736) m. Mary Groom (1700-1772)
Alexander Cooper (1730-1790) m. Mary Cooper (1730-1800)
Pvt. Alexander C. Cooper (1754-1844) m. Mary Lippincott (1755-1849)
James J. Cooper (1776-1830) m. Elizabeth Mavel (c. 1772-1882) Cherokee
Reuben N. Cooper (1810-1880) m. Martha Perkins (1813-1896)
Reuben W. Cooper (1856-1910) m. Mahala Bumbalough (1858-1890)
                             m. Sarah Huddleston (1874-1959)
Esrom Cooper (1883-1945) m. Ida Davis (1884-1969)
S B Cooper (1913-1992) m. Grace Patricks (1916-2003) Moved to California
Richard Cooper (1934-) m. Patsy Blake (1933-)
Ronald Cooper (1954-) m. Joan Wendt (1955-)
                             m. Aimee Hardy (1967-)

Aimee's Story

I come from a family of bootleggers and moonshiners. My middle name honors the legacy of my maternal grandmother Georgia Ruth Moffett (nee Williams.) She was born and raised in Crowville, a town in northern Louisiana that was so small that it wasn't even in the Rand McNally atlas. Locals called it "a bump in the road." She always talked about being poor as a child, growing up in a tin shack with a dirt floor. Her family had come from Mississippi and was English and Scottish by background. She said that she married "the first fast-talkin', good lookin' man who came through town," which turned out to be my grandfather Bill. He was also Scottish, as his mother was from the Bathgate clan and his father was from the Moffett clan. I later learned that the Moffett clan originated in lowland Scotland and had the motto "Spero Meliora" meaning "We hope for better things," most likely explaining why so many of them immigrated to America during the 1700s. The Bathgate clan was from near Edinburg and had a long history of making scotch whiskey. Their motto was "Vive u vivas", meaning "live life to the fullest," which probably accounts for my love of a good drink.

My grandmother Georgia Ruth was very proud of graduating from high school, a rarity in Crowville, and then earning a college degree in the secretarial arts. She and Bill left Louisiana and lived in a number of places before ending up in California, where they raised five children. Bill worked as a chemist for Seagram and Bechtel Oil. At one point he got kicked out of Saudi Arabia for operating a hidden still under his bed in the company dormitory while he was working at an oil refinery.

My grandmother's Southern roots were often evident in her choice of foods, ordering gizzards at Kentucky Fried Chicken or cooking pecan pies for Thanksgiving. She babysat me and my sister from time to time and her round bosom and red hair figure prominently in my concept of who I am and where I come from.

My mother was born in Shreveport, Louisiana. She grew up in California but still evidenced quite a bit of Louisiana, especially when cooking. "You've gotta make a roux!" was a favorite catchphrase of hers. She would yell it and cackle to herself madly. It was years later that I learned what the heck a "roux" was. On Sundays, she made beignets and I always associate those little sugary donuts with home.

The South is a romantic concept to most West Coast folk, but it had its dark side. I will always remember my grandmother storming out of a store, dragging me along by the wrist. She had asked the clerk to honor an expired coupon and the checker had primly informed her that the coupon was "no good." Furious, my grandmother had cried, "No good? Aren't you an uppity n*gger!" To this day I still squirm inside thinking about how awful that comment was and how, even at the age of 10 years old, I knew that it was dirty and wrong. Pile on all the excuses you like about growing up poor in Louisiana with parents from Mississippi, I had seen the ugly part of the South. I never heard my own parents use that word, but I wondered how often my mother had heard it growing up and what she thought about it. I never had the courage to ask her, but I wanted to explore the place that had fostered such extremes of love and prejudice in my grandmother.

As the child of an aerospace engineer and a schoolteacher, I couldn't really grasp what Louisiana was like. I pictured alligators and swamps everywhere, with sharecroppers working the fields. It was a ridiculous mash-up of "Gone with the Wind" and Disney's "Song of the South." It turned out to be more than I had expected in many ways. We took more than one Cajun Swamp Tour, poling around the bayous in little boats or zooming across them in airboats. The bayous were dark and lovely, dripping with Spanish moss and indeed filled with alligators and snapping turtles. It's impossible to describe the lowland bayou country in pictures, you have to smell and feel it. There is a moisture in the air and a heavy green scent of the verdure mingled with the sweet smell of decomposition. It reminded me of sitting at an old dock at low tide.

What is completely unusual about Louisiana is the culture. The people are proud of their heritage and the Cajun dialect is totally unique, peppered with French and Creole words. In many places, time has all but stood still. The food is completely democratic, influenced by French aristocracy and African slaves alike. I like to think that I inherited the good parts of Louisiana, the love of food, the appreciation of the outdoors, and the beauty of being part of a melting pot.

It was a powerful feeling to visit the places where our families had lived. It was almost as if we were standing next to them while they were alive. We sat in front of Aimee's grandmother's old schoolhouse. We laid flowers on the gravestones of my great-great-great grandparents in an old rural cemetery in White County, Tennessee. We talked to the 234 residents of Roy, New Mexico, to see if they knew my grandmother or my dad when they were growing up. The local people were always very friendly and helpful, although we could only imagine what they thought when they saw a sticker-covered RV parked at their remote country church, while two obvious out-of-towners wandered around peering at the headstones in the cemetery. But they quickly warmed up to what we were doing. We were getting a richer appreciation of our family histories by following in their footsteps as they pursued their dreams. It didn't get more American than that.

Red Scare
—Aimee—

I am very proud of my Scotch-Irish heritage. One of my favorite family photos shows my grandmother and mother standing next to me when I was nine months pregnant, everyone's hair some shade of auburn. By then, they were almost certainly dyeing theirs back to the copper colors of youth. I know this now, because my hair color has faded over the years and has acquired some terrifying steel-colored strands.

Unlike the gentle dusting of gray that men seem to acquire at their temples as they age, we women get gray hair in the most horrible ways. Consequently, I was totally dependent on my hairdresser to bring me back to the russet tones of my youth. Like most women, I was closer to my hair stylist than to many of my family members. I have whispered truths to my stylist that I wouldn't share with a priest. So, it came as no surprise that when I told her that Ron and I were taking a long RV trip, her first words were, "Who will do your hair?"

I had been pondering that issue. There was no way that I could just keep switching hair stylists on the road. My hair color was a very specific formula that combined many shades and tones. It required talent and skill to get right. I won't compare my hair stylist to a master artist, but I'm pretty sure that Van Gogh couldn't have painted Starry Night every five weeks at two o'clock sharp. I couldn't let a bunch of unknown stylists tinker with my hair. I pictured myself leaving a New York salon with an angular short dark bob or driving around Texas as a platinum blond with super tall hair. Terrifying. I was also determined that I would not sink to cutting my hair short or give up on being a redhead. Hell No. I refused to give up on my glamour.

After thinking about it, my hair stylist said, "You know, I could teach you to do your own hair. I'll pre-make your formulas in bottles and you can apply it yourself."

"Genius!" I said, and we set out to do just that. She made me a kit for coloring my hair that rivaled my high school science lab. It had everything—rubber gloves, brushes, color vials, processing compounds and several sizes of mixing bowls. We practiced my technique for months before I headed out. I was ready. I would only need to get an occasional trim along the route.

It was a great plan, but like most plans, it didn't factor in the environmental realities. Gypsy's bathroom was roughly the size of a broom closet with almost no counter space. The shower was basically a telephone booth with a skylight dome for tall people like me. If you drop the soap, you slide your hand down the wall and try to snag the bar as it swirls around your feet in the shower pan. The shower drain is a tiny crossbar, fond of clogging.

The first time I tried to color my hair in the RV, it took two hours. One hour to do it and another hour to clean up the walls, the ceiling, the floor, and me. The whole affair was accompanied by an occasional "Are you okay?" coming from the other side of the bathroom door.

I also tried coloring my hair in campground bathrooms, but campground managers frown on women dragging a bag of colorful hair dyes into their showers. Also, coloring hair takes time and people get huffy when you spend an hour in a campground shower. The only way that it worked: Midnight Hair. If no one is awake to notice, you can sneak into a bathroom at an ungodly hour and you're good. Hotels also worked when we took a night out of Gypsy to enjoy a big bathtub. I took my kit and my towels into the room and had a full spa event.

I am proud to say that I colored my hair over twenty times during our trip. I even brought my hot rollers along so that I could really glam it up once in a while. A girl needs some glam.

So, ladies, if you're planning a cross-country trip, don't forget your hair care. I suggest that you start planning now.

Tour de America
—*Ron*—

One of the best decisions that I made was to take my bike with me on our trip. And I owe it all to my brother Russell.

I had been a casual bike rider for several years when we lived in Southern California, where the mild climate made biking a convenient way to exercise at almost any time of the year. I rode four times a week, including a long ride each week with my friends. Of course, a long ride for me was anything over 10 miles. Not exactly a Tour de France competitor.

Then my family held a party for my 49th birthday. Russell was describing in some detail how he was riding his bike to rehabilitate from knee surgery. In a moment of middle-aged hubris, I interrupted him with, "How hard can it be to ride a bike? Let's do a real ride—let's go from your house to my house." He looked at me for a minute, obviously weighing whether it was a smart idea to ride 500 miles on a bad knee, then simply said, "Okay." As my grandpa used to say, I had "let my alligator mouth get ahead of my lizard brain" and now I had to live with it.

My bike was 20 years old and not built for long rides, so I doubted that it could handle a 500-mile trip. I was even older and not built for long rides either, but three weeks later I flew up to Sonoma County, bought a new bike and we saddled up. We rode 502 miles in six days, and it was the hardest physical thing that I had ever done. I got blisters on my blisters and assorted injuries from several falls on the bike. At times, I barely had the energy to eat. Nevertheless, it was a great experience. My new bike worked perfectly, so I named it Hidalgo in honor of a movie about a mustang that won the Ocean of Fire endurance race across Arabia.

A few years later, Russell suggested that we celebrate my birthday by riding my age in miles. Once again, pride won out over common sense and my birthday ride became a tradition, getting longer each year. When he heard about our trip, Russell challenged me to continue my birthday ride while we were on the road.

First, I had to find a way to store Hidalgo while we were driving. The only places big enough inside Gypsy were in the hallway, which would block access to the bathroom, or on the bed. Aimee told me in no uncertain terms that neither was an option. I thought about putting Hidalgo on the roof, as there was plenty of room to tie him down and Gypsy even had a built-in ladder. After nearly falling when I tried climbing the ladder with Hidalgo on my shoulder, I realized that if I had to haul him up and down the ladder each time I wanted to ride, I would take very few rides. Instead, I bought a small bike rack and attached it to the ladder. Hidalgo's front wheel stuck out about two feet on the passenger side, so I had to be careful not to drive too close to anything, but he was officially part of our trip.

Over the next two years, I rode over 2,000 miles in 26 states and discovered that riding a bike was a completely different way to experience America. Driving Gypsy, I mostly watched the scenery as it went by unless we stopped to get a closer look. On Hidalgo, I felt like I was part of my surroundings.

In western New York, we stayed at the Daisy Barn Campground about 25 miles east of Niagara Falls on Lake Ontario. The next morning, I rode along the lakeshore to Olcott, whose old-style amusement park, lighthouse and beautiful marina made it so picturesque that the World Fishing Network had dubbed it the Ultimate Fishing Town. Getting to these sights would have been difficult in Gypsy, but they were a breeze on Hidalgo. I rode around enjoying the peaceful feeling of fall in a small town.

Massachusetts' Berkshire mountains was another beautiful place to ride a bike in autumn, although they were a little scary. Our campground outside Westhampton was in a forest, surrounded by trees in flaming colors. The sky was blue and the temperature was perfect. The air was crisp with the faint smell of corn and ripe apples. Unfortunately, the road was narrow with no shoulder, heavy traffic and drivers who didn't have much experience with bicycles. Each time I went around a corner, I expected to end up on a poster for bike safety.

Speaking of scary, during our first October on the road I rode the 10-mile route through the forest and along the rocky seashore of Maine's Acadia National Park. The park's roads were nearly deserted, so I could relax and enjoy the nip in the air and the rich colors and aroma of the autumn leaves. Suddenly, I discovered that the park was not quite empty. I looked up and saw an Eastern timber wolf about 20 yards away from me on a hill next to the road. He was larger than a German Shepherd and seemed pretty interested in me. Suddenly, being alone on the road didn't seem like such a good idea. I wasn't sure how fast he could run, but I was pretty sure that it was faster than I could ride. Besides, I thought, don't wolves travel in packs? I had visions of ten wolves encircling my bike like Indians around a lone covered wagon. The next few miles of the ride were the fastest that I have ever gone on Hidalgo.

The bike was also a great way to see the desert, especially in the early morning. I never grew tired of watching the rapidly changing colors as the sun rose. The roads were quiet, and the wildlife was out foraging before it got too hot, although several times I had to avoid rattlesnakes that were warming themselves on the pavement.

My only real disappointment in riding my bike around America was the Florida Keys. The Overseas Heritage Trail was touted as a 106-mile trail stretching from Key Largo to Key West on which "more than 75 miles have been paved and completed." I had visions of cruising along, the palm trees swaying in the light ocean breeze of the Atlantic Ocean on one side and the Gulf of Mexico on the other side. The reality was mostly a sidewalk, broken frequently by stretches of "share the road" sections on one of America's busiest two-lane highways with no shoulder. As one bicycle enthusiast put it, riding Highway 1 through the Florida Keys is "a feat best done carefully and with plenty of daylight, especially when taking into account its historical reputation for fatal accidents." Not a way to enjoy the scenery.

I had two birthdays while we were on our trip, and Russell flew out from California to join me for my birthday ride each time. I tried to find a place that had a scenic route, but I also wanted it to be flat and close to sea level. Climbing mountains was fine when I was younger, but now I was in my 60s. If I was going to ride through the Rockies, I'd do it on a motorcycle. Even on an easy course, riding 60+ miles meant over 4 hours of pedaling. We would start out feeling fresh, talking and challenging each other with trivia questions as we rode, but by mile 30 my attention would be focused solely on getting to the finish. Still, I wasn't ready to give up on the birthday ride tradition or the hope that I could still be an athlete. Besides, the ride gave me a great opportunity to eat. I generally had to watch my calories on our trip, but I burned over 3,000 calories on my birthday ride, so I could eat anything that I wanted on that day.

The first year, we rode the Washington and Old Dominion Railroad Trail, a paved bike path that had been built on an abandoned railroad right-of-way from Washington, D.C. through northwest Virginia. Riding on a dedicated bike path let us enjoy the scenery or ride alongside each other and talk without worrying about any cars. Despite cold, rainy weather, we made good time, finishing the 61 miles in under five hours including stops for food and water. Afterwards, we drove Gypsy around D.C. to see the sights and ate at Ben's Chili Bowl, a landmark in the city's Northwest "Black Broadway" neighborhood. Since it opened in 1958, Ben's has hosted such notables as Nat King Cole, Barack Obama, and French President Nicolas Sarkozy. The Washington Post said that "No D.C. politician would dream of running for office without dropping into Ben's." We weren't politicians, but we enjoyed Ben's homemade chili and milkshakes.

The next year, we rode in New Orleans. Aimee and I had spent a week there on the first year of our trip and we loved its history, its architecture, and its food. I had also discovered that there was a paved bike trail along the levee of the Mississippi River that provided a great way to see the river and the city. The city end of the trail opened into the 350-acre Audubon Park, a converted plantation with oak trees, ponds, and a rookery where hundreds of egrets, herons and cormorants live. We rode around the park's ponds and through the trees, enjoying the shady scenery and the wildlife. The trail was flat and there were very few other riders, so we rode pretty fast despite the temperature and humidity. We celebrated our ride by hitting the New Orleans restaurants. We started at the Camelia Grill, a diner that has been a city landmark since it opened in 1946. Despite offering only counter service, it is always packed, serving omelets, burgers and its signature item, pecan pie heated on the flattop grill. Later, we visited Cowbell, a New Orleans favorite that is described as "a quirky diner with elevated comfort food." Located in a converted gas station, they offer their creative versions of traditional American favorites, including a goat pimento grilled cheese sandwich and apple pie with rum sauce. The next day, we walked around the French Quarter and ate at the Coffee Pot, another New Orleans landmark that dates back to 1894. They are especially known for their calas, a rice-filled pastry that is as much a part of the New Orleans food tradition as the beignet.

Now that our trip is over, I still try to ride regularly to stay in shape. Russell and I have kept our tradition alive, meeting somewhere each year to ride my age and explore the local restaurants. I even got my hip replaced so that when our next big road trip comes, Hidalgo and I will be ready.

The Cycle-Ology of Bike Riding

—Aimee—

I'll start by saying that I'm not a bike enthusiast. I love the concept of biking: the freedom, the sightseeing. The reality is somewhat less glamorous—sore crotch, blisters, cars whipping past, big chance of injury. It's not for me.

Instead, I support Ron's interest in riding from the sidelines. When he wanted to bring his bike, affectionately named "Hidalgo" on the trip, I said, "Sounds great, honey. It will be a fantastic way to for you to get some exercise." But when I saw him lugging it into Gypsy, I put my foot down.

"No bikes in the hallway!" I said. Maybe he was willing to contort around the bike to get to the bathroom, but I wasn't. After much head-scratching, Hidalgo ended up on a bike rack that Ron attached to the back of Gypsy. The only problem was that it stuck out two feet on the passenger side, which is my side and therefore my responsibility.

Sadly, I'm a real side-seat gasper. You know the type. That person who loudly sucks in air every time you change lanes. I had to get over myself and get used to a seeing a bike wheel in my side view mirror every time I looked back. At first, I cringed every time we drove through a tunnel or onto a bridge but eventually, I learned to treat it like a back-up alarm. If something was about to whack the bike, well, things were too tight; otherwise, it was just a part of Gypsy.

Being attached to the back of the RV meant the poor bike got dirty. Really, really dirty. Rain, snow, freeway grime dirty. As a neat freak known to my children as "The Cleaning Fairy," I felt bad for Hidalgo out there in the elements. We tried a bike cover, but it didn't work very well, so I settled for cleaning Hidalgo every couple of days. After all, it was a beautiful Bianchi road bike and I didn't want it looking like a dusty junker. I'll bet those Italians didn't have this in mind when they built the veritable Ferrari of bikes and painted it racing red. Hidalgo was built for the Tour de France, not the Tour de Wisconsin. Still, Ron loved his bike the way Han Solo loved the Millennium Falcon. He'd proudly say, "She's not much to look at, but she's got it where it counts."

Every few months, Ron would take Hidalgo into a bike shop for a tune-up. It always went like this: Ron would walk into the shop without his bike and ask the owner if he had time to tune up a bike while we were in town. The owner would say "Yes" while looking Ron over, his body language clearly saying, "Old-Fart probably doesn't ride five miles a month, but I'd be happy to charge him 80 bucks for ten minutes' work." Ron would then walk out and wheel his bike in. "Really seen some miles!" the shop owner would say with some surprise on his face, "Did you say that you're taking an RV trip around the US?" Then Ron and the owner would swap bike stories for 30 minutes before the owner would say "20 bucks" and then tell Ron about a bike trail that no one has ever heard of in a remote corner of the local county. Ron had become part of the in-crowd, that secret clan of biking enthusiasts who talk about downhill speed, the time they biked through a swarm of African bees, biking after they lost a leg, whatever.

Did Ron ride Hidalgo as much as he claims? I can testify that he speaks the truth. Many is the time that I sat in Gypsy waiting to see if he was going to survive after he said reassuring things like, "I'm gonna check out the Blue Ridge Highway. I'll try to be back in an hour." I pictured him flattened so many times that I actually staged it as a picture for our Halloween postcard to family.

I loved the time that he came back wild-eyed from a ride through a remote stretch of Acadia National Park in Maine. "I just saw a wolf!" he cried, pulling off his bike helmet and shoes. Like any good wife, I said "Are you sure? Maybe it was a coyote."

"Yes, I'm sure," he said emphatically. "That thing was really big. Tall as a German Shepherd. Huge feet, no mistaking the eyes. Coyotes don't eyeball you like that."

"I'm not sure there are wolves in Maine anymore," I said, grabbing my phone. When in doubt, Google it. Supposedly, Maine has no wolf population but there were some reported sightings. Some of them were in the area where he had just ridden. Holy crap!

So, I had to believe him. Besides, Ron doesn't get dramatic. That's my job. But now I had to worry about him being eaten by wildlife on his rides. What was next, Sasquatch? Alien abduction? This solo riding thing seemed fraught with danger.

Good thing Russell came out to do the long rides with Ron. I figured those two could get in and out of trouble together. Besides, Ron really looked forward to Russell's visits during our trip. It's great to be a couple, facing the open road together, but sometimes a guy needs "bro-time." They would talk on the phone for weeks ahead of their trips, planning the route for the ride, gauging the weather and discussing possible restaurants for their post-ride meal. I liked Russell's visits too. They were another way to stay in touch with family when everything familiar seemed like it was far away across the country.

So while I didn't cycle, it became a part of my life. Seeing Ron return to the campsite at the end of a ride covered in dirt, his legs permanently tan below his bike shorts and snow-white above and wearing crazy wrap-around sunglasses that reminded me of the Terminator movies, I was proud of him. He was MY guy.

Good Vibrations
—Ron—

On our first motorhome trip with the kids, our rig had a cassette tape player and exactly two tapes: the soundtrack from the movie "The Big Chill" and the Broadway production of "Camelot." For seven straight days, the girls echoed Julie Andrews in praising "The Lusty Month of May" and sang the Temptations "Ain't Too Proud to Beg" whenever they wanted something from me. From then on, music was always a big part of our motorhome trips.

Knowing that we would be spending two years on the road, Aimee downloaded over 5,000 songs on her iPhone so that we would have music for every occasion. We set out with everything from classical to country, musicals to Motown and reggae to rock.

I soon learned the rules of music etiquette on the road. If your spouse hates a song, don't try to convince them otherwise—just play it when you are alone. Don't tell your spouse that the cast of Glee did a song better than the original artist (even if it's true). Finally, never make up clever new lyrics to your spouse's favorite song. It may seem funny, but it isn't worth the miles of stony silence that follow.

Aimee often used music to help set the mood during the day. Every morning as we started out, she played "Renegades" as a tribute to our pursuit of freedom and adventure:

> "Run away with me,
> lost souls in revelry,
> Running wild and running free,
> two kids, you and me.
> And I say hey, hey hey hey,
> Livin' like we're renegades."

When we were tired, she played Brian Setzer's "Jump Jive and Wail" or MC Hammer's "U Can't Touch This" and soon we would be ready to go again. When we were blue, Patty Griffin's "Heavenly Day" always made us smile.

> "Oh, heavenly day, all the clouds blew away
> Got no trouble today with anyone
> The smile on your face, I live only to see
> It's enough for baby, it's enough for me
> Oh, heavenly day, heavenly day, heavenly day."

We also picked songs to help us get the feel of the areas that we were visiting. Hearing the music of a place made us feel like we were a part of it. We drove the back roads of Louisiana, bouncing to The Mudbugs Cajun and Zydeco Band's "Jambalaya" or swaying gently while Linda Ronstadt crooned about "Blue Bayou." The bluegrass harmonies of the Dixie Chicks and Loretta Lynn's growing up as a "Coal Miner's Daughter" set the tone for driving through the Appalachians. Even though we were both raised in California, the Zac Brown Band's "Chicken Fried" made Georgia feel like home.

> "Well, I was raised up beneath the shade of a Georgia pine
> And that's home you know
> Sweet tea, pecan pie, and homemade wine
> Where the peaches grow
> And my house it's not much to talk about
> But it's filled with love that's grown in southern ground
> And a little bit of chicken fried"

As we rolled through Michigan, Gypsy rocked the sounds of Motown with Aretha, Smokey, and the Temptations. Driving around the Southwest, we were kept company by Johnny Cash, Toby Keith, Tim McGraw and, of course, Willie Nelson.

"On the road again
Goin' places that I've never been
Seein' things that I may never see again
And I can't wait to get on the road again"

Sometimes we got hooked on a song about a place and changed our route to go there, which led to some great adventures. George Strait sang about "Amarillo By Morning," so we took a 350-mile detour and it was so memorable that we wrote a chapter about it. Marc Cohn convinced us to go "Walking in Memphis" and we took several days to explore its musical heritage. As we listened to the great blues music pouring from the clubs throughout Memphis's downtown district, we understood what Cohn meant by walking "with my feet 10 feet off of Beale." We visited the Elvis Presley Museum in Graceland, where I had to try singing my favorite Elvis song "Can't Help Falling in Love with You" at their karaoke exhibit. When someone asked the lady running the exhibit if it was Elvis singing, it absolutely made my day. We saw Sun Records where Elvis, Johnny Cash, Jerry Lee Lewis, Roy Orbison, and Carl Perkins were first recorded, amazed how much of rock & roll had come together in this tiny studio. We toured the Gibson Guitar factory where they make the famous "Lucille" electric guitar played by B.B. King. Aimee paid close attention to how a top-quality guitar was made, so I should have known that something was up. A few days later, she talked me into buying a Martin steel string acoustic guitar. It was a challenge to play, but had a beautiful sound when we got it right. Aimee named our guitar Sylvia after her late mother, who sang like Ethel Merman and taught Aimee her love of music. Our Sylvia was also "big, loud and demanding with a beautiful sound." We played almost every night sitting next to our campfire and while we would never be professionals, our renditions of "Wagon Wheel," Leavin' on a Jet Plane," "Peaceful Easy Feeling" and "Always on My Mind" kept us company all across America.

Sometimes, music helped us meet people at the campgrounds. In Malibu, California, we were sitting outside playing guitar and watching the sunset over the Pacific Ocean when a man came over with his guitar and asked if he could join us. Soon the sounds of Neil Young's "Heart of Gold" filled the campground and several people stopped to join in on the chorus. In Tennessee, a guy was performing for the campground guests. When he played "Take Me Home, Country Roads" we all joined in and the rest of the evening became a giant sing-along. In Idaho, a group of kids ran around the campground inviting everyone to join their potluck dinner. As it turned out, it was a church group on a retreat. We sang hymns well into the night, and the next morning, they asked me to join their choir for Sunday services.

Music helped us enjoy living on the road. It brought us to places that we would not have gone otherwise and gave us a richer appreciation of the places that we went. Whenever we miss being on the road, we pick up Sylvia, who still smells faintly of campfires, and play some of our favorite songs. My favorite is by the Temptations.

> "I've got sunshine on a cloudy day
> When it's cold outside, I've got the month of May
> I guess you'd say, what could make me feel this way
> My girl, talking about my girl.
> I don't need no money, fortune or fame
> I got all the riches baby, one man could claim
> I guess you'd say, what could make me feel this way
> My girl, talking about my girl"

It didn't get any better than driving around America with my girl.

The Singing Cowboy
—Aimee—

I'm a fairly creative person and over the years, my creativity has expressed itself in a number of hobbies. Drawing, cooking, and gardening have all consumed me from time to time. Like any good artist, I can run hot and cold on my interests; mad for craft brewing one year and then for watercolor painting the next. Some pursuits have stuck with me and others have fallen by the wayside. I like to think that I have enough talent to spread across a number of interests and hobbies.

I've always thought that I had a good eye, but did I have an ear? I've never played an instrument, unless you count three painful months of violin lessons in the fifth grade. My mom played the clarinet in college and I was always impressed with her musical ability. She sang while working in the kitchen, belting out show tunes and top forty hits in her throaty alto. I wanted to sing and play an instrument, and the instrument that captured my imagination was the guitar.

In my secret heart, I wanted to sit under the stars with the campfire smoke drifting upwards. I would be strumming a guitar and singing along softly. My fingers would find the strings and chords with surety, perhaps improvising sections to a cowboy tune. My voice would thrill those who heard it wafting over the cactus as the stars came out. The beauty of my song would attract nearby campers who would gather around the fire and add their voices. Maybe someone from another campsite would bring a guitar of their own and join in while complimenting me on my playing. I wanted that. I wanted it bad.

Like any naïve enthusiast, I was convinced that top notch equipment was the key to my success, so I not only wanted a guitar, I wanted an outstanding one. I researched acoustical guitars and the brand I kept coming back to was Martin. Martin specializes in steel string performance level acoustical guitars for serious artists…and none of them are cheap. I could just hear my fellow campers saying, "Ooh, you have a Martin!" I would nod sagely, "Yes, I do."

In Pelham, Alabama, I saw a store that advertised a huge selection of second-hand acoustic guitars and talked Ron into going in with me. He had played guitar a little over the years and sometimes talked about owning a Martin steel string guitar. This was my chance.

The store had over a hundred guitars hanging from pegs on the wall. Little guitars with high pitched voices, touring guitars with cutouts to fit over your knee while you played on a stool, guitars made from teak, guitars made from ash. I didn't know the first thing about the materials, the strings, any of it. Sure, I had researched guitars, but I had yet to play a single note on one. I had no experience whatsoever. I was afraid to even strum the guitars in the shop for fear that a staff member might say to me, "You've never played, have you?" while reaching for a copy of Guitar for Dummies. Oh, the shame!

Ron tried guitar after guitar, using a few simple chords to test their sound. One in particular caught our attention—a large Martin steel string touring guitar made of mahogany with a big, silky sound. Her strings were tight and low on her neck, which made her hard to play, but the sound was amazing. I told Ron that she reminded me of my mother, a big woman with a voice like an angel who brooked no fools. We dickered for her, paying cash, then drove away high-fiving each other on getting "Sylvia" complete with case, books and picks for half of what we would have paid anywhere else. It was kismet. That very night, I set out to learn guitar chords and start playing…

Those of you who have invested the years it takes to get good at playing an instrument can go right ahead and laugh at my hubris. I deserve it.

I now know that the steel guitar strings are also used by assassins to make wire garrotes. These strings require callouses on your fingers to play or you will experience great pain and may bleed. Beginning guitar students are encouraged to start on a guitar with nylon strings. I scoffed at starter instruments. "I should learn on the guitar that I will play. What's the point of learning on nylon strings only to have to learn again later on steel strings?"

No way was I going to start with training wheels. Desire was whipping me. I wanted so badly to play. I spent every night with Sylvia, my hands crabbed and cramping as I formed chords around her neck while I peered at the lessons on my phone. The pads of my fingers cracked and sometimes the strings stuck in them and had to be forcibly pulled away.

"How's it going?" Ron would call from the front of the rig.

"I'm working on the F chord tonight for a John Denver song," I would holler back through the closed door, my teeth gritted with pain. I didn't want anyone to see me sweating as I tried to force my fingers into chords. Anyone with a kid in band knows that the process of learning a musical instrument is not pretty.

After a couple of months, I was proud of my slow, inching progress. I often made some ear-bending noises, but I also made well-formed notes here and there. When I played through my first Credence Clearwater Revival song with only a fumble or two, I was ecstatic. Greatness awaited.

But an irritating truth also began to emerge as the nights went by: Ron had more talent for guitar than I will ever have. While I labored over chords, painfully learning to play simple songs, he picked up new tunes easily, often learning to play them in a few minutes.

Unlike areas like drawing, I had no real talent for guitar. And like many new students, I was learning a valuable lesson about music. You can't just jump in and be amazing. You have to earn it. When you see someone play a song at a coffee shop, with very few exceptions they have spent years playing the same song over and over to get it right. Apparently, I was not going to be Carlos Santana anytime soon. Bummer. I resigned myself to a longer path to greatness while Ron sat in the camp chair under the coyote moon and played "Amarillo by Morning."

Along the way I did develop my singing voice as a good accompaniment to his playing and singing. This is the part where you expect me to say, "And I sweetly sang the high notes to accompany him." Nope, cowboys and cowgirls; I sang the bass line. My singing voice is deep for a gal, really deep. It's all whiskey and gravel. Definitely Patsy Cline, not Celine Dion. It's perfect for last call at your local honky-tonk. I used to hate my voice and hide it in the family sing-alongs, but now I picture myself as an outlaw. I like surprising the other campers when I pick up the bass line on "Wagon Wheel."

Did I fulfill my dream of playing under the stars? Yes, I did. I played at night next to the campfire, nestled under my blanket with no one but Ron singing along. We traded the guitar back and forth while we sipped wine or whiskey and I loved every minute of it. The process of learning the guitar also made me more humble about my passions. In fact, the other day I told Ron that I'm thinking of taking up the country fiddle. I just love that Appalachian fiddling. It should be easy to learn it now that I've mastered the guitar, right?

Amarillo, Texas

—Ron—

When we set out to travel around America, we were determined to let the destinations find us. Leaving things to chance was part of the experience. It was challenging at times, but the surprises often led to great adventures. Amarillo, Texas was a perfect example.

It started when we flew back home from Florida to the West Coast to visit our families over the holidays. We had never seen the Panama Canal, so we decided to take a cruise back. One night on the ship, we heard a passenger sing "Amarillo by Morning" in the lounge and really enjoyed it, so we looked up the song and learned that it was credited with establishing the singing style of George Strait, the "King of Country Music" who went on to record over 60 #1 songs, the most by any singer.

A few months after we got back, we were wandering around Texas with the strains of "Amarillo by morning, up from San Antone" accompanying us in Gypsy every day. One night when we were camped in the Guadalupe Mountains, Aimee said, "We've been singing this song every day for three weeks. Let's go see what Amarillo is like. It's only 350 miles away and it's on a part of Route 66 that we have never seen." So away we went.

We took the back roads to get a better sense of Amarillo's natural setting. As we drove, Aimee did Internet research on the city. "Its name is Spanish for yellow," she said, "after the yellow soil of its local lake and creek." Knowing my love of trivia, she also told me that Amarillo has many nicknames, including "The Yellow Rose of Texas" for its abundant yellow wildflowers, "The Helium Capital of the World" because at one point it supplied nearly all the world's helium and "Bomb City" for having America's only facility for assembling and disassembling nuclear weapons.

We got our first surprise when we camped in Palo Duro Canyon State Park outside Amarillo. I had always thought that west Texas was flat desert terrain, but Palo Duro is the second-largest canyon in the U.S. after the Grand Canyon. Georgia O'Keefe painted several paintings of its 100-mile length, calling the steep canyon walls and multi-colored rock layers "a burning, seething cauldron, filled with dramatic light and color."

Driving into town the next morning, we got another surprise when we stopped at an RV dealership to get some supplies for Gypsy and found the Jack Sizemore RV Museum of vintage RVs, trailers and camping equipment that had been collected by the dealership's owner Jack and his son Trent. Its exhibits included the world's oldest Airstream trailer, the first Fleetwood RV model ever built, the 1948 Flexible bus used by Robin Williams in the movie RV, a 1967 VW van that went to Woodstock and a FMC luxury motorhome built by FMC Corporation that was used on location by movie stars like Clint Eastwood. As an added bonus, the back corner of the museum had a Chris Craft powerboat exactly like the one that I learned how to ski behind as a kid. Standing next to it, I was ten years old again, sluicing through the water without a care in the world.

Aimee researched the local restaurants and found a place called the Big Texan Steak Ranch that was famous for its 72oz. Steak Challenge. If you could eat their 72oz steak dinner, including a shrimp cocktail, baked potato, salad and bread, it was free. The contest was started to attract the cowboys who worked at the nearby stockyard when the restaurant opened in 1960. Nearly 70,000 people have taken the Challenge, with about 10,000 succeeding. The record is held by Molly Schuler, who devoured the steak in under 3 minutes and then ate two more. I was excited, thinking of the many buffets that I had ravaged over the years, but when I looked at the Challenge meal being placed in front of the contestants, my stomach sent me a clear message that my days of youthful gorging were over. I pictured myself popping Tums all afternoon to ease my bloated stomach and settled for a regular lunch.

As we drove around Amarillo, we noticed several odd signs. We learned that they were part of the Dynamite Museum, a collection of over 1,000 road signs funded by Stanley Marsh 3, a local billionaire, art pioneer and legendary prankster. When challenged about the aesthetic value of the signs, he said, "Art is a legalized form of insanity and I do it very well." One sign said "Road Does Not End" which captured the philosophy of our trip perfectly.

On the way out of town, we stopped to grab something to eat and discovered Tyler's BBQ. Its owner, Tyler Fraser, embodied all the great things about Texas. When he saw that we were from out of town, he sat down at our table and talked with us for nearly an hour. He asked about our trip and told us about his life's journey that had led him to start his own restaurant. We gave him some of our Sonoma County wine, he gave us more of his great BBQ and we left having found a new friend.

A few miles west of town, we stopped at Cadillac Ranch, a classic piece of Americana. It was created in 1974 by three "art hippie" architects who had traveled to San Francisco for the Summer of Love and decided to pursue experimental art projects. One night while drinking, they got the idea of showcasing the style of Cadillacs from 1949 to 1963. They found the perfect patron in Stanley Marsh 3, who wanted a piece of public art that would "baffle the locals" of Amarillo. They bought ten Cadillacs and half-buried them in a perfect row with their fins up. People were invited to decorate the cars, and they became a destination for graffiti artists from around the world. They are repainted every few years and new graffiti usually shows up within 24 hours. Cadillac Ranch has inspired a Bruce Springsteen song, a Garth Brooks song, a Christopher Lloyd movie and has appeared in the Pixar movie *Cars*, Brooks & Dunn's music video *The Honky Tonk Stomp* and James Brown's iconic music video *Living in America*.

We headed west toward New Mexico having learned once again about the value of chance encounters and "off the beaten path" destinations. We had gone to Amarillo on a whim, based solely on a song. We found a breathtaking natural setting in Palo Duro Canyon, an entertaining camping museum, a legendary restaurant, several quirky art exhibits and a BBQ place with great food and warm companionship. It was just the kind of experience that we wanted to have on our trip, and it helped us remember to let fate take us on more adventures in out of the way places.

Easy Bake Oven
—Aimee—

Do you remember the Easy Bake Oven that you had as a kid? It was a toy roughly the size of a shoebox. You and your friends would eagerly attempt to cook a tiny cupcake in it using its single incandescent bulb. An hour later, you shared a partially baked confetti cupcake lathered with white frosting among five slumber party guests, congratulating yourselves on your cooking skills.

Fast forward a few decades and it's back. The first time I opened Gypsy's oven door, I turned to Ron and said, "Oh my God, it's an Easy Bake Oven!"

Now that we were living on the road, standard RV kitchen appliances had replaced the Wolf range and the Subzero fridge that my chef-worthy kitchen at home had harbored. My new oven was twelve inches tall and fifteen inches wide with three grouchy propane burners on top and a small microwave oven set into the cabinetry above the burners. The fridge had about six cubic feet of interior space and a small freezer that would barely hold a bag of ice. There were two small cabinets for storing food, barely enough to hold necessities like flour, sugar and, of course, coffee.

In all fairness, our RV kitchen would have been truly a luxurious way to spend a weekend camping, sitting out in the wilderness and pulling cold milk from the fridge and heating up some breakfast sausages on the gas stove while microwaving a cup of water for tea. As a substitute for a real kitchen, it was almost unworkable. Almost.

At first, I hadn't really grasped what real RV living might look like. My picture was still mostly a vacation model, consisting of breakfast at the campsite and lunch/dinner at a restaurant or picked up to be eaten in the rig later. For the first six weeks on the road, we ate out at restaurants a lot, and despite the enjoyment of trying new places, it got old after a while. Take-out food, while convenient, came in disposable packaging and was often cold by the time we found a place to eat it. We missed having homemade dinners in the comfort of our home, with actual plates, cloth napkins and dinnerware. We missed the smell of food wafting from the oven before it was served. When you come from a family that enjoys home cooking, food is love and we needed a little more romance around our place.

I realized that I needed to cook more of our meals in Gypsy. Besides, why was I turning my nose up at one of the great challenges that our trip offered? I considered myself an accomplished cook. Why couldn't I harness the same skills to master the tiny kitchen that I was using? Food trucks did it all the time.

First, I had to figure how to set up Gypsy's kitchen so that real cooking was possible. We bought a cutting board that fit snugly into one of the sinks, then used the extra counter space for a toaster oven that became one of my handiest tools. Now I had a way to make toast, reheat foods and even cook smaller items when my regular oven was occupied. By the way, accumulated breadcrumbs under the toaster oven have a nasty habit of catching fire. Be warned.

Ron was a whiz at using the cabinet space efficiently for stacked dishes and things that needed careful, tight storage like sugar and flour. He also figured out ways to stock the refrigerator so things like eggs didn't suck up too much space or end up smashed. That man could really stuff a shelf! He made sure to find room for my big cast iron skillet, which is roughly the weight of a bowling ball, but was good for cooking damn near everything. I could start a recipe on the stovetop and switch it to the oven. As long as my arms held out, we were in business.

If you love to cook, then you probably have a huge hoard of obscure spices. Say yes if your cupboards have any of the following: Cardamom? Fennel? Cream of Tartar? Well, pick your favorite ones now because no RV is going to have enough storage for those twice-a-year goodies. Gypsy had a single shelf capable of holding a dozen spices that would become the key to my meal flavors.

I learned to shop locally. Not locally in a "Hey, let's go to the Farmers market and buy lavender soap" sort of way, but more like "If you're in Florida, eat fish." We devoted serious road time searching for local markets and foods. We also learned that some areas of the country don't carry much produce. You'd better buy ahead if you want to have a fresh salad in South Dakota.

Cooking in the RV had some unique challenges. If the ground wasn't level, pots on the stovetop had to be closely monitored or they would slide off. I once lost an entire skillet-full of scrambled eggs that sloshed over the edge of the stovetop onto the couch. My tiny oven worked for just about any regular recipe, but it took about 20 percent longer than the recipe called for and the oven's temperature gauge wasn't very accurate, so we mounted a thermometer in the back of the oven.

I had some interesting failures in my learning process, like my rather ambitious fish fry in Mississippi. I had bought a bunch of fresh local catfish and decided to deep fry them with homemade hush puppies. Filling my iron skillet with a couple of inches of oil, I managed to turn out some truly tasty catfish and crunchy hush puppies, all without burning down the kitchen or setting off the smoke alarm. I was terrifically pleased with myself. Taco trucks, watch out! The next day, however, Gypsy reeked of fish. The day after that, Gypsy reeked of fish. A week later, despite several serious doses of Febreze and driving with the windows wide open, Gypsy still reeked of fish. Ron started saying things like, "Whew! Low tide!" I hadn't considered the fact that our ceiling, like most RV ceilings, is carpeted. Despite a small exhaust fan over the cooktop, our carpeted ceiling had trapped all the atomized fish oils, leaving me smelling my catfish fry for about three weeks.

Over time, I got pretty adept at turning out everything from meatloaf to enchiladas in Gypsy's tiny oven. I even made a full Thanksgiving dinner including a turkey breast (sorry, but the legs would not fit), homemade cranberry sauce, stuffing, potatoes, and gravy. It took every stovetop burner, the RV oven, the microwave, and the toaster oven, plus my watchful eye and a bottle of wine……but it was fantastic. Sure, the turkey breast had to be measured for fit into the tiny oven and defrosted overnight in the RV shower, but we spread out our Thanksgiving feast onto our little kitchen table and toasted our success.

Truly, nothing beats home cookin'.

Motorhome Meals

—*Ron*—

Aimee has described the difficulties of cooking in Gypsy. Let me just say that once she decided to test the limits of what she could cook in a motorhome, Aimee was more than up to the challenge. Many of the best meals that we ate as we drove around America were ones that she made in Gypsy.

Aimee started by figuring out how to make my favorite dishes in Gypsy's tiny RV kitchen. I grew up in a town that was known for its authentic Italian foods, and soon, the aroma of spinach-stuffed chicken parmesan filled the air. As we drove through Montana, she adapted her lasagna recipe by using local buffalo instead of beef. With local sourdough bread, it felt like we were in a Healdsburg ristorante.

Driving through Wisconsin, we tried the local brats in a restaurant and Aimee decided that we needed to make some ourselves. She did some research and had me buy Usinger's brats along with some apples and a large can of "the cheapest beer that you can find." When I asked why we were going to use low-end beer on high-end brats, she reminded me that she was the lead cook. We boiled the brats in water, beer, and apple slices, then grilled them over our campfire until their skin was crispy and served them on toasted rolls with sauerkraut and mustard. Yum!

Our first autumn as we drove across upstate New York, we were surprised by the number of produce stands that we saw along the road. We stopped at several of them to chat with the farmers and bought whatever they recommended, which Aimee made into delicious soups and shepherd's pie.

Thanksgiving was our first big holiday away from home and I missed our big family gathering, with food stretched out as far as the eye could see. Seeing my concern, Aimee surprised me with a traditional Thanksgiving turkey dinner, including roast turkey, stuffing, gravy, mashed potatoes, homemade cranberry dressing, and fresh berry crisp for dessert. There were even leftovers to make turkey sandwiches and turkey pot pie.

Driving around the country, we sampled a lot of the popular local foods and Aimee often tried to make them in Gypsy. In Florida, we really liked the grouper, so she searched the Internet to find the best fish markets, then set about to match the quality of the local restaurants. Grilled grouper, teriyaki grouper and fish tacos, all served with homemade mango salsa were some of the best meals that we had anywhere on our trip.

In Louisiana, Aimee wanted to honor her family roots by making some traditional local dishes. Soon, strange ingredients like okra and crawfish showed up in our grocery store shopping cart. Aimee would cackle, "First, you have to make a roux!" while smoke wafted from Gypsy's kitchen, then foods that I had never eaten before would appear on the table in front of me. We ate shrimp etouffee, crawfish over pasta and boudin balls of rice, sausage and spices fried in hot oil. Afterwards, we sat outside listening to zydeco music and sipping Bayou Rum made from local sugar cane.

Mexican food was always a favorite of ours. During our trip, I drove Gypsy through the narrow streets of old downtown Houston so that Aimee could eat at the original Ninfa's, the restaurant that introduced fajitas into American culture. Driving around the Southwest, Aimee made a large variety of Mexican and Tex-Mex dishes using local ingredients. We went to Hatch, New Mexico, famous worldwide for its chiles and bought a bag big enough for a dozen dinners. In the ensuing nights, the aroma of green chile chicken enchiladas, stuffed poblano peppers, street tacos and huevos rancheros filled Gypsy and we got more than a few envious looks from nearby campers as the scent drifted around the campground.

Aimee didn't find too many things that inspired her as we drove across Canada, but Quebec was a clear exception. In a small town outside Quebec City, we stopped at a farmer's market that offered fresh meats and produce. The first night she made bison filets with fresh asparagus and tomatoes, accompanied by warm crusty bread from a local boulangerie. The next night was bacon-wrapped chicken with fresh tomatoes and green beans. It was like dining at an inn in the French countryside.

We have a lot of photos from our trip, but we also came back with memories of foods from different parts of the country. Now, when Aimee makes them at home, it is like being back in Gypsy, exploring America one great meal at a time.

Sisterhood of the Traveling Ants
—Aimee—

One day they just showed up. Ants. I found ants crawling on the linoleum in the morning. I found ants wandering inside my kitchen cabinets when I was making dinner. When I found them in the bathroom sink while I was brushing my teeth, enough was enough. I pride myself on keeping a spotless home and Gypsy would be no different.

Normally, I have a certain Zen-like tolerance for critters that I find in Gypsy. Spiders love to take shelter in our little spaces and I escort them out the side door in a dishrag. My favorite creature discovery was in Flaming Gorge, Wyoming. Our neighbor had trouble starting his engine one frosty morning. As I stood nearby, prepared to offer sage advice, he popped the hood and peered into his engine compartment, then made an squeak/scream noise and leapt backwards. Apparently, a marmot (picture a oversized ground squirrel) had spent a cozy night on his engine. The marmot went one way, and the guy went the other. Needless to say, we opened our engine hood cautiously that morning.

Crossing Kansas, we ran afoul of the stockyards that dot the landscape. Close your eyes and picture five million cattle and then picture ten billion flies floating around them in what must be fly heaven. I spent two days shooing flies from the rig, only to get ten new flies for every one that I sent out a window or door. It's all hilarious until you turn to give your husband directions and a fly zooms into your open mouth. Ick! I finally bought a fly swatter at a truck stop in Kansas—

and there were LOTS of fly swatters to choose from. After that, I was squinting like a gunfighter and wielding my fly swatter with deadly accuracy. Probably not a Zen Buddhist that day.

Anyway, when the ants appeared, I let bygones be bygones at first. They were much easier to deal with than flies. Unlike the flies, however, they persisted across four states. As near as I could tell, we had picked up an ant colony when we parked in Florida for a few days. Somewhere inside Gypsy there was a hidden queen, sending out her loyal subjects to find leftovers in my cupboards. When I started to find them in our bedding and my bathroom, it was time for action.

We stopped for two days near New Orleans, and I took everything out of the cupboards and sealed up any possible food access. No dice. I read RV blogs on the subject and tried every bit of advice, but to no avail. I am somewhat ashamed to say that I even bought ant traps and Raid. (We will probably get cancer later.) The ants just kept coming. It was a war of attrition, and they were winning. Two humans against the queen's army? We had no chance. I pictured her in repose on a tiny divan under my RV, listening with disdain to the reports of her scouts.

"Your Majesty, the humans have cleaned their fridge and cupboards, but they left these beignet crumbs under the couch," her lieutenant said, holding up a tasty morsel.

"Foolish humans!" she said, waving her antennae and stuffing a crumb into her mouth. "I shall breed an army worthy of this motorhome, and then we shall see who stays and who goes!"

Suddenly, they just disappeared. One day it was all-out war, then the next day there wasn't an ant in sight. When I described the event to our daughter Kim, she said they were just hitching a ride to New Orleans. Then she laughed and said, "They were the Sisterhood of the Traveling Ants!" Our little miseries had totally made her day and since then I've never looked at an ant without thinking of Kim's comment.

Sometimes I picture the queen of the traveling ants with a string of her attendants carrying her Louis Vuitton suitcases as she eyes each million-dollar A class motorhome in the park to pick one to move into. She is heading to Los Angeles to follow her dreams of stardom and needs a huge rig with a full pantry and more storage for her growing entourage. Our Gypsy just wasn't nice enough anymore…

Horse Country
—Ron—

I could not have lived for two years on the road without horses. That may sound strange, but it's true.

Moving almost every day, with no permanent home to provide a sense of roots, we often got homesick. When this happened, we tried to find things that reminded us of home. For me, it was horses. I had grown up with horses, starting with an Arabian mare named Tiffy who was given to us when I was 5 years old. My parents bought other horses to keep Tiffy company and over the years we had Quarter horses, draft horses, Thoroughbred racehorses, Shetland ponies and even a wild-caught mustang from the open range. It was a lot of work to take care of them, but they were more than animals. They were my friends. Many of my best childhood memories involved horses, so it was a treat to find them when we were on the road.

The horses that we saw as we traveled around America were as diverse as the country itself. In the Amish country of Pennsylvania and upstate New York, horses are still an important part of the workforce. Outside Lancaster, we camped next to a farm and fed the draft horses carrots and apples after watching them working in the fields all day. In nearby New Holland, horses-drawn buggies were as common as cars on the downtown streets. We saw many houses that used their backyard as a pasture and their garage as a barn.

In Kentucky, the thoroughbred racehorses were tall and sleek, looking like equine runway models. They were treated like royalty, with horse barns that looked like mansions and pastures like manicured parks. The horses must have known that they were elite, as they were generally aloof, but their power and grace as they moved were a joy to watch.

In Texas, there were horses on all the ranches and in quite a few towns as well. When we visited Round Top, its annual Antique Fair was under way and the town of 90 people had attracted over 100,000 visitors. The roads and parking lots were completely clogged, but their police force had no problem getting around on horseback. We wondered if the fire trucks and ambulances were pulled by teams of horses as well.

We saw wild horses several times in the desert scrub of Utah and Arizona. The horses were small, probably from the scarcity of food and water, but they looked healthy. They were very curious about us and unafraid of our presence as long as we weren't right next to them. I got within 20 feet of one herd before the lead stallion moved them away. I tossed apples near them, then retreated to Gypsy to watch them puzzle over what was clearly a new food to them. In Arizona, the wild donkeys were even more comfortable with us. One mom and her baby stood on the shoulder of the road and waited for us to throw food to them, which they happily ate while we watched.

Chincoteague Island on the Delmarva Peninsula had packs of wild ponies. The general belief is that they trace their lineage to a Spanish shipwreck off the coast. The ponies are still considered wild, but they clearly know how to win the affections of passing visitors and got a lot of treats from us.

Driving through rural Idaho, every farm seemed to have dozens of horses. After seeing over a thousand horses in one day, I started asking questions like, "How many horses are there in the US?" and "Is the horse population growing these days?" Aimee obligingly searched the Internet to satisfy my curiosity. After dropping from 25 million in 1925 to roughly 3 million in 1960, the US horse population has grown to over 9 million, more than any other country in the world. (I was surprised to learn that China is second with seven million horses.)

Driving around the country, I was pleased to see that America's love of horses is still thriving. Our country's heritage is more closely associated with the horse than any other animal. Like many Americans, horses were immigrants who adapted to virtually every part of America and were a vital part of building our country. Without horses, we could not have worked our farms, herded our cattle, or moved across America's vast distances to knit its various parts into a single nation. Maybe I'm biased, but I believe that many of America's most powerful images center around horses, from the Pony Express to draft horses plowing the family farm to cowboys working a cattle drive. When I see the Budweiser Clydesdales, it makes me happy to be an American. Visiting horses during our two years on the road cost us some carrots and apples, but it kept me going by reminding me of home.

Talking Trash
—Aimee—

RV manufacturers sell people on the concept of having the total freedom to camp along rivers and see the National Parks in relaxed comfort. Their commercials always depict a happy family serving up hamburgers and hot dogs from a Coleman grill to an adoring set of kids sitting around a campfire. There is never a dumpster in the background, and they never, ever mention taking out the garbage.

As Americans, we generate a lot of trash. For everything you cook or eat in your RV, there will likely be a wrapper, plastic baggie, cardboard box, milk carton or yogurt cup to be thrown away. It's inescapable. And since RVs generally do not have a space for a trash receptacle in their design, everyone who takes an RV out on the road has to come up with a system for their trash.

Many folks like to place a giant lined garbage can just outside the door to their rig when they arrive at a campsite, which offers the advantage of holding several days' worth of trash. I find that approach off-putting. There you are at your picnic table enjoying the evening breeze while sitting next to a huge garbage can. Unsightly? I think so. We preferred to keep our trash in a scented trash bag shoved under the kitchen sink cabinet. It only held about one day's worth of trash, thus necessitating a daily trash disposal chore performed by—me.

Getting rid of your trash sounds like a boring job, right? Quite the contrary. It can be both exciting and aerobic.

Getting rid of trash usually involved taking it to a dumpster located somewhere in the campground. The hike could be very stimulating, depending on how hard it was to find out where the dumpster was located. Hopefully, it was a ways away from our campsite, because no one wants to camp right next to a dumpster for obvious olfactory and aesthetic reasons. This is where your puzzle-solving skills come into play. Just where is that dumpster? Maybe it's shown on the campground map. Maybe it's not. Maybe there's a sign pointing toward it. Maybe not. You may have to brush up on your social skills and ask another camper, although other campground denizens can be somewhat unhelpful.

"Do you happen to know where the trash is?" I have asked on many occasions.

"Somewhere near the office," was the most frequent response.

"Gosh, I sure hadn't thought of that after 100 campgrounds. Thanks!" I might have said if I'd been totally honest about my thoughts.

"Thanks, have a nice day!" was what I really said.

When no one was around to ask directions, I just walked around carrying a Hefty bag like I was a hobo, cursing under my breath like I had Tourette's Syndrome. Hopefully, I'd stumble upon the dumpster before Ron sent out a search party.

Of course, you must always factor in weather when on trash duty. I have been caught outside by monsoon-like rain, with big drops rolling over my eyelashes. I have dashed to the park dumpster in a lightning storm to get rid of some Louisiana crawdad shells that were stinking up Gypsy. I once grabbed our trash on the way to the community shelter while a tornado warning blared at our Texas campground. I know that sounds ridiculous, but I had been planning to take it out anyway and the dumpster was on our way to safety. Besides, I pictured Gypsy half smashed by a tornado and the locals rummaging through my trash strewn everywhere. "Shameful!" my mother's voice said in my mind, and so I grabbed the bag as we scrambled out the door. Ron often thinks I'm nuts, and maybe he's right.

If we arrived at the campground late enough that it was dark outside and our trash was full, things could get exciting in a hurry.

I'll bet that when you take your trash out at night, you don't need to bring a flashlight and a buddy in case you meet wild boar, bear or coyotes. I got in the habit of taking the trash out as part of my morning walk. Mornings were serene and lovely, full of all the natural beauty that the world has to offer.

Picture yourself hiking over to the dumpster at dawn. Birds are chirping, it's a beautiful morning. The other campers are still in their bunks, so you are practically alone. Morning dew covers your shoes as you walk down the trail. You casually lift the dumpster lid, about to toss your bag inside, when a squirrel leaps out of the dumpster, runs up your arm and jumps off your shoulder, all in the time it takes you to inhale enough air to shriek. Stimulating!

I have seen raccoons sleeping in a dumpster, a porcupine eating leftover hot dog buns inside a dumpster and a family of armadillos living underneath a dumpster. I've had ravens fly out of a dumpster where they had been trapped overnight.

I learned to approach all dumpsters like they might contain man-eating tigers. Look, listen, and then slowly lift the lid. Be prepared to run.

There you have it. Please think of me fondly the next time you take out your kitchen garbage in your slippers and bathrobe. You know where the can is. You don't need a map. It's probably less than fifty feet away. You don't worry about being attacked by wild animals or struck by lightning as you dump your old pizza box into the recycle bin. It's so civilized.

New Orleans

—*Ron*—

Even though it is considered a top destination, I was not enthusiastic when Aimee said that she wanted to spend several days in New Orleans. I had been there twice on business trips and mostly remembered it as hot, humid, dirty, and noisy. I also didn't relish the idea of driving Gypsy through the French Quarter. I had used a rental car around New Orleans during my earlier visits and between the narrow streets and the crowds of drunken revelers, it was more about survival than enjoyment. Parking was another scary thought. New Orleans has some very questionable neighborhoods and I had visions of finding Gypsy stripped to the frame and covered with graffiti when we came back after walking around seeing the sights. But Aimee had never been to New Orleans and wanted to explore its spooky nature, so I kept my concerns to myself. I researched RV parks and surprisingly found one that was located on the edge of the French Quarter. It was expensive, but the pictures and reviews looked good. Best of all, it would allow us to walk to anything that we wanted to see. Excited that I wouldn't have to leave Gypsy in some remote parking facility and pay for a hotel in the French Quarter, I reserved their last available spot.

As we drove toward New Orleans, I wondered if Mother Nature had other ideas. Heading along the Gulf coast through Alabama and Mississippi, we watched the weather turn increasingly dark and gloomy. We were working out at a gym about 30 miles outside New Orleans when suddenly the power in the building went out and hail the size of golf balls started falling outside. We ran back to Gypsy, hoping to outrun the storm and get settled into the RV park. We hadn't realized that we had to drive across Lake Pontchartrain to get into the city. After watching several 18-wheeler trucks weave back and forth in the high winds on the main bridge, we opted for the smaller Maestri Bridge on Highway 11 that had less traffic. We found out later that the bridge was 92 years old, considered unsafe for large vehicles and would need major repairs after the storm. Sometimes ignorance is bliss.

Exiting the freeway, we came to an eight-foot-tall concrete wall covered in graffiti with rolls of barbed wire on top. It looked like the outside of a prison. It was situated next to a centuries-old cemetery and an abandoned supermarket that had a bunch of questionable-looking vehicles in the parking lot. We pulled up to a locked iron gate, wondering what awaited us inside. When the gates slowly opened, we got the biggest campground surprise of our entire trip. The French Quarter RV Park may have been ominous on the outside, but inside it was beautiful. The sites were level and brick-paved, with neatly trimmed greenery between each one. The laundry and fitness center were modern and spotless. The spa area could have been a high-end resort, with a large pool and hot tub set in beautiful decorative tile. Amazed by the extraordinary contrast between the inside and the outside, we thought that it was the nicest RV park that we had ever seen.

The next day we wandered around the French Quarter, walking down its narrow cobblestone streets underneath flower-covered balconies, and soaking up the New Orleans vibe. Perhaps its atmosphere comes from being a melting pot of cultures, starting with its roots as a French and then a Spanish colony, adding a liberal dose of Cajun and Caribbean spice, all set to the smooth rhythm of jazz music. Whatever it is that gives New Orleans its unique feel, it has been celebrating it for over three centuries and shows no signs of slowing down.

We knew that New Orleans was famous as a food destination, but we had to find out for ourselves. The first item on our list was oysters, and we tried them at several places as we walked around the French

Quarter. For variety, it was hard to beat Felix's, which offered oysters prepared raw, chargrilled, Rockefeller (with mixed greens), Bienville (with broiled shrimp) or whatever else they had dreamed up that day. Still, our favorite place was the Acme Oyster Company. We went there four times and each time there was a line down the block and around the corner, but it was worth the wait. Their chargrilled oysters served in herb butter sauce and topped with Parmesan cheese may be a heart attack waiting to happen, but we would be dying with a smile.

Next, we went hunting for beignets. They had been her mom's specialty when she was growing up, so Aimee had high standards. It was hard to beat the classic setting of Café Du Monde on the Mississippi River across from Jackson Square, but for pure flavor the Morning Call in Metairie was by far the best. A classic hole in the wall that we heard about from the locals, they offered fresh-baked delicious beignets 24 hours a day. We spent over an hour there, getting buzzed on sugar and caffeine while we relived Aimee's youth.

Walking down Decatur Street, we stepped into a little Italian delicatessen to buy some water and discovered that we were in the historic Central Grocery, the store that launched the muffuletta. Along with the po' boy, the muffuletta is New Orleans' most famous sandwich. Created in 1906 by a Sicilian immigrant, it has several Italian meats and cheeses with an olive-based spread on a round loaf of bread roughly the size of a pizza. The crunchy bread, authentic Italian fillings and unique olive flavor made such a delicious combination that I found it difficult to share.

Red beans and rice, jambalaya, shrimp creole, po' boys—the list of "must try" foods went on and on. New Orleans had small cafes hidden in courtyards on every block. We tried at least a dozen different places and didn't feel like we had even begun to sample the range of delicious foods that were available.

My sister Robin flew out from California, and we spent several days touring the city. We rode around the French Quarter in a horse-drawn carriage, then took a tour of the city's Garden District on the St. Charles Streetcar, the world's oldest continuously operating streetcar. Built between 1850 and 1900, the Garden District has one of the best-preserved collections of historic mansions in America. As a lover of architecture, it was one jaw-dropping view after another for me as we passed through the historic neighborhood at the streetcar's leisurely pace. Later, we drove Gypsy up the Mississippi River to visit the Oak Alley Plantation, famous for its double row of southern live oak trees that stretch 800 feet from the river to the estate's main house.

We enjoyed our visit to New Orleans so much that we returned the following year and met my brother Russell for my annual birthday bike ride. Pedaling down the paved bike trail that runs on the levee alongside the Mississippi River, I pictured myself riding on an old-time paddlewheel riverboat, its steam whistle blowing as we reached the 350-acre plantation that is now Audubon Park. After we finished our 62 miles, we sampled more New Orleans restaurants.

In total, we spent nearly two weeks in New Orleans, the longest time that we stayed anywhere on our trip. Unlike my earlier overnight visits, we immersed ourselves in the city's food, architecture and atmosphere and learned that New Orleans can't be visited—it must be experienced to really appreciate its charms.

Can I Buy Your Ghost a Drink?

—*Aimee*—

Of all the interesting places that we visited around the US, the French Quarter of New Orleans has to be my solid number one for the strange and unusual.

How to explain the French Quarter? Like most people, I knew it only based on film footage of Mardi Gras that showed wild, feather-covered papier-mâché floats in a rainbow of colors, accompanied by college kids puking from balconies. While these images are real, they don't do it justice. The French Quarter has been a bustling trade port near the mouth of the Mississippi since the early 1700's. Its French influence permeates the architecture and food. African slaves added their cooking and culture to the city's melting pot and gave it a subtle Caribbean and African flavor. The old French Quarter of the city became synonymous with both culture and piracy as aristocrats from Europe came to the New World and built the huge plantations that surround it. The French Quarter is packed with voodoo shops, bars, upscale Michelin restaurants and back-alley dives, street performers and antique shops all rubbing shoulders in buildings that date back centuries. Driving is nearly impossible on the cobbled streets that were originally built for horse-drawn buggies. Everyone walks.

I was agog at the "feel" of the place. I'm generally a reserved skeptic about paranormal phenomenon, but you can't be a skeptic in the French Quarter. Walk around and feel the "weird" before you call me crazy. The dead are as much a part of the city as the living.

Into all this, we added Ron's sister Robin. It was her 60th birthday and she had always wanted to visit New Orleans, so we arranged to meet her for a few days of sight-seeing around the city. We went everywhere: eating beignets covered in powdered sugar at Café du Monde, sampling jambalaya and oysters, riding the Green Line streetcar through the Garden District to see the old mansions. We spent an afternoon riding around the French Quarter in an open horse-drawn buggy with an eccentric tour guide that we hired in front of St. Louis Cathedral. He told us ghost stories and pirate stories while stopping at places like Lafitte's Blacksmith Bar, the oldest structure in New Orleans. His horses, (actually, mule-crosses), were patient as he stopped frequently and loudly expressed his political views (very conservative) and his thoughts on the Quarters' paranormal activity (very open-minded).

Robin seemed entertained and a bit startled by all the talk of murders, pirates, hauntings, and voodoo. Robin is a dependable, pragmatic person with a wonderful heart. She attends church regularly and I'm pretty sure that she brought her Bible with her to New Orleans. This had to be a real eye-opener.

That evening things only got more interesting. We walked along the streets of the city in the deepening twilight, smelling the jungle-like aroma of jasmine while watching the full moon rise over the Quarter. You could hear the partying down on Bourbon Street, but we were blocks away in the older section. We decided to try a little bar and grille on the north end of the Quarter for dinner. It was relatively new but had a wonderful rating on TripAdvisor for small plates and seafood. We couldn't get a table but a few stools at the bar were clearing out, so we settled in and ordered from the menu while chatting with other folks at the bar. Ron got into an animated conversation about global warming with a couple of visiting marine scientists at the far end of the bar while Robin and I chatted about our kids and generally enjoyed the bar's atmosphere. Robin doesn't drink, so the experience of sitting along the brass rail of a legit wooden bar was pretty novel to her.

After a while, she asked the bartender "What's that up on the wall?" She pointed to a small shelf high above the bar that was adorned with an incense holder, candles and a variety of beads, crosses and charms dangling from it.

"It's an offering to the ghost," the bartender said seriously. He was clearly not joking.

"You mean there's a ghost in this bar?" she asked, looking everywhere at once.

"Yep, the charms must not be working because we've had about ten bottles jump off the shelves in the last two days for no reason. It's very frustrating," he said in that slow Louisiana drawl. "The owner says the building had a reputation for issues when he acquired it. Sometimes our offerings work, sometimes weird stuff just happens." He shrugged and started collecting empty glasses.

"Hold up a sec," I said, and turned to Robin. "Give me ten bucks" I said to her, pulling money from my wallet.

"Why?" she asked, but she was already reaching for her purse. That's the kind of nice person she is.

I turned to the bartender.

"We want to buy a jigger of your best whiskey to appease your ghost," I said and smiled at Robin, who looked completely shocked while still in the process of handing me her ten bucks.

"Wow, cherie, that's a new one," he said with approval in his voice while reaching for a bottle. "Nobody has bought the ghost a drink before. Sometimes we leave an offering, but no patron has ever done that."

"Well, maybe she just needs a friend or two," I said, smiling and lifting my glass in salute. Robin followed suit with her ice water while we watched the bartender gently set a jigger of whiskey high on the shelf.

I know that this is the part where you expect something paranormal to happen. It didn't. We laughed as we walked with Robin back to her hotel in the moonlight. It was just the kind of thing that happens in the Quarter, and maybe nowhere else in the States.

I often wonder if Robin ever told anyone about the night that she bought a ghost a drink. I think it was fantastic that, when the moment came, she didn't hesitate.

The Great Oyster Shooter Incident
—Aimee—

Getting sick on the road sucks. You can't see your family doctor and you have limited options for care.

Before we started the trip, we arranged a set of doctor visits and updated all of our vaccinations. As the family medic, I planned ahead as much as possible, packing my enormous "black bag" medical kit with a wide selection of over-the-counter medicines, some antibiotics that I had acquired on our overseas trips and every conceivable first aid item. I took all of the available first aid training, including Advanced Survival First Aid, CPR, Suture Training and a variety of classes on fun things like removing ingrown toenails, giving stitches and administering IVs. Sounds crazy, right? But I thought we should be prepared for anything up to and including a zombie apocalypse.

Things went pretty well for the first 18 months on the road as I treated toothaches, ear infections, a torn foot ligament, back strains and one garden variety case of bronchitis. The true test awaited us in New Orleans. Not a heart attack, not a broken leg…just oysters.

Oysters are served in nearly every bar and restaurant in New Orleans. We ate them charbroiled, baked, sauteed and raw. We loved every one of them. That is, until Ron got sick. It started just like you'd think, with GI distress. Nothing too serious, but it never stopped.

He had already made plans to meet his brother Russell in New Orleans to do their annual bike ride on the levee that runs along the Mississippi River. When Russell arrived, Ron had already been sick for three days but thought he'd gut it out and just stay hydrated. He finished the ride but was running a fever, and alarmingly, the GI stuff was only getting worse. We started heading west toward Texas, but each day he would drive less and sleep more.

Four days after leaving New Orleans, we stopped for groceries in a Texas strip mall, and I refused to move any further until we visited the Urgent Care that just happened to be located in the same shopping center. (That might seem like quite the coincidence, except that I handle Google Maps and the navigation.) I was convinced that Ron was battling the Vibrio bacteria that are sometimes found in oysters that were harvested from warm waters. Vibrio are a nasty little bacteria that can make a person dramatically sick, causing diarrhea that can kill by dehydration.

Ron was feverish and his body was basically shutting down. He had just enough strength to do what any good husband would do: protest this ambush.

"I'll be fine if you would just let me nap for an hour and then we can move on," he said in a somewhat blurry voice.

"If you don't go in, I'm taking over and driving you to the hospital instead of this handy Urgent Care that we are parked next to right here. Then you can enjoy an overnight visit in a Texas hospital," I told him curtly. We weren't moving until he got looked at. I didn't want to tell the kids that their father had died of stubbornness.

After much stalling, Ron finally agreed to go inside. They took his temperature (102 degrees) and did some blood work, then told us that it was indeed a food-born bacteria and that he needed an IV. After another round of protests, he lost that battle too. Fifteen minutes later, after absorbing a bag of saline with a bevy of drugs, he was a new man. He perked up and asked the Urgent Care tech for "another round" since the first IV had improved matters so much.

Suffice it to say that Ron turned the corner following the treatment and improved steadily over the next several days. Afterwards, we referred to the experience as "The Great Oyster Shooter" incident. He hasn't eaten a raw oyster since. I really can't blame him.

Holidays on the Road
—Ron—

Holidays have always been a big deal for me. Growing up, my family lived nearby, so grandparents, aunts, uncles and cousins all gathered together for holidays. Thanksgiving was a huge turkey dinner and hours of card games. Christmas was a marathon of festivities, starting with a family potluck on Christmas Eve that included carols and a visit from Santa. On Christmas Day, we ate breakfast at home and opened presents, then met at my grandparents' house for another feast and more games until Dad drove back home at midnight with us kids asleep in the back of the station wagon. On Memorial Day, 4th of July and Labor Day, we all met at the local park to play kickball and poker, tell family stories and have a potluck so big that it took several tables to hold all the food. Holidays were our way to celebrate being a family through a shared love of food and games. I worried about missing them when we were driving around America, but I discovered that holidays on the road were special in their own way.

Our first holiday on the road was the Fourth of July. At home, we would have held a family barbeque at my brother Rick's house, then watched our town's fireworks show. Now, we had no family or friends nearby, but we learned that Americans join together to celebrate the Fourth wherever they are. At the Granite Lakes RV Resort in Clarkston, Washington, our campground hosts held a barbeque for the guests. We ate and shared stories while we watched the fireworks over the Snake River. The next year, we spent the Fourth of July near Bend, Oregon. The campground hosts handed out ice cream and put on fireworks show. Soon the air was filled with the sound of children screaming as skyrockets shot into the sky. The smoke set off Gypsy's smoke detector, so we pulled out its battery to stop the noise, but we didn't think that would work on the sugar-stoked kids.

Halloween is Aimee's favorite holiday. At home, she would spend a month planning the décor. We would carve a dozen pumpkins, me scooping out their insides and Aimee turning them into dragons, ghosts, haunted houses, and other wild designs. Our costumes ranged from elaborate Renaissance Faire outfits complete with swords to regulation Star Trek uniforms. We greeted the kids who came to our door with huge bowls of candy while "Thriller" or "Monster Mash" played in the background.

On the road, we were delighted to find that Halloween was celebrated at the campgrounds. It felt very authentic and even a little spooky sitting under the pine trees with the campfire flickering and pumpkins glowing in the night. The kids were in trick-or-treating heaven as they zoomed between campsites that were filled with people who loved to hear their squeals of joy. Aimee also created a Halloween postcard each year to let our family and friends know that we were alive and thinking of them. My favorite was when she put a twist on the famous American Gothic painting. We dressed up like farmers and stood in front of Gypsy holding a pitchfork and a Halloween pumpkin.

We were in the Southeast during November both years on the road, too far away to share Thanksgiving with any of our family. Fortunately, some friends graciously invited us to join them. We spent our first Thanksgiving with Walt and Suzan Strader at their home on Lake Norman in North Carolina. Walt and Suzan have an intense love of life and it certainly showed in their

celebration of Thanksgiving. They rolled out a meal fit for a Michelin restaurant, and we ate, drank, and talked deep into the night. The next year, we joined Rick and Diana Roof in Charlottesville, Virginia, another perfect location for Thanksgiving with autumn leaves carpeting the grounds of the University of Virginia and Thomas Jefferson's Monticello home. We had a traditional Thanksgiving dinner at the historic Boars Head Inn and talked for hours, realizing that time spent with family and friends was what we were most thankful for.

Aimee and I had never spent Christmas away from our families. For many years, we loaded the kids into the Desert Weasel and drove 450 miles to Sonoma County for the family Christmas celebration. We often went to four different homes to share Christmas Day with all our families and friends, then drove all night to get back home, tired but happy.

For our first year of living on the road, we decided to try something totally different by spending Christmas in the Florida Keys. It was strange swimming in a pool on Christmas Day and seeing palm trees instead of Christmas trees, but it was fun to see the rigs at our campground decorated with Christmas lights, inflatable snowmen, and candy-cane walkways. Aimee made a traditional Christmas card using a picture of us at Rangeley Lake in Maine to send to our family and friends, but the truth was that we were wearing flip-flops and tank tops on Christmas Day.

The next year, we flew back to Sonoma County to be with our families. After nearly two years on the road, we had a lot of stories to share. Besides, Christmas with Mom was something special.

Thanksgiving with old friends, Halloween in campgrounds full of sugar-wired kids, Fourth of July joining other Americans to celebrate our country's heritage, Christmas lounging on a tropical beach or flying home to be with family. Living on the road gave us new ways to enjoy and appreciate the holidays.

Quilt Junkie

—Aimee—

I am a confessed quilt junkie. I have a thing for linens of any kind, but blankets are where my addiction really got started. My first security blanket, "Mr. Blanky," was a yellow cotton crib blanket with a matching satin border. I dragged him everywhere and threw him over my head at night to protect me when I thought that the monsters might get me. Four years and five hundred washes later, Mr. Blanky had faded to an indistinct mustard color and the satin border was long gone from my repeated nuzzling. When my sister and I ripped Mr. Blanky during a tug-of-war fight, my mother tried to toss him out. To her, he was an outdated and shabby security object. No mom wants her five-year-old dragging a torn crib blanket to school. Her suggestion prompted a bout of me crying so fiercely that I was allowed to keep him for bedtime only. A year or two later, Mr. Blanky moved into the closet, and I moved on to bigger and better blanket addictions.

I have collected quilts and blankets from all over the world. On our honeymoon, I scoured the market stalls in Tahiti for a Polynesian wedding quilt. On motorhome trips to the Southwest, I dragged Ron onto Indian reservations in search of authentic native American blankets and rugs. I drove up mountain roads in the remote villages of the South Seas Cook Islands on the barest rumor of an elderly native who still made colonial blankets. Early on during our RV trip, I talked Ron into visiting the original Pendleton woolen mill and scored three wool blankets direct from the factory. I have the zeal of an explorer and the hot desire that any devoted collector feels upon seeing a rarity.

When we entered Pennsylvania, I had a plan. This was Amish country. Where else in the world could you get a handmade quilt rivalling the kind that you see in American museums? Amish country! For a quilt collector, this was Mount Everest. I did not share my plan with Ron because we already had blankets and quilts decorating every flat surface in Gypsy. How could I justify the need or the expense? Handmade Amish quilts often cost thousands of dollars.

I tried mentioning it obliquely as we camped for the night. "You know, we are right in the middle of Amish country. This is where some of the best quilts in America are still made by hand. I wonder if there are any farms around here selling them?" Subtle, right?

He wasn't biting. After nearly twenty years together, he knew what I was up to.

The fencing match was about the begin.

"Don't we already have a bunch of quilts in the rig?" he asked. A classic parry.

"I know we do, but when we will ever be back here? I'll never get a chance like this again. Maybe we can just go see some," I replied. Riposte!

"Aren't they expensive?" Retreat and Parry.

"My birthday is coming up in two weeks." Advance and Lunge!

"I know I'm not going to win this one. We can look tomorrow." Point and Match. He knew when to quit.

The next day, we set out driving the back roads and asking random folks where we could buy quilts. I was counting on Ron here. He's absolutely fearless when it comes to talking to strangers, even those as reserved as the Amish. Picture our RV parked on the side of the road while an Amish buggy drawn by horses pulls alongside. Ron sticks his head out of the window and asks the bearded driver for help in finding a place that sold quilts. Totally weird, yet it always seems to work.

Eventually, we pulled into a classic Amish farm with a huge white farmhouse and matching barn. The lady of the house was quite shy and spoke almost no English, but Ron charmed her into opening up the little store that she operated in her basement. There were over a hundred quilts and pillows hanging from wooden hooks, each one with a hang tag indicating who had made it along with its astronomical price. To a quilt junkie like me, it was heaven. I wandered around in a haze of desire while Ron chatted her up about living on a farm.

I finally picked a quilt with a complicated multi-color pattern and Ron had the temerity to ask if she would negotiate on price. After much back and forth and a side-bar discussion of her secrets for making jam, she eventually agreed to give him a fifty-dollar discount on a seven-hundred-dollar quilt. If you know the Pennsylvania Dutch, that kind of discount is totally unheard of. Her husband came in from the farm as we were settling up and berated her slightly for giving us a discount. Ron told him that his wife was a great salesperson and a tough negotiator. "We weren't planning to buy a quilt at all until she convinced us that we needed one." Sly dog that husband of mine.

Still not satisfied, the farmer walked us out into the yard, hands on his suspenders, hair tucked under a straw hat, his white beard neatly trimmed. Every inch an Amish elder.

"That your RV?" he asked stoically.

"Yep, we are taking two years to drive around the country, seeing America," Ron replied.

"The wife and I want get an RV and do just that." he said. "We only get out for vacation about twice a year right now. Just finished a visit to California. Took that wine train through Napa."

Well, there you go. Ron and the fellow spent ten minutes discussing California wines and the various pros and cons of trailers versus RVs while standing there in the Amish farmyard. Normally, it would have seemed surreal, but I was busy pulling a Pendleton blanket off the bed in Gypsy and installing my new treasure.

God help Ron if we ever take an RV trip around Scotland and Ireland. He will be wearing a custom tartan kilt within a week…and isn't Ireland known for its hand-knit fishing sweaters??

Truth or Consequences

—Ron—

New Mexico was a place that we kept returning to during our trip. We both loved the stark beauty of the desert, the ever-changing colors of the rocks, the subtle patterns of life in the harsh setting and the wild patches of color when the desert wildflowers were in bloom.

Like most people who visit New Mexico, we spent a lot of time exploring Albuquerque, Santa Fe and Taos. We toured the Georgia O'Keefe Museum, bought homemade soap at the Cherokee Soap Company, and walked around Taos soaking up the artistic vibe. We ate our way through Albuquerque, from blue corn enchiladas at the Range Café to green chile apple pie at the New Mexico Pie Company. As big sci-fi fans, we had to visit Roswell and its Extra-Terrestrial Museum. We went to the village of Roy (population 211) where my dad and grandma had been born. For us, however, the biggest surprise in wandering around New Mexico was Truth or Consequences.

There are three major highways that go through New Mexico. Interstate 10 runs east/west through the southern part of the state, passing through Las Cruces on its route from El Paso, Texas to Los Angeles. Interstate 40 goes east/west across the northern part of the state, following historic Route 66 and passing through Albuquerque as part of its path between Oklahoma City and Flagstaff, Arizona. Going north/south, Interstate 25 connects Las Cruces to Albuquerque and Santa Fe, then continues north to Denver. The portion of I-25 from Albuquerque to Las Cruces is the least traveled of New Mexico's freeways. It follows the Rio Grande River, but it's not very scenic. Even Elephant Butte Lake, the largest lake in the state, is mostly brown water surrounded by dry earth and scrub. You need a really good reason or a touch of crazy to drive this 229-mile stretch of road.

Beyond our normal "why not" attitude, we went for two reasons: Hatch chiles and Truth or Consequences.

Located 40 miles north of Las Cruces, Hatch is known as the "Chile Capital of the World" because it grows a wide variety of chiles including the New Mexico chile. Aimee loves chiles and Hatch chiles are her favorite, so we had to see the place. Hatch only has a couple of main streets, so it didn't take us long to find chiles. In the restaurants, every item seemed to include chiles and we discovered that fresh-picked chiles were a delicious addition to most dishes. Stores sold dried chiles in hanging clusters or in big burlap bags. When we left town, we were stocked with enough chiles to last for many, many meals.

Driving north from Hatch, we reached Truth or Consequences, a small town of 6,000 people on the banks of the Rio Grande River. The town started as a resort destination named Hot Springs and had over 40 natural hot spring spas at one point. The town acquired its current name when the game show Truth or Consequences offered to broadcast from the first town that would change its name to match the show. The town changed its name on March 31, 1950, and the program was broadcast from there the next day. I had once been a contestant on Family Feud and Wheel of Fortune, so I couldn't resist visiting a town that named itself after a game show.

As we entered Truth or Consequences, we got our first surprise when we saw Riverbend Hot Springs, a spa resort perched on the banks of the Rio Grande. Its rooms ranged from a traditional single room to a 3-bedroom suite and were beautifully decorated in southwestern style. They also had eight RV sites, so we camped there and walked across the street to soak in the pools overlooking the river. The grounds were perfectly landscaped and the water from the artesian spring was clean and hot. We lay there enjoying the luxury of a hot soak as we watched the animals come down to the river to drink at dusk.

Truth or Consequences

The next morning, we walked around, enjoying the town's history and artsy vibe. There were still a dozen working spas, all connected by a walking path decorated with art works by local artists to showcase the town's hot springs history. The spas themselves ranged from basic to artistic. Our favorite was the Blackstone Hot Springs Lodging and Bath, which offered private in-room soaking tubs in TV-themed rooms like The Twilight Zone, The Golden Girls and, of course, Star Trek. Walking down the main street, we stumbled upon the Passion Pie Café. (OK, maybe I had looked up bakeries in town.) It had been in business for only a few years, but it was already a local landmark, with a menu that featured an assortment of artistic edible delights. We especially liked The Fat Elvis, a waffle covered with bananas, peanut butter, whipped cream, and maple syrup. We sat there, trying to eat with our eyes rather than our mouths. Judging from the number of local people who sat talking while ogling the display case, we weren't alone.

We took one more soak in the hot spring pools, packed up Gypsy and headed out of town. While we were driving, Aimee looked up from her Internet research and said "There's a side road up here that goes to the Very Large Array and a place called Pie Town. Are you interested?"

"The world's most powerful radio telescope and a town dedicated to pies? Absolutely!"

Mobile Wild Kingdom
—Aimee—

Walking through Graceland RV Park in Memphis, I passed an enormous top-of-the-line A Class motor coach with its sun awning deployed against the evening glare. Under the awning lay a tidy arrangement of outdoor furniture worthy of Pottery Barn and a giant flat-screen TV set on Animal Planet. Sitting outside and watching this entertainment extravaganza from the comfort of their custom perch were several macaws, chatting away and grooming each other as parrots do. They were clearly enjoying watching their TV show. Their owner, a Canadian singer, came out with a fruit tray for them and chatted with me about his birds for a short bit before I continued my walk. Was I surprised to see $500K worth of motorhome outfitted for the comfort of three birds? Nope. Totally normal. RV enthusiasts love to take everything with them, replicating the comforts of home. This means their pets, common or exotic, come along too, sometimes in the most ingenious ways.

Dogs were absolutely common, and they came in all shapes, sizes and quantities. We encountered a husband and wife in Virginia who had ten shelties milling around their campsite behind an elaborate set of baby gates. We were fascinated and asked how they managed to travel in an RV with ten dogs, chatting with them while the black and white shelties sniffed various fingers. Apparently, the couple took their shelties to dog shows around the country and had a whole system for their care. The wife walked them in groups of three or four every morning and again each evening while the husband set up their pens and laid out their meals. They said that RV parks usually let them stay as long as they paid a little extra for the privilege. Walking back to Gypsy, I thought, "Wow, that's commitment—or wow, that's nuts. Take your pick."

We saw lots and lots of dogs of various breeds and dispositions, but our favorite was a pair of dogs living in an enormous A Class RV in Grand Junction, Colorado. While walking past the RV, we noticed a sign taped inside the passenger window stating that "If there is any problem or the dogs are too loud, please call XXX-XXX-XXX. Thanks Bob and Sheri." The dogs themselves were the most mismatched pair you could imagine: a purebred boxer and a tiny toy mix with long shaggy hair. Barking at us through the dashboard window, the toy fit perfectly on the dashboard and the huge boxer stood with its paws over the steering wheel to slather the windshield glass with snot and a volley of barks as we walked by. It might have been scary except that after every two or three barks the toy mix turned on the boxer and made a growling attack on its ears. This repeated over and over; bark, bark, snarling ear attack, bark, bark, snarling ear attack......hilarious.

It seems to me that dogs would take better to the mobile lifestyle than cats, but you would be surprised at the number of feline-friendly RVs we saw on our trip. Walk around most RV parks and you will almost certainly see a couple of kitties looking back at you from the dashboards of their rigs. You might even meet a few cats being walked on leashes. I even saw campers who used wire, tubing, and miniature ladders to build cat exercise areas around their RV.

We also saw a lot of reptiles, especially iguanas. Peer into an RV driving by in Florida, and your chances are pretty good of seeing an iguana perched on a driver's shoulder. Personally, I am not a fan, having once been chased around my living room by a large green iguana that my mother had agreed to babysit for a friend, but campers seemed to love them and we would often see them being walked around the campground on small leashes. Reptile lovers have snakes as well. I saw one large Burmese python sunbathing in a tank on a picnic table, but I am sure many more hang out inside RVs.

Even barnyard animals made the leap to the mobile lifestyle. I understand the appeal of walking a cute little pot-bellied pig on a sequined halter around a park, drawing lots of interest from the other campers. However, I shudder to think of how a pig might ride with you on the open road and the possible cleaning chores involved. Driving through Arkansas, I spotted a square wire contraption hanging off the back of an older motorhome. Urging Ron to get closer, I realized that we were looking at a chicken coop. This one clearly allowed the chickens access to a cage outside of the RV when it was stopped. I hoped that the hens were crated inside when they were moving but my inner child pictured a bunch of hens wandering free throughout the RV like an episode of the Beverly Hillbillies.

I am sure somewhere in America there is a motorhome rolling down the highway with a tiger sitting in the passenger seat. Or maybe someone has a Jersey cow in their Prevost A Class that they milk every morning. It could happen.

Romance on the Road
—Ron—

When we told our families that we were going to be living in an RV together, they questioned whether we would get along in such close quarters. However, we were overdue for some extended time together. We had been together as a couple for over 15 years, but our jobs required extensive travel, so we were rarely home at the same time. When we were, we usually had to "divide and conquer" to catch up on chores. Our time together was usually focused on being parents. We loved being with our kids and were very aware that they would soon move out, so we tried to spend as much time with them as possible. But it was hard to find time for romance—that candlelit dinner at a fancy restaurant is somehow different when your teenage daughter and her boyfriend are sharing your table.

We saw our trip as an opportunity to make up for all the years of being apart. We would explore America together, with no agenda other than spending time with each other. It seemed like the perfect setting for two people in love. In retrospect, perhaps we should have wondered why no one has ever described their RV trip as a romantic getaway.

We soon discovered that finding romance in a motorhome presented some challenges. First off, it's hard to be mysterious when you are together 24/7 in a 29x8-foot metal box. Want to surprise her with flowers or her favorite chocolate? Good luck sneaking them into the grocery cart as you shop together. Want to have a gift mailed ahead for a special occasion? Difficult to do when you don't know where you will be two days from now. Oh, and by the way, that perfect present has to fit in your tiny storage space. Eventually, we figured out that the best romantic gift was to take a break from living in Gypsy for a more traditional couple's getaway.

Our first October on the road, we were heading from Maine, where we had been visiting our daughter Kim, to Long Island to visit with our daughter Wende. We had been living in Gypsy for six months and were a little road-weary, so when we saw the Mystic Inn perched atop a hill overlooking the harbor in Mystic, Connecticut, we decided to celebrate our wedding anniversary by pampering ourselves. We got a room with a wood-burning fireplace, an oversized jacuzzi tub and a wonderful view of the water. For three days, we took long baths and naps together, ate dinner in front of our fire, walked around the town holding hands and just enjoyed being in love. It was so nice that we went back the next year to celebrate our anniversary there again.

For Aimee's birthday one year, we booked a room at the luxurious Hotel Marlowe overlooking the Charles River in Boston. We ordered room service for dinner and watched the sunset over Cambridge and Harvard University. The next morning, we borrowed one of the hotel's kayaks and paddled along the Charles River watching the fall colors and feeding the ducks. In the afternoon, we walked around Boston's Inner Harbor and ate lunch at a waterfront Italian restaurant. Our waiter, an older Italian gentleman in a tuxedo, played his part perfectly, promising Aimee the meal of her dreams and then making it come true with an assortment of fresh-caught shellfish served over a bed of black pasta.

When the mandolin started playing in the background, I half expected the tune to be "Bella Notte" from the movie "Lady and the Tramp."

Aimee is a huge fan of classic horror author H.P. Lovecraft, so we went to his hometown of Providence, Rhode Island for her birthday the following year. We stayed in the Biltmore Hotel, a city landmark that was built in 1922. Aimee loved its history and architecture, and the fact that it housed the largest Starbucks in New England was an unexpected bonus. We spent the day enjoying the fall colors as we wandered through the old neighborhoods, admiring the Victorian houses, stopping at the local bakery. The next day, we drove to Swan Point Cemetery, a prominent cemetery where H.P. Lovecraft was buried. We couldn't find RV parking, so I sat in Gypsy while Aimee wandered among the 40,000 grave sites. Sometimes my wife has a strange sense of what is romantic.

We didn't always wait for a special occasion to have a getaway. In the spirit of the Twilight Saga movie series, we stayed at the Quinault Lodge, a beautiful historic inn on the shores of Lake Quinault in Washington's Olympic National Forest. Built in 1926, its open-beam architecture and huge fireplace made us feel like we were in a country estate house. After breakfast, we took a long walk through the rainforest, pretending to be star-crossed lovers. We also stayed at the Columbia Gorge Hotel, a historic hotel on the Columbia River in Hood River, Oregon. Built in 1925, it was a world-famous destination whose visitors included presidents and movie stars. We had drinks in the Rudolph Valentino Lounge, ate dinner in the dining room overlooking the river, then walked through the hotel's gardens and 200-foot waterfall with a carpet of summer stars shining brightly above us.

Not every romantic getaway went as planned. Aimee had never been to San Antonio, Texas, and I thought that its scenic Riverwalk would be the perfect setting for some leisurely time together. I booked a room at the Hyatt Hotel located right on the Riverwalk and we spent the afternoon strolling around the quiet shaded walkways before settling down for a quiet night of luxury in our hotel room. Little did we know that the San Antonio Spurs were playing their most important basketball game of the year that night. It was so loud that the hotel put earplugs and a white noise app in all the rooms. Not quite the peaceful experience that I had envisioned.

While we looked forward to our getaways, we found most of our romance in our daily routine. After being apart for many years, it was a pleasure to share Gypsy's close quarters, bumping into each other as we did our chores. We took walks together almost every day, enjoying the scenery and each other's company. When we were driving, we talked about anything and everything, Aimee telling me about the strange places that were just up the road and me driving her crazy with my constant requests for Internet research on some obscure topic. At night, we sat around the campfire, playing the guitar, and watching the stars. Best of all, we got to sleep together every night, fighting over who was hogging the covers. If that isn't romance, nothing is.

Rest Stop

—Aimee—

I think that Ron and I have a pretty frisky sex life, much to the everlasting dismay and general discomfort of our children. However, even the most adventurous couple can find it a challenge to be passionate in the cramped quarters of an RV.

RV sites are not very far apart at campgrounds. The notion that we were camping, all alone in the wilderness, was rarely true. It was a real turnoff to think that our RV might be moving rhythmically, or worse yet—squeaking—while someone was outside walking their dog or admiring a sunset. In addition, sounds of passion ran a real chance of being heard and we were not exhibitionists. Sex in Gypsy became a stealth proposition, punctuated by "Shh, I hear someone walking by!" or "Did you hear that?" Not sexy. We had to work at ways to make it exciting and fun.

Every so often on our daily drive, we would pull into a rest stop to take a nap or eat lunch. Rest stops are wonderful if you're in an RV. They are easy to access from the freeway and offer amenities like bathrooms and walking trails. A few big rest stops have restaurants, gas stations and even museums. They generally have dedicated parking for RVs and big trucks, which was an absolute relief after the challenges that we normally faced in parking our twenty-nine-foot vehicle.

Rest stops could also be really entertaining. They were often filled with enormous long-haul trucks and RVs of every size, color, and style. Parking between the idling rigs made you feel like you were part of a truly American experience. It reminded me of the movie "Convoy" with engines revving and generators running.

Parked between two eighteen-wheel semis one afternoon, I got a crazy idea. Their idling noise and running generators were super loud and their sheer size hid Gypsy in the shade between them. It didn't take much to lure Ron into the back bedroom. It felt a little tawdry but also titillating. One thing led to another and in a post-coital moment of hilarity, I said, "Hey, let's have sex at a rest stop in every state!"

We proceeded to do just that. It was kind of a cheap high school thrill or a road game if you will. We'd pass a sign that said "Welcome to Georgia" and Ron's head would turn slowly toward me from the driver's seat and he'd raise his eyebrows.

"You're not serious!?" I'd say, smiling.

Just like that, we'd swing into a rest stop for a little love making and a lot of laughter. There's nothing like an inside joke with your lover.

And now that I've shared this very personal fact about our trip, I'm pretty sure you'll never look at that map of the states on the back of Gypsy the same way again.

Texas Hill Country
—*Ron*—

Texas is so big (nearly the size of America's original 13 colonies combined) that we weren't sure where we should start in trying to see it. Big Bend National Park on the Rio Grande? The Guadalupe Mountains at nearly 9,000 feet high? The Gulf Coast with 400 miles of shoreline, sand dunes and hatching sea turtles? A desert that is bigger than the entire state of Maine? Ninfa's Mexican restaurant in Houston, where the fajita was first introduced to America? San Antonio and its Alamo? The possibilities seemed endless. I had been to Texas many times, but only to the cities. During my visits, the locals had spoken of their "hill country" in reverential tones usually reserved for Matthew McConaughey or Tom Landry. As Texans have been known to exaggerate, we decided that we needed to see the area for ourselves.

The Texas hill country covers an area larger than South Carolina, which seemed pretty big to us until we learned that it represents less than ten percent of Texas' total area. It is roughly kidney-shaped, stretching diagonally from Austin in the east to the Rio Grande near Laughlin Air Force Base in the west. Texas hill country people have always been political rebels. In the Civil War, they were the only part of Texas that did not vote to leave the Union. Following Reconstruction, they voted Republican for over 100 years while the rest of the state was staunchly Democratic. It seems only fitting that the TV character Maverick was from Texas hill country.

We started our tour in Round Top, Texas, a tiny town of 90 people that claims to host the largest antique fair in America. For a week each spring the locals are overrun by thousands of rabid antique hunters.

The vendors and their exhibits stretch for several miles. The day that we visited, the two-lane road through town was so congested that law enforcement had to be done on horseback. The closest parking space that would fit Gypsy was two miles away from the exhibits, so we decided to simply watch the action as we inched our way through town.

We headed on to Austin, the state capital and one of my favorite cities. How could we not like a city whose motto is "Keep Austin Weird"? Austin is an oasis of liberal beliefs and eclectic tastes in otherwise conservative Texas, bonded with the rest of the state by its love of great BBQ. Austin encourages people to let out their inner artistic passion, and the results are never dull. We spent several days wandering around the city's funky old-time commercial areas and the parks that line its river, enjoying the city's off-the-wall vibe.and sampling Austin's dazzling array of food trucks. We started at South Austin Trailer Park & Eatery, located in an old trailer park. It had a covered pavilion with picnic tables and a large-screen TV so that we could watch the NCAA tournament basketball game while we ate Torchy's Tacos, a local favorite. From there, we headed to Biscuits and Groovy, which offered creative combinations of ingredients on homemade biscuits and gravy. My favorite was the Gloria, made with eggs, sausage, bacon, cheese, and jalapenos, accompanied by a Mexican Coke made with the original formula using cane sugar. Next up was barbeque, as some of Austin's best barbeque came from food trucks. Austin seemed to have an ongoing competition for who makes the best barbeque, and top-rated places like La

Barbeque or Franklin have a fame that rivals the state's best athletes. After trying the brisket, ribs, and smoked turkey, I decided that I had it backwards. Texas has so many great athletes because their BBQ attracts them from all over the country.

Despite our gorging, we somehow managed to leave room for the local desserts. It was worth the trip to Austin just to discover Tiny Pies and Amy's Ice Cream. Tiny Pies is a little bakery run by a mother and daughter that make hand pies using their family recipes. They got the idea when their sons wanted pies to take in their school sack lunches, proving that while necessity may be the mother of invention, hungry boys are not far behind. Their signature item is the Texas Two Step, a pecan pie with brownie chunks and chile chocolate, topped with a pastry cut in the shape of Texas. They had over fifty different pies available, but we had to limit ourselves to five so that we could stop at Amy's Ice Cream. We tried over a hundred places during our trip looking for the best ice cream in America, and Amy's Ice Cream in Austin was our top choice. Their Mexican Chocolate was the best chocolate ice cream that we had ever tasted and the Mexican Vanilla, a blend of Madagascar vanilla and Mexican orchid flavors, was close behind.

Heading west from Austin, we stopped in Driftwood, home of Salt Lick BBQ, often cited as the best BBQ in Texas. It was also a great family story that began in 1867 when a young Mississippi girl promised to marry a man even though "she wasn't sure that she would ever love him" if he agreed to take her to Texas. During the journey there by wagon train, she made meals using an old family BBQ technique of searing, then slow cooking meat over coals. A hundred years later, her great-grandson was still cooking meats for family gatherings using the same method. He decided to try selling to the public, so he built a huge barbeque pit that is still going strong over 50 years later. Their most popular dishes are brisket and sausage, but for us the real treat was the buffalo ribs. They were as tender and smoky as pork ribs, but with the unique sweet taste of buffalo.

We continued west on Highway 290, known locally as the Wine Road. Texas' hill country has a thriving wine industry, with over 50 wineries and the second-largest growing region (AVA) in the United States. We tried a couple of places, and they were quite good, but overall, we remained loyal to our Sonoma County wine heritage.

We headed into Fredericksburg, the hub of Texas hill country's world-famous wildflowers. We drove the Willow City Loop, a 13-mile private two-lane road. Its multi-colored carpets of bluebonnets, Indian paint brush and other wildflowers set among oak and mesquite trees with creeks, limestone escarpments and rugged hills in the background were breathtaking. Afterwards, we wandered around town, which reminded us of Healdsburg with its wineries, quaint B&Bs, pretty parks along the town's creeks and lots of great restaurants. Best of all, it had a family bakery called the Fredericksburg Pie Company.

We finished our tour through hill country by heading southeast to San Antonio. The oldest city in Texas, San Antonio is a beautiful blend of its old-time west roots with more modern areas like the Quarry Market, a shopping center built on the site of an old cement factory using the original façade and smokestacks that looks like a work of art. The centerpiece of San Antonio's scenic beauty is the Riverwalk, a walking path that follows the San Antonio River as it wanders through the heart of town. Set ten feet below street level with plants and flowers providing shade all along the water, it is lined with restaurants and shops, inviting casual relaxation with the feel of a pre-air conditioning era. We got a room at the Hyatt Hotel on the Riverwalk and spent the afternoon strolling around before settling down for the night. The next morning, we headed to Magnolia Pancake Haus, which turned out to be the best breakfast place that we found on our entire trip. Its waffles, eggs benedict and homemade corned beef hash were so good that we went back the following year. One of the Trip Advisor reviews said it all: "I'm glad this is not a buffet, or I'd die of gluttony in this place."

Great food, beautiful scenery and two centuries of quirky, interesting people. By the time we had completed our drive through Texas hill country, we understood why it holds such a special place in their hearts.

And a Color TV!

—Aimee—

Sure, we were camping while leading an exciting lifestyle filled with travel and adventures, but honestly, who doesn't want cable TV at the end of the day?

Both of the RVs that we had previously owned were capable of receiving antenna TV, but we had never actually tried it. Our trips were dedicated to spending time with our kids, and TV was a strict no-no. The one exception was the Finals of the 2001 NCAA Men's Basketball Tournament. We were driving north from our home in Southern California, and it was killing Ron that he was missing the title game. He stopped and bought a TV that was roughly the size of a toaster oven, then had me hold it on my lap so he could listen and take completely illegal peeks at the screen while zooming along at 65 miles an hour. I had to continually adjust the rabbit ears antenna to catch the signal and switch channels as we drove through different network affiliate broadcast areas. (For you Generation Z and Millennials, ask your parents what I'm talking about and prepare to be astounded by the answer.) At the time, we thought we were totally cool as we drove down the road watching a blurry, snow-filled broadcast.

Our new rig, Gypsy, came with a flat screen TV that swung out of the upper bunk on an arm so you could watch TV from the couch or the dining room table. She had an antenna on the roof that we could raise up using a crank handle in the ceiling to catch a few grainy channels of the local NBC, CBS, or ABC broadcast. Woe to the traveler who forgets to crank down their antenna before driving away. We saw campers running and screaming after an RV that was pulling away with its antenna at full mast, dragging tree branches and park banners, its occupants blissfully unaware that they were one low bridge away from disaster.

If we wanted more channels or better reception, Gypsy had internal wiring to hook up to campground's cable TV (if they offered it.) Some RV parks made watching TV even more challenging by providing a cable converter box that you had to connect to your TV system if you wanted to access their cable channels. Picture a giant nest of annoying wires and a box dangling from the overhead loft with two new remote controls to figure out. Since I was considered more tech-savvy than Ron, it was my job to reboot unfamiliar cable systems and scream things like, "Is the connection tight!?" out our window while he attempted to screw in some strange new cable connector. It often took me over an hour to get it all set up and working, only to unplug the whole thing when we left the next morning. We also discovered that Gypsy's internal cabling had been chewed by mice and was no longer working, so we bought a new cable and ran it from the TV down the inside wall and out the kitchen window. I know, it was a totally ghetto move, but you do what you have to do to pick up the E! channel.

One morning, during one of the few times that we were staying in one place for more than one night, I heard the buzz and chug of the RV park's lawn maintenance men mowing the grass around our site at a campground in Las Vegas. Suddenly, Good Morning America disappeared, and I was left with a blank TV screen displaying the two tragic words: "Signal Lost." I went outside to investigate, and sure enough, they had mowed right through our cable line. All that was left were two frayed ends laying in the grass. Was this the end of our cable TV? No way. With some help from Google, I learned how to splice cable TV wiring. Sounds nuts, right? Don't judge until you have been on the road long enough to yearn for the local news or even a Turner Classic Movie.

Now, if you're wondering why we didn't just watch TV on our computer, you have never tried to download a movie using the campground's Internet or your cell phone's hotspot. We once sat in a truck stop for two hours in South Dakota attempting to download a full episode of the TV series Sherlock with Benedict Cumberbatch. That episode probably cost us $50 in excess data charges.

Some fancy RVs have their own TV satellite dish. Before you think that must be the way to go, picture having to raise your satellite dish at every park and rotate it around while searching for a satellite link like you are some messed up NASA employee, all the while hoping that you aren't under a tree or in a gully. Plus, the whole thing costs serious coin. I'll admit to some envy here, but Ron wasn't going for it, so I just had to work with what I had.

Suffice it to say, when we wanted real TV, I learned to fight for it. Antennas, cables, converters, hot spots. I can get you Jeopardy in a snowstorm in the Rockies. Call me if you need some old-school tech help—I am a WIZARD!

Cross Country Routes
—Ron—

We drove nearly 100,000 miles on our trip, on every kind of road from freeways to jeep trails. Normally, we stayed on the smaller roads, where it was more fun to wander, but there were some occasions where we had to drive directly across the country. We came back to the West Coast each summer to visit family, and one year we drove from Oregon to Massachusetts for our daughter Kim's wedding. We went from one coast to the other six times and drove at least part of every cross-country route.

There are only four roads that completely cross the United States. US Highway 20 and US Highway 50 were part of the 1926 U.S. Highway Plan that provided a national numbering system to previously existing roads. These roads had been built to connect towns, so they tended to have more history and roadside attractions. Interstate 10 and Interstate 90 were part of the national freeway system that began construction in 1956. The interstate freeways were designed to allow the rapid movement of vehicles over long distances. They were direct and fast, making it easy to set the cruise control, turn on some tunes and watch the scenery as the miles went past. To us, each type of road had its own personality and appeal.

Interstate 10

The shortest route across the United States, Interstate 10 runs 2,500 miles across the southern part of the country from Santa Monica, California to Jacksonville, Florida. Its western half travels through three major deserts between California and Texas, while the eastern half provides a tour of bayou country and the Gulf Coast.

We always looked forward to driving the desert, seeing how the plants and animals found creative ways to live in the harsh environment. Most of all, we loved finding wildflowers in bloom. They came in all shapes and sizes, from single flowers nesting among the cactus spines to strings of flowers on woody tendrils stretching across the desert floor, their blossoms a rainbow of colors set against the reddish-brown soil. Finding wildflowers was a challenge, as they were only open for a brief time, and it varied from place to place and year to year. It was like being on a safari, stalking the elusive blossoms in a location that required effort and had some amount of personal danger to get the perfect shot. I would be driving along on I-10, pleased with the "easy miles" that I was making, when Aimee would spot a splash of color in the distance. The next thing I knew, we were off the freeway and on a steep, winding, narrow desert road. I would pull off onto the non-existent shoulder and Aimee would clamber through the arid landscape, avoiding the snakes and scorpions to take a close-up photo. I don't know if the flowers were endangered, but she certainly was. Somehow, she survived and got some beautiful pictures.

Aimee favorite cactus is the saguaro, the largest cactus in America. Featured in nearly every cowboy movie, the saguaro cactus can grow 80 feet high, with over 50 arms reaching to the sky. The saguaro's flowers can grow on all of its arms, but each flower is open for less than 24 hours, so every day the cactus has a different set of flowers in bloom. The saguaro is also covered with 3-inch spines, so Aimee had to be careful to get a photo without getting hurt. In 1982, a man was killed by a saguaro when he fired his shotgun into it and one of its limbs fell on him. Fortunately, the cactus survived the attack, and the man received a Darwin Award for improving the human race by removing himself from the gene pool.

Our most unusual stop on I-10's deserts was the White Sands National Park and the White Sands Missile Range outside Las Cruces,

New Mexico. The Missile Range is the largest military installation in the US and the site of the first atomic bomb test in 1945. They were testing a missile that day, so we got to watch it. They closed off the highway, then a few minutes later a siren sounded and the missile took off. Its vapor trail looked pretty erratic as it sped across the sky, and we later found out that two missiles have crashed during testing. Happy that this one missed us, we headed on to the National Park, home of the world's largest surface gypsum deposit. The gypsum crystals were formed in an ancient seabed, then trapped in a basin and piled up into 50-foot-high dunes by the wind. Weathering has made the gypsum crystals as soft as flour and perfect for sledding. We bought a plastic disc, put on our shades, and went sliding down the dunes like we were kids.

In Louisiana, I-10's enters the bayous of the Gulf Coast, one of the most interesting settings that we encountered on our trip. Unlike a swamp or marsh, a bayou has a gentle tidal current that makes its water clear and slightly brackish. Everything there seems to thrive on silence. Spanish moss muffles everything as it hangs from the tree branches. Alligators and turtles blend into the background as they sun themselves or drift in the water. Riding through the shadows in a canoe, we swore that we could hear things growing. As for the Gulf itself, the water was so warm and calm that it seemed like a giant bathtub. We could have spent months there just watching the wildlife, with rays, whales, dolphins, over fifty species of sharks and five of the world's seven species of sea turtles.

Interstate 90

Interstate 90 is America's longest and northernmost interstate freeway, over 3,000 miles from Boston to Seattle. Its eastern half connects America's major industrial centers of Syracuse, Rochester, Buffalo, Cleveland, and Chicago, while the western portion showcases the scenic beauty of Montana, Idaho and Washington.

Some of our favorite stops were on I-90. At the Basketball Hall of Fame in Springfield, Massachusetts, we soaked up the history of the game as it developed from peach baskets to Golden State's Splash Brothers. In Cleveland, Ohio we spent several hours at the Rock & Roll Hall of Fame, wandering through the music exhibits and listening to everything from Pink Floyd's "The Wall" to Sam Cooke's "A Change Is Gonna Come." Even the long stretch across the northern Great Plains had some memorable places. At Badlands National Park in South Dakota, erosion from water and wind has transformed an ancient seabed into fantastically shaped formations that became a paradise for the local wildlife. In one hour, we saw sage grouse, prairie chickens, burrowing owls, bighorn sheep and prairie dogs. We took turns using the binoculars until our eyes wore out. Thirty miles away, the drug store in tiny Wall (pop. 814) is an international destination that attracts over 2 million visitors each year. After they purchased it during the Depression, the owners put up road signs offering free ice water to entice travelers to stop. The signs were very popular and expanded to include slogans, trivia and jingles. There are over 3,000 signs all over the world, many of them created independently by the store's fans.

Highway 20

Highway 20 passes directly through the town where we had bought a house in Oregon, so we drove it several times during our time on the road. America's longest cross-country road, Highway 20 stretches 3,365 miles from Newport, Oregon to Boston, Massachusetts, and it is filled with outdoor scenic beauty. Heading east from Newport, we went through the verdant Cascade mountains, covered by forests, and cut by rushing rivers and waterfalls. Fifty miles later, we entered the high desert of eastern Oregon and Idaho, where patches of green only exist where water is available from the Snake River. In the middle of Idaho, we stopped at the Craters of the Moon National Monument, the largest post-Ice Age lava field in the U.S. We spent an afternoon exploring exhibits and walking the trails that pass through its 600 square miles of over 60 different types of lava. The Apollo astronauts trained there, learning how to operate in a harsh, unfamiliar environment. We then followed Highway 20 as it headed north along the spine of eastern Idaho and turned east into Yellowstone National Park. We had never been to America's first National Park, and we were amazed. Sitting atop an enormous volcanic chamber, Yellowstone is home to half of the world's geysers, including Old Faithful and Steamboat Geyser, the world's largest active geyser. Yellowstone's wildlife was even more impressive, with over 30,000 elk and 3,000 bison along with large numbers of bears, mountain lions, wolves, mountain goats, deer and even wolverines. We visited Yellowstone three times during our trip and still felt like we had barely scratched the surface of its natural wonders.

Highway 50

No road trip would be complete without experiencing Highway 50, which stretches 3,017 miles from Sacramento, California to Ocean City, Maryland. Passing through 12 states and the District of Columbia, it is a showcase of extremes. The 500-mile stretch of Nevada's Great Basin is deservedly called "The Loneliest Road in America." It made us feel fortunate to be in Gypsy rather than settlers crossing it in wagons at 10 miles a day. Driving Highway 50 over the Rocky Mountains was like taking giant roller coaster with its tight bends, steep climbs, and hair-raising drops. At one point the road is so curvy that the locals claim that "you can see yourself coming." Once we got through the mountains, we stopped to explore Pueblo, Colorado's Old West Historic District and discovered Bingo Burger, whose custom burgers were the best that we found anywhere in America. From Pueblo, we drove through the enormous stockyards of western Kansas, with billions of flies trying hitch a ride on Gypsy. Further east, we drove Highway 50 through downtown Washington, D.C., where it passes directly in front of the White House. Covered with stickers from our various stops, Gypsy got a lot of attention, including some suspicious looks from the Secret Service. The remaining part of Highway 50 was one of the prettiest drives of our trip, passing through Annapolis, crossing over the Chesapeake Bay to the Delmarva Peninsula, then winding through miles of windswept marshes and picturesque little towns until it reached the Atlantic Ocean.

Highway 2

Unlike the previous four, Highway 2 doesn't go continuously from coast to coast, but it was our favorite cross-country route. Highway 2 runs near the Canada border and is divided into two sections, with a 700-mile gap at the Great Lakes. The western part stretches 2,115 miles from Everett, Washington north of Seattle to Saint Ignace on the shores of Lake Huron. It begins again in Rouses Point, New York and runs 460 miles to Houlton, Maine. Both sections are breathtakingly beautiful.

Driving east from Everett, Highway 2 is a National Scenic Byway as it passes over the rugged, rain-laden Cascade Mountains. Driving through the National Forests and Wilderness Areas, we had the sense that we might see Bigfoot around any corner. Halfway across Washington, we came out of the mountains onto a flat, semi-arid plain and crossed the Columbia River at the Grand Coulee Dam, one of the most fascinating stops on our entire trip. The Grand Coulee was an ancient riverbed formed by floods during the Ice Age from Lake Missoula, which had twenty times the volume of Lake Tahoe. When its ice dam broke, the lake emptied at 65 mph, releasing more water per hour than the combined volume of all the rivers in the world. Once the water level had dropped, the ice dam built back up. This cycle occurred at least 40 times, all during periods of human habitation. I wondered how the people living there felt, knowing that roughly every 50 years they were going to experience a flood of Biblical proportions.

The human effort required to build the Grand Coulee Dam during the Depression in the middle of a desert was equally impressive and a tribute to American grit and ingenuity. In a location that had harsh conditions and little infrastructure, seven thousand people built the largest power plant in the country and the largest concrete structure in the world. Their effort transformed the surrounding desert into fertile farmland and was critical to winning WWII by providing electricity to Seattle's aluminum mills and aircraft plants. My favorite exhibit was the workers' diaries where they talked about their living conditions, including one entry that described how when it rained, "the main street was full of floating rattlesnakes."

Crossing into Idaho, we followed Highway 2 along the Priest River to Lake Pend Oreille. During WWII it was used as a naval training ground and is still used for testing submarine prototypes, although we wondered why they put a submarine base 500 miles inland from the ocean with no navigable river. Secrecy, maybe? We walked around Sandpoint, whose quaint streets and year-round recreational activities earned it the title of Most Beautiful Small Town in America from Rand McNally and USA Today. From there, we drove Highway 2 north on the Selkirk Loop, which has been designated an All-American Road for its scenic beauty.

In Montana, our favorite stop on Highway 2 was Glacier National Park. Glacier gets half the visitors per year that Yellowstone does, so most of its 1 million acres of mountains, alpine meadows and lakes are still in their natural state. We stayed in Lake McDonald Lodge, a National Historic Landmark that looked like a huge Swiss Chalet with a three-story lobby all made of wood. The next morning, we drove around the park and swam in a couple of the lakes, enjoying their quiet scenic beauty.

East of Glacier, Highway 2 left the mountains and entered an ocean of grassland in the Great Plains. At one point, we watched ten giant combine harvesters mowing a field, clearing over an acre a minute. When I joked that it was a classic "combined" effort, Aimee hit me. Crossing into North Dakota, we dodged the trucks that were careening wildly through the Bakken oil fields and breathed a sigh of relief when we reached Lake Sakakawea and Lake Oahe. Formed by dams to manage flooding on the Missouri River, they are the two largest reservoirs in the U.S. with a combined length of over 400 miles. We stayed in lakeside state parks, swimming, hiking, and watching the local wildlife, then continued on Highway 2 into Minnesota's "Land of 10,000 Lakes." Formed by glaciers that flattened the area and left small depressions that filled with water, it looked like a giant green canvas with blue spots scattered everywhere. I thoroughly enjoyed swimming in the calm water of the small lakes until Aimee informed me that they also have leeches.

After detouring around the Great Lakes, we picked up Highway 2's eastern leg on the shores of Lake Champlain and took it through the Appalachian Mountains in Vermont, New Hampshire and Maine. Driving the quiet country roads through rugged beauty of the mountains, brilliantly colored by the autumn leaves was a truly spiritual experience. Even the small towns, which often had to be built around a river or granite outcropping, reflected the enduring power of the natural environment. We completed our tour of Highway 2 in Bangor, Maine, where we stopped to see the home of Stephen King, Aimee's favorite author, before we headed to the coast at Acadia National Park.

If you are planning to drive around America, our advice is to favor back roads, but don't avoid the cross-country routes. Tour the Grand Coulee Dam. Visit the Rock & Roll Hall of Fame and the Basketball Hall of Fame. Ride an airboat through the bayous. We'll meet you in Pueblo, Colorado for burgers at Bingo's.

O Canada

—*Aimee*—

One of our goals was to drive the Trans-Canada Highway from Maine to Vancouver. What held us back was the fear of losing our Sonoma County wines. We had stored four cases of wine in the loft above our cab and routinely had more drop-shipped to places along our route for resupply. To our dismay, we learned that while Canada might welcome visitors into their country, they only allowed one bottle of wine per person. We were not about to turn over fifty bottles of fine wine for the privilege of driving into Canada, so we waited and debated about how much wine we were willing to donate to the border police.

Eventually, our chance arose. Our daughter Kimberly announced that she was getting married in Massachusetts. Perfect! We would contribute our wine for the wedding reception, get the girl married off and head up into the Great White North.

Like any American, my general knowledge of Canada was fuzzy. I pictured it as a small, mostly empty country, located above the much more impactful USA. All Canadians probably played hockey and listened to Rush at parties, drinking beer in their woolen hats while it snowed. Mounties on horseback would ride by and tip their red hats to the crowd as they patrolled the wilderness for moose and bear.

The morning we left Caribou, Maine, I was excited to cross into Canada. I had boned up on Canadian terms the night before, pestering Ron with my comments.

"Guess what a Canadian one-dollar coin is called?" I hollered toward the back of Gypsy as he lay reading something on his iPhone.

"What?" he replied laconically.

"A Loony! And the two-dollar coin is a Toony!" I exclaimed.

"Great," he said, although he didn't sound too enthusiastic.

"And the big food there is called 'poutine.' It's gravy over fries."

"Okay," He replied faintly.

Undaunted, I raised my voice. "And anyone who is trying too hard is called a 'Keener.' Isn't that wild?"

"Mmm." His replies were getting shorter.

"Don't worry, I'll handle the French. My French teacher in high school was Canadian, so I've got this."

Turns out, I didn't have "this."

I was certain that we would receive a warm welcome at the border crossing. Canadians love Americans, right? Maybe not. First, an unsmiling border guard waved us into the inspection area and proceeded to search every inch of Gypsy while Ron and I leaned on the hood like a pair of perps at a drug bust. The guard even wanted to search my purse. Sacrilege! A woman's purse is like the Pentagon. You need several layers of clearance to go in there. Even Ron only has limited visitor privileges. Now here's this total stranger rooting around in my private stash of lip gloss, old nail files, eyeglass cases and loose tic-tacs. Infuriating.

Finally, we were cleared and given our passports back. I consoled myself that this was Quebec, mostly French and had therefore probably inherited France's disdain for uncouth Americans.

The next day, we took a bus into Quebec City and walked around, enjoying the architecture and the cafes. We took a tour of the Cathedral-Basilica of Notre Dame de Quebec, which was over four hundred years old and the oldest church in Canada. In the States, anything over a hundred years old is ancient. They were very nice, especially after Ron sang a hymn in Latin for them in the cathedral.

I took Ron to J.A. Moisan, the oldest continually operating grocery store in North America, where I bought baguettes, charcuterie (meats) and French cheeses. I also bought their shopping bag, envisioning the comments this might provoke at future farmers markets. "Where did you get that lovely bag?" people would ask. "Oh, I got it at a French grocer in Quebec" I'd respond casually, sounding like a worldly foodie, the kind that visits cheese caves and bakes croissants on Sunday morning.

I loaded up our goodies into my new shopping bag until it weighed as much as a husky toddler and then handed it over to Ron. He carried my loot as we walked along the cobbled streets for about two miles uphill back to the bus, getting lost in the pouring rain and arguing over which street to take while getting soaked underneath the one umbrella that we had between us. In the make-up phase of our bickering, I promised Ron that dinner would be a fabulous French affair and that he would be delighted that he had hefted that bag back to the campground. Sadly, I had not factored in the effect of the rain on my beautiful French baguettes. As I pulled them from the shopping bag, they slumped over, forming a sorrowful u-shape that looked for all the world like an ad for erectile dysfunction. Ron laughed so hard at my stricken expression that I started laughing as well and damn near peed myself. Dinner that night was cheese and salami served with copious amounts of French wine. Oh, well.

As we drove west through the province of Quebec, I felt like we were wandering through the French countryside. We stopped at a little farmers market to buy strawberries, fresh herbs, local honey, and fresh bison meat, all of which I carried back to Gypsy in my new bag. At night I practiced my French cooking and Ron loved it. "I never knew that Canada had such great food!" he exclaimed. What I didn't know as we drove out of Quebec was that we were leaving most of what I consider good food behind. The French influence quickly disappeared. Fresh food got scarce, and we started to see a lot of Tim Hortons restaurants.

If you've never been to Canada, you may not have heard of Tim Hortons. It's kind of a cross between Starbucks and McDonalds. They serve lots and lots of hot coffee and donuts at reasonably low prices, which is handy since Canadians eat more donuts per person than any other country on Earth. We tried a couple of Tim Hortons and didn't really understand the appeal, but it's a Canadian institution. It's like the Waffle House chain in the southeast part of the U.S. You may not eat at a Waffle House much, but you can be sure that there is a Waffle House open at three o'clock in the morning somewhere within twenty miles of you. It's comforting and very American. Tim Hortons is the same way to Canadians.

So, onward we drove across the province of Ontario. Strangely, camping was not a problem. There were campgrounds around every little lake and signs all along the highway for upcoming camping spots, each one claiming to be the perfect place for family fun. The campgrounds offered a variety of recreational activities to attract people, from playground equipment to water toys. At one place, Ron found a pontoon raft powered by a bicycle on top. Dubbing it a "Canadian Jet Ski" he proceeded to pedal this monstrosity all over the lake, scattering geese in all directions.

If you decide to go camping in Canada, bring your bug spray. I thought that I had experience with big, biting mosquitos in the Midwest, but I was not prepared for the clouds of bloodthirsty prehistoric mosquitos awaiting us at every campground. When you look out your window and dozens of mosquitos are sitting on the window glass, it makes you think twice before opening the door. What amazed me was the general disregard that the locals had for mosquitos or "Mozzies" as they are affectionately known. One night, I was walking past a campsite and a husband and wife called out, "Nice night, eh?"

I responded, "Sure is, but what about the mosquitos? They're biting pretty bad."

"Aw, just a little nip or two. Just watch out for the blackflies," the wife replied with a smile as I walked past.

Blackflies? I thought, whipping my head around, looking for trouble. What in the hell are blackflies? Then, on my way back to our rig, I felt a huge, stinging chomp on my inner thigh. Diving into Gypsy, I saw a red, raised welt where I had been bitten. This must have been the aforementioned blackfly. From then on, I did not leave the confines of Gypsy near the lakes of Canada without applying a deadly, glistening layer of DEET to every exposed surface of my body and my clothes. If you've never applied this level of DEET before, I warn you that you can taste it in the air around you.

We continued west, driving beyond Quebec and Ontario. Now I say, "driving beyond Quebec and Ontario" like it took a few hours, but it actually took nine days. Crossing through Quebec and Ontario is over halfway across the entire country. But eventually we were past the lakes and forests and Canada's Great Plains rolled out before us, larger and vaster than the U. S. Great Plains. We drove for hours, our only company the enormous round rolls of hay in the fields.

I think that it's time for a geography lesson. Canada is bigger than the US. Yes, it is. Look it up. Canada has ten provinces and three territories. So, class, if the US has fifty states and Canada has thirteen provinces/territories, then how many US states fit into a typical Canadian province or territory? Nearly four states! They are huge! However, Canada's total population is about 35 million people. Picture if you took the population of California and spread them over all of the U.S., including Alaska, and you get a sense for why you can drive for five hours in Canada and see one town. By the way, that one town will have the following food choices: a Tim Hortons, an Indian restaurant and a food truck that is selling Poutine.

Ah, poutine. Poutine is a uniquely Canadian food. In its simplest form, it is French fries smothered in brown gravy, but there are many twists on poutine. You can get it with barbecue and gravy, cheese curds and gravy or peppers and gravy. If you're sensing a theme here, you're right. Poutine is basically anything "and gravy." We tried about ten different types of poutine at various locations throughout Canada and I never really found one that spoke to me. Good news though, every poutine truck also sells regular fries. Who doesn't like hot fries with salt and ketchup? Oh wait, it's Canada! You have to ask for ketchup or you will get malt vinegar, mustard and mayonnaise as your condiments. Apparently, the practice of slathering ketchup on everything is also uniquely American.

We drove through the endless prairies of Manitoba and Saskatchewan, stopping in RV parks run by couples catering to people who were headed for one coast or the other. No one picks Manitoba or Saskatchewan as their vacation destination unless they have a thing for looking at fields of tall waving grass that stretch to the horizon.

I had heard that there was a Heritage Center for the Royal Canadian Mounted Police or "Mounties" near Regina, Saskatchewan. I pictured it filled with stories of Mounties patrolling the vast wilderness, protecting settlers from wild animals and hostile Indians. The reality was somewhat more educating and altogether disturbing. According to the Center, the Mounties were formed to keep Americans from crossing into Canada with their illegal liquor and molesting Canadians and the indigenous Indian population. More than a few exhibits showed American hooligans drinking and bothering women in border towns. The Mounties were always depicted as the heroes of these tales, saving the virtue of the women, and booting the uncivilized Americans back to their side of the border. True or not, the Heritage Center painted citizens of the United States in a hugely unfavorable light. For me, it was quite a wake-up call. Even a country as friendly as Canada has stories that don't jibe with our cultural self-image as the good guys. I left feeling somewhat ashamed about how Canada viewed Americans. As Americans, we were taught to feel superior to Canada. Well guess what? It was clear that Canadians felt superior to us.

Our windshield covered with bugs, we drove westward, passing through Regina and other little towns like Moosejaw (Yes, it's a real place). Our company on the highway was mostly made up of truckers bringing their goods across Canada. We were headed for Banff. If you see a postcard of the Canadian Rockies, it will almost certainly show

Banff, with picturesque Lake Louise set like a blue gem under snow-capped peaks. If you are wondering how to pronounce Banff…well, just say it like a comic-book noise "Banff!" and you'll get the sense of how it rolls off the tongue. We camped in Banff National Park up at about 5,000 feet (in Canadian, about 1,525 meters.) It felt a lot like Aspen, Colorado in the summer, very beautiful and very, very busy. Banff is on the edge of British Columbia and fairly accessible to folks from the West Coast and Vancouver. Alone no longer, we jockeyed for position in parking lots and alpine towns with every kind of international tourist. Bye-Bye Canadian drawl and hello Mandarin, German and French. When we hiked along Lake Louise, the scenery included a stream of tourists. If a bear wandered across the highway, a thousand vehicles stopped to gawk. The food in town was very good but astoundingly expensive. We tried a local fondue restaurant that specialized in game meat and it was more than $100 US for a single entree.

We had noticed a haze of smoke over the valleys during the day and learned that summer forest fires had been ravaging the Northwest US states and British Columbia, so we decided to cut short our cross-Canada trip. Besides, after nearly a month in Canada I felt the pull of home. I needed a Starbucks and McDonalds fix and the US border was just four hours south of us.

Approaching the border, I was anxious. Our last crossing into the US had been super-stressful. I kept harping at Ron.

"Have our passports ready and look relaxed," I said tensely. "Don't make any jokes. Let's keep the radio off."

Ron just eyeballed me. He knows to clam up when I panic-babble.

"Don't tell them that we were planning to go from Maine to Vancouver. You remember how weird the Canadians were about us wanting to drive all the way across Canada," I continued.

"Where's our registration, in case they ask?" I said, frantically digging through our console storage compartment.

"I have it. Take it easy," he said, smiling at me.

"Do you think this is funny?" I asked. "Remember when they wanted proof that our youngest daughter was actually our kid?" I was getting really wound up.

"That was going INTO Canada," he said. "And it's just the two of us this time."

"Oh, yeah?" I said. "Remember that time coming back into the US at 2am when we got searched and they confiscated our firewood and the dog food?" I was really getting some steam in the kettle now. "Oh, crap! We still have firewood! Tell them we forgot about our firewood!" I was such a cool international traveler.

We came over a ridge and saw a sign that read "US Border One Mile." There was a kiosk with a gate and cameras. We were the only vehicle on the road. We rolled up and I tried to look as cool as I had told Ron to be. Ron rolled down his window and said, "Hey, it's sure great to be back in the States."

The border guard said, "Coming out of Banff?"

"Yes, we are, officer!" I said…perhaps a bit too loudly. Ron looked at me sideways. I always feel like a drug mule when we're questioned by Customs officials. Clearly, I should stop watching "Locked Up Abroad."

The guard waved us through the border with a smile saying, "Welcome back to the US, and have a nice day!"

Without…even…checking…our passports!

"See, I told you it would be okay," I said to Ron as we drove into Montana. Ron wisely said nothing.

Signs, Signs, Everywhere the Signs

—Aimee—

When you drive three or four hours each day, you start to make a game of darn near anything. One of our favorite things to watch for while we were rolling along were the many strange and unusual signs. On previous road trips with the kids, we had gotten used to wacky signs like "Tsunami Warning Area" which depicts a tiny human running in terror from a giant tidal wave.

Our trip, being more far-flung, gave us ample opportunity to find unusual signs. Here are a few of my favorites:

This sign had no caption, but I really appreciated the detail, including the twisted bicycle and the rider's head that is actually coming off. I think it's a warning about loose debris, but it could be about steep grades or even falling rocks.

This sign demonstrates how confusing the English language can be. Are the hitchhikers in question actually prisoner inmates? Or are the hitchhikers escaping the inmates and so we should pick them up to save them? I pictured Swedish college kids on summer break, with long blond braids and carrying rucksacks but now running for their lives from some knife-wielding prisoners.

This shop in Michigan took straight-forward marketing to a whole new level. It's a name, a slogan and an advertisement all rolled up into one. I wish Victoria's Secret knew that this is EXACTLY what women want: Bras that Fit!

Just when you think fishing isn't a big deal in America anymore, you run across a large sign on a road in Michigan's Upper Peninsula. This part of America is practically its own country, and I shouldn't have been surprised by their enthusiasm for identifying which species of trout they had caught. After all, these are people who fish in tiny little houses on frozen lakes all winter.

Ron loved this sign in Montana. It's a warning and a challenge all rolled up into one. It's signs like this that remind me that most of America still has a sense of humor. I appreciate the little touches, like the tennis shoes on the bull and the faint path through the field to the finish line. Someone really took their time creating this warning to the unwise. I wonder if anyone has ever tried to beat the bull?

Two years on the road and this is my absolute favorite sign. It was near a research facility on Cedar Key in Florida. I can imagine fishermen dropping off unusual sharks here, I get that. But who is picking up sharks? I envision sharks in trench coats and fedoras trying to be inconspicuous while waiting to catch a bus and get out of town.

And lastly, this line carved on a seaside bench in Louisiana, said it all for us.

Companionship on the Road

—Ron—

When we told people that we were planning to live on the road, almost everyone warned us that we would be lonely with just the two of us. Family members even made bets on how long Aimee would be able to stand not being with anyone that she knew other than me. Fortunately, we got a lot of support from our family and friends who made a special effort to spend time with us while we were on the road. We also found that meeting new people was easier than we thought and led to some great experiences.

We stopped for lunch at a little diner outside of Cody, Wyoming and met Ed, who grew up in Chicago near where I had gone to graduate school. We sat and talked about Chicago, Wyoming and almost everything else. Ed told us that climate change was due to the reduction in logging in California. His theory was that letting the trees grow had led to greater wind resistance, which had shifted the jet stream to the north. Why not?

In Annapolis, Maryland we stopped in a little French-style café. We had been living on the road for eight months and were a little weary of our new lifestyle. The lady who owned the café decided that we needed some mothering along with our soup and fresh-baked bread. She made us feel like we were back home, eating comfort food on a cold winter day.

In Amarillo, Texas we stopped at a BBQ restaurant for dinner on our way out of town. The owner, Tyler Frazer, sat down at our table and asked about our trip. It turned out that he was quite the road warrior himself. He grew up in Amarillo, worked at a BBQ stand during college, then spent four years catering events all around the country before coming back home to start his own place. After an hour of sharing stories, we gave him some Sonoma County wine as a thank you for his warm hospitality. In classic Texas fashion, he gave us several days' worth of food for the road.

In western Florida, the campground where we were spending the night held a Super Bowl party. Forty people met in a low-ceilinged room that looked like an old dining building at summer camp. Soon the tables were filled with an array of foods. We sat around eating and sharing stories about why the dish that we brought was our favorite while we watched the game on a 19-inch vintage 1980's TV. We couldn't really see much of the action, but we laughed at the commercials and felt like a big noisy family.

On a Saturday night in northern Idaho, a group of kids ran around the campground inviting everyone to join in their potluck dinner. I went over and discovered that it was a local church group on a retreat. We ate and sang hymns well into the night. The next morning as we were getting ready to leave, the whole group came to our campsite and invited us to sing with their church choir for Sunday services.

When it came to meeting people, Gypsy was our best icebreaker. We collected stickers from the places that we visited and soon had a gallery of bumper art on the back of our rig. Aimee bought a map of America, with stickers for each state. She added a sticker each time we entered a new state, making a visual display of where we been so far. People would stop and ask us about our experiences and give us suggestions on the places that we should see while we were on the road.

Driving around America was a golden opportunity to reconnect with friends that we had not seen for a long time. It shouldn't take a two-year road trip to visit friends, but our freedom from having a schedule somehow made it easier.

Our most frequent companion on the road was Charley Brown. I had met Charley in 1982 when we played basketball together. He is

6'8" tall, so my job was mostly to pass him the ball. Charley and I were friends throughout our business careers and worked together on several occasions. We also raised our families together, renting a lake cabin and a boat each summer with our kids for a week of playing games, water skiing and unbridled eating. When Aimee and I got married, Charley was the best man at our wedding. During our trip, Charley invited me to do a project for his company. I did most of the work by phone while we were driving and every month or so we stopped and took a plane to meet with his team. It was a great way to balance our carefree lifestyle with some structured business activity and to spend time with Charley.

Walt and Suzan Strader hosted us twice at their home in North Carolina. I had met Walt in 1982 when I was consulting for the company where Walt worked. Fifteen years later, when I was appointed President of a troubled business, I tracked him down by finding someone who had compiled a listing of every person named Strader living in the America. They read me the phone number of every Walter Strader, and I started calling until I found him. Two weeks later, he joined me, and we spent two years together getting the company back on its feet. It just goes to show that time and distance cannot keep kindred spirits apart. When Aimee and I arrived at his house in North Carolina, I had not seen Walt in over ten years, but our friendship quickly fell back into place. He started hollering directions about how to back Gypsy into his driveway and I found myself listening or ignoring him depending on how I felt, remembering the passion for perfection that had drawn us together when we first met 33 years earlier. Over the next few days, we enjoyed that passion again as we shared great food, wine, conversation, and companionship.

We stayed with our friends Spencer and Sonia Clark on their farm outside Lebanon, Kentucky. I met Spencer in 1991 when we both worked at General Electric. We became friends and he joined me when I joined Black & Decker. He met Sonia, who was also working with me there, and they fell in love and got married. We remained close friends even though we moved to different parts of the country, so getting to see them was a real treat. During our visit, Spencer took me to the Varmints Dinner, a weekly stag poker game and "eat what we shot or caught" meal that has been going on continuously for over 60 years. After two hours of drinking and playing strange poker games, my wallet was twenty dollars lighter, and I was unofficially part of the local men's club. Spencer and Sonia also took us on a tour of Maker's Mark, where Sonia taught me how to put the red wax seal on a bottle of Spencer's favorite brand of bourbon. She seemed quite adept at it, and I didn't ask how she had developed her expertise.

Deb Keller was another friend who had worked with me at General Electric. It had been 20 years, but soon we were as comfortable as we had been years ago as she took us around Maryland's Eastern Shore where she lived. The highlight of our tour was the Delmarva DockDogs, where dogs compete in various water events. Our favorite was the aquatic canine long jump, where the handler would get their dog as excited as possible, then throw a toy out over a pool of water. The dog would run and leap into the air, trying to catch the toy before it hit the water. Some of the dogs could leap over 30 feet. It looked like a perfect game to play with my grandkids. First, work them into a complete frenzy, then have them sprint after something and land in a pool of water. Then give them back to their parents.

Being on the road also let us visit our kids, who lived in various parts of the country. We stopped in Denver twice to see our son Michael and got the VIP tour of the Denver Museum of Nature and Science from his fiancée Jean, who worked there. Michael also helped me on my work projects, so we got together every month in different parts of the country when we met with the client team.

We went to Long Island twice to visit our daughter Wende and her husband Kyle. We toured the farms on the eastern end of the island and got hooked on apple cider donuts. We sampled the traditional Italian delis in Queens and Brooklyn. Wende took me to get a shave at an old-school barbershop, where a seventy-year-old man with shaky hands held a straightedge razor to my throat. During our trip, Wende had our first grandchild, a little girl who soon had us wrapped around her little finger.

Our youngest daughter Dakota and her fiancé Josh took care of our house and the dogs, so we went back to visit them each summer. They also joined us at a cabin on Flathead Lake in Montana for several days of swimming, fishing and just hanging out together.

Visiting our daughter Kim fit our mobile lifestyle, as she moved three times during the two years that we were on the road. Our first summer, we met her in Wisconsin where she was working at a wildlife rehabilitation center. In October, we visited her and her fiancé Mark after they had moved to Maine. When they moved to Massachusetts and Kim got a job with the Boston Museum of Science, she gave us the insider's tour when we came to visit. The next summer, we went back for their wedding, which let our entire family spend time together.

My sister Robin and my brother Russell made special efforts to join us during our trip. Robin met us in New Orleans to celebrate her 60th birthday. We took a carriage ride around the French Quarter, visited a historic plantation and ate dinner at a bar where Aimee and Robin bought a drink for the resident ghost. We talked nonstop the entire time and I felt like I got to know her better than I had in years.

Along with our annual trip to the World Series of Poker, Russell also flew out twice to join me for my birthday bike rides. Each time, he came with several interesting topics to discuss while we were riding: "If you could only watch 5 movies for the rest of your life, what would they be? If you could eat whatever you wanted for 24 hours, where would you go and what would you get?" He also brought a list of interesting local restaurants so that we could replace the calories that we had burned during the ride.

Thanks to our family and friends, we were rarely lonely during our more than two years of driving around America. Rather, the trip let us rekindle old friendships and make new ones along the way.

Idiot Light
—Aimee—

Gypsy's "Service Engine Soon" light came on as we were driving somewhere along the Pacific coast. I asked Ron to pull over and in a cloud of stress, we popped the hood. Looking at the engine, nothing was obviously wrong. No billowing smoke, no strange smells, no leaks, drips, or other ominous signs. We walked the length of Gypsy, checking everything and nothing seemed amiss.

Ron shrugged. "I don't see anything wrong. It might just be a light on a timer for an oil change." Our prior RV had a nasty habit of turning on the "Service Engine Soon" light every so often to demand an oil change. Some genius on the RV design team had the bright idea to engineer it so that the most terrifying warning light in the vehicle snapped on when it was time for garden variety maintenance. I can only hope that the designer is now residing in a circle of hell filled with useless warning lights while he writes intensely private emails that accidently route to "All Recipients" every time he hits the Send button.

Anyway, I was willing to acknowledge that the light, which had remained on but not blinking, might be something small. Those of you who are experienced in automotive repair know that a steady light can mean one of a thousand errors have happened, some serious, some not. On the other hand, a blinking "Service Engine Soon" light is a cry for help from your RV's dying engine. It means "Pull over immediately and pray that your repair bill will be less than five thousand dollars." Since our light was a steady yellow and the engine was purring along, I agreed that we could wait for the next automotive supply store and use their diagnostic tool to see what the error indicated.

We stopped in Grants Pass, Oregon to have the light checked out and the service person said the code was "something electrical, a fuse maybe?" It was not exactly reassuring that his statement ended in a question mark.

After much debate and crawling around the engine compartment, Ron and I decided to replace most of our fuses, including the fuses in a second and apparently super-secret fuse box hidden at the side of the engine block. Several hundred curse words later, we fired up Gypsy and the light…wait for it…was still on.

You're probably starting to wonder why we didn't just find a repair shop. That sounds totally reasonable, except that RV repair shops are a different creature. Rare as hen's teeth. Slow as molasses and never, ever open on weekends. Unless you are planning to take a week to get your repair, it's best to be your own mechanic on the small stuff. In Aurora, Colorado, we once spent two hours in a parking lot with a rivet gun, re-installing our side entry door to the sound of "Snap-Bang!" as each rivet was replaced. The door had been rattling and whistling loudly as we rolled down the highway. Upon inspection, we discovered that only three of the fifteen rivets holding the door onto the coach were still in place. Whoops! Auto-Zone repair plan enacted.

So, back to our story. The Idiot Light stayed lit for the most part. Sometimes it would go off for a week and then come back on for a month. I am sorry to say that I got used to it being on. There's a lesson in human psychology here. As nothing went wrong, I got more comfortable that nothing WOULD go wrong.

That's not to say that I stopped thinking about it. I spent hours on the Internet researching the operation and repair of the Ford V10 engine. Then I would share my ideas with Ron as we drove along. "Do you think it's the fuel rail assembly or the fuel tank float? A cylinder misfire perhaps? The fuel pump? The injectors? Here's what I'm thinking." I'd be reviewing fuel injection systems and error codes while intermittently eyeballing the little yellow light that had become my obsession. I was sure that when whatever Gypsy was trying to warn us about really happened, we would be on Highway 50 in Nevada and our desiccated bodies would be found months later. The story on the news would be that we had been unable to flag down a passing motorist when our cell phones failed to work in the remote desert canyons. The news anchor would shake his head while describing the inevitable disaster that awaited motorists who failed to heed the "Service Engine Soon" light.

Every once in a while, we would pull into a service bay and have someone use their diagnostics tool. The error code always said that it had something to do with fuel and electrical. We spent an entire day in Laramie, Wyoming having the fuel rail replaced. The light stayed off for two weeks and then "blink" it was back.

The light went on and off for over a year as Gypsy took us around the country. Smooth sailing. No worries. Until Wisconsin.

We were driving from Oregon to get to our daughter Kim's wedding in Massachusetts. Passing through the middle of the Wisconsin farmlands along a two-lane highway, all the dashboard warning lights suddenly snapped on and Gypsy rolled to a silent halt along the edge of the road. No fanfare, just dead. Ron couldn't restart her. With my adrenaline level through the roof, I grabbed my cell phone. Surprisingly, there was plenty of service.

I Googled the Ford Dealership near me, sure that it would say "150 miles from your current location and closed on Sunday, you fool." It actually said, "Three miles from your current location and open until 6pm." I handed Ron the phone and he called the dealership. Miraculously, they answered. Even more miraculously, they knew a tow service that could handle our RV. Wow!

A half hour later, an eighteen-wheel tow truck pulled alongside and hooked up our rig. We rode in his cab to the dealership with Ron sitting next to him and me jammed into the sleeper cab.

Midwest friendly to the core, the dealership offered to let us camp in their parking lot until the service shop opened on Monday. They even tried to arrange for electrical hook-up off a nearby lamppost. We demurred and decided to take a room at a motel in town and wait for the bad news.

The next morning, they called us and the news was mixed. The good news was Gypsy's engine was a standard Ford V10, so they could service it despite not being an RV repair shop. The bad news was that our fuel tank pump had indeed failed and replacing it would require pulling the entire fuel tank, which was located underneath 14,000 pounds of RV.

I thought that we were done. We would be still living in our motel a month from now. Kim would get married and send us a picture with a caption that said, "Sorry you missed my wedding, but you should have listened to Gypsy's warning light."

Ron talked at length to the service manager, explaining that we were on our way to our daughter's wedding and that we had to be there or forever be the parents who missed the wedding. He really laid it on thick. I knew that we could probably take a plane, but Ron was never going to leave Gypsy behind, so he waxed lyrical about our sweet daughter Kim and her relationship with her loving dad. Kim is indeed wonderful, but Ron's picture of a little girl in pigtails fishing with Dad on Sundays would have made her barf.

A few hours later, the dealership called us again. They had located a replacement fuel tank pump and could get it delivered the next day and probably have it installed by Wednesday. Growing up in California, my mind simply could not grasp this level of customer service. I was suspicious, but if all went well, we would only have to make up three lost days of driving.

Wednesday morning dawned, and I anxiously awaited the call from the dealership that would basically say, "Nothing worked, we buried your rig and gave her a proper funeral." Probably followed by, "And you owe us $5,000 dollars."

Then the actual call came. "Hey guys, your rig is ready and we managed to keep the cost under $2,000. We decided not to charge you for the Sunday tow. We hope you say hi to your daughter for us!"

I felt like I was having an out-of-body experience as we settled the service bill and climbed into Gypsy. The service bay staff came outside to see us off, the whole group waving to us as we turned out of their parking lot. Never in my life have I had such an amazing experience with vehicle repair. Gypsy ran like a top and the dashboard lights stayed dark. I looked at Ron in disbelief. He smiled back.

Ron lives in a world where the best can and often does happen. He expects things to work out and they do. In his mind, Gypsy had picked a safe place to break down.

I had to stop and consider my pessimism. We hadn't been lost or murdered or spent a week in a canyon hoping for rescue. Things had actually worked out and strangers had gone out of their way to help us.

So, we motored onward to Kim's impending nuptials, the idiot trusting in his karma and the skeptic wondering if she should reevaluate her world view. After much deliberation, I decided that karmic balance would be achieved if the idiot had a skeptic to keep an eye on him so that he didn't end up dead in a ditch.

Still, I love his optimism. Idiot.

And the folks at Homan Ford in Ripon, Wisconsin have my undying gratitude.

The Best Of...
—Ron—

The question that people most often asked us about our trip was, "What was your favorite place?" Honestly, our favorite place was the one that still ahead. The mystery of the unknown and the surprise of discovering things along the way were a big part of the experience to us. Still, we did try quite a few things during our time on the road. We ate at over 1,000 places, stayed at over 500 places, and did hundreds of activities, so while we can't say that we found "The Best" we did find some pretty amazing things. Some of them were so good that we would adjust our route to go back again. Here are our favorites.

Best Places to Eat

Glen's Mountain View Café, Florence, Montana

Maybe it was the fact that the burgers came from the owner's own cattle, or that his daughters walked in with homemade pies hot out of the oven, but Glen's was our favorite café in America. The hardest part about eating there was trying to decide what to order. For breakfast, should I get an omelet with a homemade cinnamon roll or huckleberry pancakes with homemade biscuits and gravy? For lunch, burgers and homemade chili or soup and a sandwich? The homemade pie is a must, but which one? The strawberry rhubarb, huckleberry, cherry, and lemon meringue were all delicious. Even though Florence, Montana was a long way off the beaten path, we went there three times.

Salt Lick BBQ, Deadwood, Texas

We were driving around the Texas Hill Country when we heard about the Salt Lick BBQ. How could we resist a going to a place called Deadwood that offered traditional Texas BBQ? The story of Salt Lick began when a Mississippi girl promised to marry a passing surveyor if he would take her to Texas. During the trip in their wagon, she adapted a family recipe to cook meats outdoors at night. Many years later, her grandson wanted to start a local business, so he and his wife, who was from Hawaii, opened a restaurant featuring a huge open pit for searing meats, surrounded by rows of picnic tables. The combination of his family meat grilling technique and her tropical sauces was a hit. We each got a combination platter and between us we got to try their brisket, pulled pork, chicken, turkey and bison ribs. Our favorite was the bison ribs with their tender meat and earthy flavor.

Chicken De-lite, Thomasville, Georgia

We were making our way from the Georgia coast to Tallahassee, Florida and looking for interesting things to see along the way. As we passed through Thomasville, a little town known for its architecture and roses, I saw a sign for Chicken De lite. It didn't look like much from the outside, but my favorite fried chicken place when I was growing up had the same name, so I decided to check it out. We learned that it was one of the last Chicken De-lite franchises, which at one point had numbered over 1,000 locations. The owner had been there for nearly 50 years, personally frying chicken that he bought from local farms each morning. I guess practice made perfect, because it was the best fried chicken on our entire trip. We took a detour the next year to see if it was as good as we thought. It was.

The Agoura Deli, Agoura Hills, California

We had lived in Agoura for several years, so this was not a place that we discovered during our trip, but it was so good that we went there four times while we were on the road. I love delicatessens and have tried over 100 of them in America, including all the major ones in New York and Los Angeles. The Agoura Deli beat them all. Everything on its enormous menu was delicious, including classic New York style bagels, matzoh ball soup, enormous sandwiches, and truly fantastic desserts. Our favorite dishes were the spinach omelet and bagel for breakfast, their signature Santa Maria style skirt steak for dinner and an éclair any time of the day or night. Based on extensive personal research in over 50 countries, I can say with some authority that they make the best éclair in the world.

Gus's Fried Chicken, Memphis, Tennessee

Gus's was a great food joint and a classic piece of Americana. Started 1953 by Napoleon and Maggie Vanderbilt and carried on by their son Gus, it was the standard by which fried chicken was judged. A notable food critic wrote about Gus's in GQ magazine, calling it "perhaps the best fried chicken in the world." What made it so good was its combination of crunchy skin and juicy, spicy meat. At Gus's original Memphis location, we waited in line with over fifty people, many of them dressed in their Sunday best and felt like we were in church ourselves. Gus's was more than great chicken; it was a Southern soul food experience.

Magnolia Pancake Haus, San Antonio, Texas

We usually ate breakfast inside Gypsy, trying to start the day on our diet, but when a family member told us about a great breakfast place in San Antonio, we decided to give it a try. It was a little hard to find, but when we did, we faced the bigger challenge of doing justice to its extensive menu. How could I choose among Eggs Benedict, Apfelpfannkuchen (a traditional Bavarian plate-sized apple pancake), homemade corned beef hash, French toast made with homemade banana bread, Texas pecan waffles or homemade biscuits and sausage gravy? We got four entrees and took several doggie bags back to Gypsy, then went back the following year to eat there again.

Lazy Days, Islamorada, Florida

We looked forward to having fresh fish when we visited the Florida Keys and were not disappointed. We found several good places, but the one that stood out was Lazy Days in Marathon Key. The building looked like a weathered old fish shack, but the food and the setting were outstanding. We sat on the edge of the beach, eating delicious grilled grouper and fresh key lime pie while watching the pelicans demand their share of the daily catch as the boats came in. Afterward, we bought several pounds of fresh grouper, which Aimee turned into fantastic fish tacos.

Tyler's BBQ, Amarillo Texas

We found Tyler's through a series of accidents. We heard a song about Amarillo and took a 350-mile detour to see the town. After a day of wandering around, we were heading west when Aimee noticed that a barbecue place just off the freeway had good reviews, so we stopped in and ordered several items to go. The owner came out and started talking with us about our trip in our RV and his own journey in the restaurant business. He had worked in restaurants all over the country developing his own style of BBQ, a combination of classic dry rub Texas BBQ, wet Kansas City BBQ, and spicy Southwest BBQ. We swapped stories for over an hour as we ate, enjoying the great food and his warm hospitality.

Malibu Seafood Fish House, Malibu, California

We were staying at the Malibu Beach RV Park when we noticed a roadhouse-style seafood place just down a walking trail from the campground. When we got there, its outdoor picnic tables were all full and a line of people snaked through the parking lot. After making our choice from the display case filled with freshly caught fish, we watched the sunset over the Pacific Ocean as we gorged on cod and mahimahi. The only bad part was climbing the hill afterward to get back to Gypsy.

Amy's Ice Cream, Austin, Texas

We are ice cream fanatics. We were regulars at the local ice cream parlor in any place that we have ever lived. When we travel, we generally stop at any place that has a sign for homemade ice cream. Driving around America, we sampled the ice cream in over 100 places, but our favorite was Amy's Ice Cream in Austin. Founded by Amy Simmons in 1984 and still privately owned, Amy's offers a huge selection of handmade ice cream flavors. We went to the original location on Guadalupe Street in Austin's funky old commercial district. The shop was small but easy to find because there was a line out the door and around the corner. We tried several flavors, and our favorites were the Mexican Chocolate, which had the slightest hint of spice and the Mexican Vanilla, a combination of Madagascar vanilla and Mexican orchid. We ate our cones while walking around Austin, then took several pints back to Gypsy to enjoy while we were driving across Texas.

Acme Oyster House, New Orleans, Louisiana

We thoroughly tested New Orleans' reputation for great food and were not disappointed. Beignets, jambalaya, muffuletta sandwiches, pralines—we tried it all. The most memorable food was oysters, and Acme Oyster House was our hands-down favorite. We went there five times on our two visits to New Orleans. The first time we tried several of their menu items, but their oysters were so good that they became the only thing that we ordered. We had them raw, Florentine with spinach, barbecued and chargrilled with cheese, and they were all delicious.

Biscuits and Groovy, Austin, Texas

Located in a food truck in an older part of town, Biscuits and Groovy was a great example of how simple ingredients can be used to make food perfection. They start with homemade biscuits and gravy, then add eggs, bacon, sausage, potatoes, cheese, jalapenos, and chives in different combinations to create a wide variety of delicious dishes. Our favorite was the Gloria, but they were all fantastic. Try one with a Mexican Coke for a perfect blend of salty and sweet.

Crazy Norwegian Fish and Chips, Port Orford, Oregon

We drove Highway 101 up the coast of Oregon several times during our trip, going between visiting family in Sonoma County and our house in Oregon. One time, we stopped at a rustic shack that had been recommended to us by our daughter's boyfriend Josh. We never did get the story behind why it was named the Crazy Norwegian, but it became our favorite seafood restaurant north of San Francisco. It had perfectly prepared clam chowder, delicious homemade pies and the best fish and chips that we found anywhere in America. And when Josh asked for our approval to marry our daughter, we said yes.

Carmen's Pizza, Evanston, Illinois

I believe that Carmen's made the best Chicago-style deep dish pizza anywhere. It was so good that it got us the last spot at a campground on Lake Michigan. We were driving from House on the Rock when we called ahead to book a camp site at the only campground on Lake Michigan. They told me that the spots were first come, first serve and asked how far away we were. I said that it would be 3 hours as we were stopping in Evanston to get pizza. "Carmen's?" asked an excited voice. "Why, yes," I replied. The voice got even more excited, "I used to work in Evanston and Carmen's is the best pizza in the world!" "Well," I said, "If there is still a campsite when we get there, I'd be happy to share." We got the last campsite. Sadly, Carmen's is now closed, but we have included it in the hope that it may re-open soon.

Best Places to Stay

RV parks are so different that it is difficult to really compare them. Do you want to be on a beach or in the mountains? Do you prefer a paved site with cable TV and a pool, or would you rather be in more natural surroundings? Our favorite places were usually ones that captured the beauty and feel of the local area.

Wind River View Campground, Boulder, Wyoming

Located 90 miles southeast of Jackson Hole, this campground was fairly basic, with gravel sites and few amenities, so we didn't expect to be impressed. Then we settled in and watched the wildlife come out around us. A mother osprey was hunting, returning regularly to feed her two chicks in the nest at the edge of the campground. Below us, we watched the pronghorn antelope came out to drink in the Green River. Nighthawks swooped overhead, eating the mosquitoes that were trying to eat us. Later, we sat around our campfire and marveled at the serenity and stark beauty of Wyoming's high plains.

Acadia Seashore Campground and Cabins, Sullivan, Maine

Acadia National Park is Maine's rugged New England Coast at its best. We went in October when the air was nippy but not freezing and the leaves were falling. At this small family campground on the water, we could watch the fishing boats going through the channel on their way home from their day's work. It has a small beach where I swam in the cold salty water of the harbor, then ran back to Gypsy for a hot shower. We picked up fresh lobster at a local place and ate dinner outside while listening to the seagulls and the foghorns well into the night.

Blue Spring Park, Orange City, Florida

We stayed at several nice campgrounds in Florida, but none captured the natural beauty of its inland waterways like Blue Springs Park. It has only 12 RV sites and they are pretty basic, but the park's mile-long boardwalk along the river gave us a close view of the wildlife, especially the manatees as they left the hot springs in the morning to feed in larger rivers, then returned at night to sleep in the warm water. The best part was when we rented a kayak to explore the waterways and a baby manatee came over to play tag with us.

French Quarter RV, New Orleans, Louisiana

The French Quarter RV is a fantastic combination of facility and location. Its high concrete walls look a little scary, but inside it has level paved sites, pretty landscaping, a nice fitness center and a beautiful outdoor pool and spa. It is located at the edge of the French Quarter, so we could walk everywhere. A little pricey, but absolutely worth it.

Buckskin Mountain State Park, Parker, Arizona

Located on the Colorado River about 200 miles downstream from Las Vegas, Buckskin Mountain State Park is a pocket of beauty, with mountains on three sides, a grassy picnic area overlooking the Colorado River and a long sandy beach. An island in the middle of the river slows its current and creates the nicest swimming area that we found on the Colorado River. We played in the water for hours, then sat outside at night watching the stars and enjoying the cool breeze from the river.

Oceanside RV Park, Charleston, Oregon

Located west of Coos Bay, Oceanside was our favorite beach campground. Several of its sites back into the sand dunes less than 50 yards from the waves. We walked for a mile along the flat sandy beach and never saw more than 10 people. The nearby little harbor town of Charleston has several nice seafood restaurants and a very good café for morning coffee and pastries..

Lost Dutchman State Park, Phoenix, Arizona

Located at the base of the Superstitious Mountains, Lost Dutchman State Park offers tranquility and beautiful views of the red rock. For the more adventurous, there are hiking trails through the mountains and the chance to search for the fabled Lost Dutchman gold mine, but I chose to relax and enjoy the scenery. We set up cots outside and spent three days reading and napping during the day and watching the stars at night.

Malibu Beach RV Park, Malibu, California

We knew that we were in a high-end park when we saw an RV with a Jaguar as its tow-along vehicle. Our site was expensive, but the location was worth it. Set on a bluff overlooking the Pacific Ocean, it has a phenomenal view of the water with Los Angeles off in the distance. Just down a hillside path is The Malibu Fish House, a fantastic seafood restaurant and fish market. We sat outside and watched the whales, dolphins, and pelicans cruise by us in the ocean below.

Giant Redwoods RV Park, Myers Flat, California

We stayed in several RV parks that were located in the redwoods of northern California and southern Oregon. Our favorite was Giant Redwoods RV Park on the Eel River about 50 miles south of Eureka. We swam in the river, picked wild blackberries, played horseshoes and lounged among the redwoods, relaxing and enjoying the grandeur of the giant trees.

We lived in Gypsy most of the time, so we didn't see a lot of hotels. However, some of the hotels were so special that we had to include them as well..